Violence as Obscenity

Constitutional Conflicts
A Series by the Institute of Bill of Rights Law
at the College of William and Mary
Edited by Rodney A. Smolla and Neal Devins

VIOLENCE AS OBSCENITY

Limiting the Media's First Amendment Protection

Kevin W. Saunders

DUKE UNIVERSITY PRESS   *Durham and London 1996*

© 1996 Duke University Press
All rights reserved
Printed in the United States of America on acid-free paper ∞
Typeset in Minion by Tseng Information Systems, Inc.
Library of Congress Cataloging-in-Publication Data
appear on the last printed page of this book.

Contents

To my wife, Mary Scott,
and our daughter, Molly Saunders-Scott

Acknowledgments

My initial interest in the topic of this book grew out of a comment made in a course I took as a University of Michigan law student. In James Boyd White's class on rhetoric, law, and culture we read Sophocles' *Philoctetes*. In discussing the violence that occurred in the play, Professor White commented on the Greek view that violence was obscene and that "obscene" meant "off stage." That comment led me to wonder how the law had come to view sex rather than violence as obscene. While my initial question was whether or not sex could be considered obscene, I later came to realize that an equally important question is why violence is considered not to be obscene.

The topic remained of interest to me in the years following law school, as I slowly gathered material on obscenity law and the history of drama. I also developed some understanding of First Amendment theory while teaching constitutional law. That exposure to various policies argued to motivate the protections of speech and press, and a reading of the statutes and cases said to justify the obscenity exception, convinced me that the exclusion of violence from the category of the obscene was unwarranted.

The actual development of any written work on violence as obscenity was precipitated by the 1993 Workshop on Constitutional Law sponsored by the Association of American Law Schools, again at the University of Michigan. I submitted a proposal to present the topic at a small group session on topics of current research. When the proposal was accepted I decided the time for serious effort was at hand. At the time, I did not know just how at hand it was. As I was preparing for the conference, the topic of media violence made one of its periodic resurgences. To avoid missing the opportunity to make a contribution while the debate was of popular, as well as of scholarly, interest, I wrote two articles. The first article, "Media Violence and the Obscenity Exception to the First Amendment," appeared in the *William and Mary Bill of Rights Journal,* and the second, "Media Self-Regulation of Depictions of Violence," appeared in the *Oklahoma Law Review.* Those articles, along with other material gathered later, grew into this book.

I want to express my thanks to several individuals for the help they have provided in the development of this work. James Boyd White is due thanks for providing the initial spark. Rod Smolla of William and Mary is also due thanks for his comments on the first law review article and his suggestions on material that had to be added and arguments that should be refocused or expanded in enlarging that article into a book. Several colleagues in legal education, Fred Schauer of Harvard's Kennedy School of Government, Harry F. Tepker of the University of Oklahoma, and an anonymous reviewer for Duke University Press also provided valuable comments and counterarguments that helped shape the final outcome. That outcome is not one with which they necessarily all share agreement, but arguments offered against my position were very helpful in forming responses to potential criticism. Comments made by participants in response to my original presentation of the thesis at the Workshop on Constitutional Law and at a later meeting of the Law and Society Association also proved helpful. Valuable assistance in providing entry into and comment on topics in psychology and communications research was provided, respectively, by Tony Nunez of Michigan State University and Haejung Paik of the University of Oklahoma.

I also want to thank law librarian John Michaud and law student Craig Sanders for the research assistance they provided during a visiting year at Thomas M. Cooley Law School, and law students Greg Heiser, Beth Espy, Ryan Hauser, and Russell Abbott for their research assistance at the University of Oklahoma. Thanks are also due the people at Duke University Press for their efforts in putting the manuscript into print. Finally, thanks to my wife and daughter for their support and understanding, when I was particularly busy with, or tired from, the preparation of this book.

Introduction

In 1961 Federal Communications Commission Chairman Newton Minow called American television a "vast wasteland." Mr. Minow was concerned that television would provide nothing of substance for his children. Thirty-some years later, many would be happy with a benign wasteland. Instead of concern that children would not benefit from television, Mr. Minow's 1991 concern was that children would be harmed by it.[1] Much of the public agrees; a 1992 *Times Mirror* poll found that seventy-two percent of Americans think television is too violent.[2]

The concern would appear to be well-founded. The 1986 American Psychological Association's task force on television and society produced startling estimates on the exposure of children to televised acts of violence. They concluded that by the time the average child finishes elementary school, the child has viewed more than 8,000 murders and more than 100,000 other acts of violence.[3] Depending on viewing habits, a child may have seen as many as 200,000 acts of violence before becoming a teenager.[4] Even those statistics don't measure the true scope of the exposure of children to media violence. The American Psychological Association estimates are based on incidents of violence on broadcast television and omit exposure from cable programming, movies, videotapes, and video games.

The increasing availability of the entertainment media and the violence it portrays have been accompanied by an increase in violence in the real world. In the fifteen years following the introduction of television, homicide rates almost doubled.[5] While the increase in the murder rate appears to have slowed, violence is still of epidemic proportion in American society. In 1991 there were over 24,000 intentional, non-justifiable homicides in the United States; the total for all categories of violent crime surpassed 1,900,000.[6] Gunshot wounds have become the leading cause of death for teenage males.[7] Other violent crimes, such as rape and aggravated assault, are also on the increase.[8]

The degree of violence in both society at large and in the media naturally gives rise to the question of causation. Do television and the other media simply mirror society, or does media violence contribute to the violence in the nation's streets? A significant number of professional and public interest organizations have concluded either that television does cause violence or at least that there is a sufficiently significant risk of such causation that something must be done. The American Academy of Pediatrics, the American Medical Association, the National PTA, the National Education Association, and various issue-specific public interest groups have called for action ranging from counseling parents on the effect of television to governmental regulation.

The concern over the effects of media violence is not new. The issue has been examined with regularity, by various entities, since television became so central to our culture. Psychologists began to study the possibility that television might cause violence in the early 1960s.[9] By 1968, the National Commission on the Causes and Prevention of Violence surveyed the psychological studies and found a link between television violence and violent behavior in viewers.[10] As the Staff Report to the Commission made clear, mass media portrayal of violence has an effect on society. The report concluded that, at least under some circumstances, exposure to media violence stimulates violent behavior.[11] In 1982, the National Institute of Mental Health took a fresh look at the issue, also finding a causal link between media violence and aggressive behavior in viewers.[12] The 1982 position, although not without its critics, survives and is reinforced by more recent studies. At this point, more than 1,000 studies, reviews, and reports "attest to a significant link between heavy exposure to television violence and subsequent aggressive behavior."[13]

Despite the conclusion that media violence has led to a more violent society, the various levels of government have been unable to limit such depictions. Congress has been willing to take only weak action. Some states and municipalities have been more aggressive, but their efforts have been held violative of the First Amendment protections accorded speech and the press. Depictions of violence have been held protected and any restrictions on such material are forced to meet a difficult standard of justification. While the protection of public safety might justify an infringement, the scientific evidence has been held to be insufficiently specific to identify the precise variety of material that causes real world violence, and such precision is demanded where material is protected by the First Amendment.

While violent material is protected and difficult to regulate, sufficiently explicit and offensive sexual material has been held to be unprotected by the Constitution. The Supreme Court of the United States, in *Roth v. United States*,[14] recognized an exception to the First Amendment, under which obscene material is left outside the ambit of the freedoms of speech and press. Since such material is unprotected, there is no need to provide the scientific data clearly demonstrating any harm flowing from specific types of obscene material.

The thesis of this work builds on the obscenity exception recognized for sexual materials. The obscenity exception is not without its critics. Those who believe that the First Amendment provides protection to all expression, or all expression short of criminal solicitation, conspiracy, and perhaps libel, find no justification for the obscenity exception. The arguments against the exception are not without force. They are the well-reasoned views of serious scholars. They are not, however, the law. The obscenity exception is a part of First Amendment law and, although there have been changes in the test to determine what is obscene, it has been part of constitutional law for almost forty years.

This work accepts the existence of the obscenity exception, but it will be argued that the exception is misfocused, or at least too finely focused, on depictions of sexual and excretory activities. Violence is at least as obscene as sex. If sexual images may go sufficiently beyond community standards for candor and offensiveness, and hence be unprotected, there is no reason why the same should not be true of violence.

In nonlegal discourse the term "obscene" is often applied to actions and materials that are nonsexual. A corporation may make obscene profits or an individual may be obscenely wealthy. In ordinary language, depictions of gluttony or of violence may be as obscene as depictions of sex. What strikes us as obscene, in this nonlegal sense, are actions or depictions in which people are afforded subhuman treatment or treated as nothing more than physical entities with no consideration of the human spirit. While depictions of the purely physical side of sex may fit within that description, so also may depictions of carnage, where even the word itself indicates the treatment of people as nothing more than meat.

The concept of obscenity is also informed by the history of drama. One suggested derivation of the word "obscene" is from the Latin for "off the stage." If depictions that are obscene are those that are barred from the stage, here too, violence is, historically, just as obscene as sex. A look to drama in classical Greece shows a greater toleration for sexual depictions than for violence. In other periods sex and violence both vary in acceptability. In some eras one or both are obscene; in other eras, neither is obscene. Importantly, neither sex nor violence enjoys an exclusive title to the concept.

The point that, in ordinary language or dramatic history, violence may be obscene is not sufficient to support the development in constitutional law argued for here. What is required is an argument that the same is true as a legal matter. The *Roth* Court offered a legal history to support the First Amendment exceptions for sexually obscene materials. The same sort of legal history can be constructed to provide equal support for a First Amendment exception for violently obscene material. The law in the era of the Bill of Rights established that not all material was protected; that is, the freedoms of speech and press were not absolute. The law in the era following the Bill of Rights established that obscene material was within the class that was unprotected. What the law of either era failed to do is to define obscenity with the specific focus on sex or excretion that it has come to have.

The focus of obscenity on sex is a product of the Victorian era of the late 1800s. Only then did the courts begin to so limit the concept. In reaction, many states passed new statutes banning publications focusing on crime and violence. Some states continued to describe such materials as obscene. Other states were unconcerned about labels and simply drafted statutes parallel to their obscenity laws. Except for the label, the legal history of violence as obscene is then just as long and as unbroken as sexual obscenity, at least until the era following *Roth*. Even more importantly, the late 1800s monopolization of the label can not speak to the meaning of the First Amendment. If the law at the time of the Bill of Rights justifies an exception for obscene material, it would be for material viewed as obscene at the time. A redefinition of the concept in the late 1800s should not serve to change the exception as it existed, during the era of the framing.

In addition to the failure of the statutes and case law of the colonial era to distinguish between sex and violence for obscenity purposes, the policies that justify such an exception to the First Amendment also do not successfully distinguish between the two. Once again, there are arguments that there should be no obscenity exception, but these arguments, while popular in academic circles, have not convinced the Supreme Court. If the conclusion of the Court is given the authority it is due, the policy arguments that are of interest are those that justify an obscenity exception. If those arguments are examined, sex and violence again cannot be distinguished. There are no theories of the First Amendment that justify an exception for sexual obscenity that can not be reasonably extended to justify an exception for what might be described as violent obscenity.

The effect of recognizing that sufficiently explicit and offensive depictions of violence may be legally obscene and unprotected by the First Amendment would allow the various levels of government to regulate such depictions. Violence that reaches the level of obscenity could be banned. Even if Congress or the states did not want to ban such material, certainly limitations on the distribution of such material to minors could be adopted.

A further important effect would be the recognition and application of a variable obscenity standard for violence. Just as material that is not sexually obscene for an adult audience may be held to be obscene when distributed to youth, the recognition of violent obscenity will entail a variable violent obscenity doctrine. Films that are aimed at a youthful audience or that are distributed to youth could be judged by a stricter standard than those intended for and distributed to adults.

Lastly, the power of the federal government to regulate the content of broadcasts would grow to include more authority over violence. The Supreme Court, in *Federal Communications Commission v. Pacifica Foundation*,[15] held constitutional the power granted the Commission by Congress to regulate indecent material. Even if it is argued that material may be indecent only on grounds that are similar to, but falling short of, the grounds on which material is adjudged obscene,[16] the recognition that the obscenity exception extends to violence also leads to the conclusion that lesser levels of violence may be indecent.

Over the next several chapters, the bases for these claims will be examined. Chapter 1 will examine the public debate on the issue of media violence. The positions of various professional and public interest groups calling for action will be presented as will the positions of the media industry and the American Civil Liberties Union, counseling against any official regulatory action. The chapter will also examine the congressional response and the media attempt to thwart any action by promising to self-regulate and at least provide warnings as to violent content. The potential for action by the Federal Communications Commission will also be examined, as will the recent attempts by some states to limit the access of minors to violent videos. Last, the current debate and media response will be placed in historical perspective. The historic cycle of complaints over media violence, promises by the media to self-regulate, the failure of such self-regulation, and a resurgence of complaints indicates both that self-regulation will again fail and that the debate will not disappear.

Chapter 2 presents the psychological and social science evidence for media, in particular television, causation of real world violence. The evidence appears to be strong. Laboratory studies, field studies, and correlational studies all point to such an effect. To be sure, each variety of study has its critics, as do many of the individual studies. Nonetheless, looking at the conclusions that may be drawn from the collection of all such studies demonstrates a very statistically significant effect, although the size of that effect and the level of contribution of media violence to real violence may be questioned.

The following chapter examines the operation of the current obscenity exception to the First Amendment. The corollary doctrines of variable obscenity, applying a different standard for material aimed at youth, and indecency, allowing for federal regulation of the broadcast of such material, are also examined. The standard for justifying infringements on speech in protected areas is also presented, and it is shown why the recent attempts to impose limitations on violent material have failed to pass constitutional muster. The inability to establish with sufficient specificity the types of material that present a danger to public safety and thus justify regulation indicates the need for a fresh approach provided by a reconsideration of the scope of the obscenity exception.

Chapter 4 looks to the concept of obscenity in other than legal contexts. In ordinary language, the extension of the term is much broader than it is in recent legal contexts. The work of several philosophers and the analyses they provide for the concept are examined. The etymology of the word, and the insights gained from the derivations commonly offered, are also presented. Those insights from human nature and from the history of drama lead to the conclusion that obscenity encompasses violence as thoroughly as it includes sex. In fact, it may well be that the ordinary use of the term, and its meaning drawn from the history of drama, extend beyond violence and sex to other areas as well. The chapter concludes with an argument that, in those other areas, the constitutional meaning cannot follow the ordinary language meaning to allow restrictions on areas that are given specific protection by the Constitution.

Chapter 5 turns to the history of obscenity law up until the Supreme Court's recognition of the obscenity exception in *Roth*. This history is important, because the ordinary language meaning of the word "obscene" will not necessarily control the scope of the obscenity exception. If the law has historically recognized an exception for materials said in the various eras to be obscene, as the *Roth* Court says it has, it is the legal definition of "obscene" in those eras that is important. The ordinary language definition becomes important to the degree that the law fails to establish a different legal definition.

It will be shown that, in fact, the legal history does fail to provide a definition for obscenity, until constitutionally recent times. The statutes and cases of the colonial era will be examined to show that not all speech was viewed as protected. It will be shown that the law in the era following the Bill of Rights included obscene material as such an unprotected category. However, it will also be shown that it is not clear, either from American law or from English law in the years preceding or shortly following the Revolution and framing of the Constitution and Bill of Rights, what was contained in that class. Lastly, the development of obscenity law in the late 1800s and beyond to focus on sex and excretion and the lack of constitutional import of changes in that era will be discussed.

Chapter 6 looks to the pre-*Roth* history of legal attempts to regulate depictions of violence. Since the law did not distinguish sex and excretion from other categories of obscenity prior to the late 1800s, it is the law of the end of the nineteenth century and the first half of the twentieth century that is the focus of the chapter. The statutes passed by various states, in the era in which the law of obscenity developed its focus on sex, will be examined, as will the later case law treatment of those statutes. The legal treatment of depictions of violence, since *Roth,* will also be examined.

In Chapter 7, the policies that explain and motivate the First Amendment will be considered. Particular emphasis will be placed on those policy arguments that serve to justify the exception for obscenity. While there are arguments that speak against the obscenity exception generally, those arguments are not emphasized, because they do not explain the law as it is but themselves argue for change. The theories that justify the obscenity exception do explain existing law, and it is these theories that are examined to determine whether they can justify an exception for sexual obscenity without equally justifying an exception for violent obscenity.

Chapter 8 examines another recent attempt to withhold First Amendment protection from a class of objectional material. That attempt was both broader and narrower than the present effort. The feminist attack on pornography, defining such material as combining erotic images with themes or depictions that include violence against women or the subjugation or degradation of women, will be examined. The failure of such attempts to stand up to constitutional challenge will also be explained. It will be shown how that approach taken here provides at least some of the relief sought. While violent obscenity does not address all images that may hurt the status of females in our society, at least those images that include violence against women will be included within any regulation of depictions of violence generally.

The last substantive chapter examines the difficulties that would be faced in drafting a violent obscenity statute and the implications of such a statute. The lessons drawn from the years of effort in defining and refining the sexual obscenity exception are exploited for guidance in more quickly developing a violent obscenity standard. The development of variable obscenity and indecency as the basis for regulation of material aimed at youth or for broadcast are also seen to provide guidance for the development of parallel extensions. Lastly, concerns that such a statute would present for the arts and for broadcast news are examined.

The Public Debate over Media Violence

Public Interest Group Concern

Much of the public has become convinced that violence in television, films, and, more recently, video games causes violence in the real world. A 1993 *Times Mirror* poll found that 72 percent of the American population believes that there is too much violence on television, and a 1990 Gallup Poll found that 63 percent believe that such violence causes actual violence.[1] While there may be some room to question such a cause and effect relationship,[2] the belief that media violence is at least *a* causal factor in societal violence has led groups of health care professionals to look toward attempting to mitigate any such causation.

The American Academy of Pediatrics, concerned over several negative effects it found to be the result of television, has recommended that pediatricians explain to parents the effects of television and advise them to limit children's television viewing to under two hours per day and supervise the choice of programs.[3] Among the negative effects that concerned the Academy was violence. Their Committee on Communications found sufficient data to conclude that "protracted television viewing is one cause of violent or aggressive behavior."[4] In addition to suggesting roles for pediatricians and parents, the recommendations also included a suggestion that the government play a role by making broadcast license renewal dependent on the airing of high-quality children's programming. Testifying before Senate subcommittees, Dr. William Dietz, of the American Academy of Pediatrics, stated the Academy's view:

> Artistic license does not absolve writers, producers and broadcasters of the responsibility to address this problem. The Communications Act declares that broadcast airwaves belong to the American public. Broadcast licenses . . . are required to serve the "public interest, convenience, and necessity." The Academy contends that the *de facto* promotion of violence on and by television is not in the public interest. . . . Holding broad-

casters responsible for their portrayals of televised violence represents an essential step in the reduction of violence in our society.[5]

Among other organizations of health professionals the American Medical Association has stated its "vigorous opposition to televised violence" and has sought to increase the awareness of patients and physicians that "television violence is a risk factor threatening the health of young people."[6] The American Psychological Association has also called for a reduction in televised violence.[7]

Outside the health care field other advocacy groups have also taken a stand against violence in television. The National PTA in 1989 reaffirmed a 1975 resolution calling for the television industry to reduce violence in hours when children are likely to be watching. The PTA noted that the Surgeon General had reported a cause and effect relationship between televised violence and aggressive behavior on the part of young viewers. Further, the Association considered the voluntary industry self-regulation codes to be ineffective and found them to be regularly violated. As a result it was resolved that "the National PTA *demand* from networks and local stations reduction in the amount of violence shown on television programs and commercials."[8] While the demand addressed the entire day, the association wanted particular emphasis given to the hours between 2 P.M. and 10 P.M. and weekend mornings, when children were most likely to be watching. The PTA issued a further "demand" that, if industry self-regulation did not lead to less violence, the Federal Communications Commission issue and enforce regulations limiting violence.

The National Foundation for the Improvement of Television has, for more than twenty-five years, been a leading advocacy group on the issue of reducing televised violence. The Foundation has taken a three-pronged approach to the problem. Since its founding in 1969, it has been involved in legal proceedings before the Federal Communications Commission and the federal courts in an attempt to persuade the Commission to exercise regulatory control over television violence. The Foundation has also attempted to raise public awareness regarding the effect of televised violence on children. Further, an attempt has been made to insure the awareness of corporate CEOs as to the violent content of the programs on which their companies advertise and to develop corporate guidelines for the purchase of advertising and thereby to encourage less violent programming.

The Children's Television Resource and Education Center has expressed similar concerns with regard to both violent television programming and violent video games. Dr. Parker Page, the center's president, testified before a joint hearing on violent video games held by the United States Senate's Juvenile Justice and Government Affairs Subcommittees. He found the research on the effect on children of television violence to show that "watch[ing] a steady diet of violent programming increase[s] their chances of becoming more aggressive towards other children . . . , more tolerant of real life violence and more afraid of the world outside their homes."[9] While expressing concern that similar results would spring from the use of violent video games, he did not call for regulation. His recommendations for government action spoke only to research and increasing public awareness of the problem.

The National Education Association has also expressed concern over media violence, but has suggested that the family is the best defense against the effect of such media on children. While the NEA supports adequate warning or notification of violent content, the Association rejects legal suppression of such materials. Arguing that a strong First Amendment is necessary to the academic freedom and free inquiry central to the Association's concerns, the NEA vice president, Robert Chase, concluded that he did not want any governmental body determining what was appropriate for his daughter to see. He saw that as his job as a parent but agreed that Congress providing, through the establishment of an independent rating council, the tools necessary to make such judgments would be appropriate.[10]

The National Coalition on Television Violence has also proposed federal regulation of televised violence but has not suggested the general suppression of such material. The NCTV approach includes ratings and warning labels to air prior to broadcast and in ads and publicity for such television shows. The proposed warning label goes beyond a simple statement of content but would, instead, state: "The TV show you are about to watch may be hazardous to your psychological and/or physical health due to its highly violent content."[11] The similarity to the warning on cigarettes carries over to recommendations on public service announcements on the harmful effects of violence and a school-based public health campaign addressing violence. The only ban called for is on offering violent programming in government institutions. While that ban could provide an economic incentive to programmers to reduce violence, the incentive would be through the government as a consumer rather than the government as a regulator and could therefore lessen any First Amendment problems.

Perhaps the most persistent voice on the issue of media violence over the past several decades has been that of Dr. Leonard Eron. Dr. Eron is not the spokesperson for any particular public interest group. He is a research scientist at the University of Michigan Institute for Social Research and Chair of the

American Psychological Association Commission on Violence and Youth. His advocacy has come through various publications and through his testimony before state legislatures and congressional committees. In Dr. Eron's view there is no scientific doubt over the aggression-causing effect of media violence. In recent congressional testimony he told the Senate that, after twenty years of the television industry's unwillingness or inability to regulate itself, it was time for the government to act. He cited an epidemic of youth violence as a public health problem and impending disaster in which television plays a causal role. While recognizing a distaste for censorship, he concluded that "drastic steps that we do not favor may have to be taken to curb the epidemic." [12]

The most noted nonindustry group speaking out against government action to limit or otherwise regulate media violence has been the American Civil Liberties Union. The spokesperson for that position has most often been the ACLU's legislative counsel Robert Peck. As an example, Mr. Peck testified before a Senate subcommittee considering the establishment of a National Independent Council for Entertainment in Video Devices.[13] He argued that material containing depictions of violence is protected by the First Amendment and any attempt to regulate such speech would cut to the core of the amendment. Even requiring warning labels as to content was said to violate the freedom of speech. The First Amendment is designed to prevent the government from serving as the guardian of the public mind, and mandated labels would allow the government to determine what sorts of speech must be accompanied by warnings that would discourage public access. In the ACLU view, a view certainly backed by numerous constitutional case law decisions, government must not be allowed to make such content-based decisions. While manufacturers and producers are certainly free to adopt voluntary content warnings, the threat of government action seen as implicit in the bill under consideration made any such adoption less than voluntary.

In response to these public concerns, various governmental entities have examined the issue and debated what action to take. Congress has considered the problem of media violence but has been reluctant to take any forceful action. The Federal Communications Commission has shown similar reticence. Some states have enacted legislation banning distribution of violent materials to minors, but those attempts have faced challenge and defeat in court.

The Media Response

The entertainment industry has also been active in the debates engendered by media violence. In that debate, the industry has sometimes been willing to recognize a problem but has consistently argued that any solution must be adopted voluntarily by the media. Any government attempt to impose a solution is seen as a violation of the First Amendment.

Jack Valenti, president of the Motion Picture Association of America, testified before the same Senate subcommittees addressed by Dr. Eron and Dr. Dietz. In a prepared statement, Mr. Valenti admitted that there was some gratuitous violence on television and that broadcasters and programmers have a responsibility to reduce such violence. On the other hand, he seemed to question the role of media violence in causing actual violence and just how prevalent violence is in television. He stated the intent of the MPAA to meet with the Directors Guild, Writers Guild, Actors Guild, and other important industry groups to address the problem. In counterpoint to that intent, he also raised the issue of creative freedom, finding it clear in the First Amendment that "[a] creative story-teller, in this land, tells a story the way he or she chooses and the only coercion constitutionally available to force a change in that choice is within the original creator, and no one else."[14] Somewhat more bluntly, Mr. Valenti also warned the subcommittee, "If you push and shove people, they're going to shove back. And remember, they have the armor of a thing called the First Amendment."[15]

Thomas Murphy, chairman of Capital Cities/ABC, similarly invoked constitutional protection, while accepting that the industry also had equally important responsibilities. He, too, questioned the prevalence of violence on network television and noted general principles regarding violence that his network had adopted. Those principles, he said, bar gratuitous violence, require that the consequences of violence be depicted so that violence not be glamorized, require the depiction of alternatives to violence in the resolution of conflict, and prohibit material that would instruct the viewer as to how to commit crimes or do violence. He concluded with two "cautionary thoughts." First, he noted that there would always be stories containing violence that would be worth telling. Secondly, he stated that "the government must exercise restraint in interfering with the content of the programming the media portrays. Our founding fathers had the wisdom to recognize the importance of freedom of expression to democratic self-governance. We must guard that freedom zealously."[16]

Stephen Palley of King World Productions also invoked the First Amendment. While stressing King World's awareness of its responsibilities and how it was meeting those responsibilities, Mr. Palley made it clear that he was also aware of King World's rights. He concluded: "We believe that we have exercised the editorial discretion accorded us by the First Amendment responsibly and thoughtfully. We believe that, in the last analysis, it is the constitutionally protected exercise of editorial judgment that affords the best means of resolving the concerns that have led to these hearings."[17]

Various other network and studio heads have been less direct in their invocations of the First Amendment. Testimony before the Senate subcommittees has often stressed how much nonviolent entertainment is being presented and the self-regulatory practices of the entities involved. It has also been suggested that Congress needs to be aware of where the problem arises, for example it must distinguish among network television, syndicated television, and cable programming, when bringing to bear criticism of violent content. Such testimony often contained only brief references to keeping in mind the freedom of speech in addressing the problem of media violence.

The broadcast stations have also addressed the issue of media violence and have similarly invoked the First Amendment. The National Association of Broadcasters has adopted programming policies regarding violence. Under those policies violence, which encompasses both physical and psychological violence, must be portrayed responsibly, consistent with creative intent, and not in an exploitive manner. Furthermore, the consequences to the victims and perpetrators should be presented. Excessive, gratuitous, and instructional violence are to be avoided, and depictions should not dwell on physical agony or brutality. Special care is required where children are involved in the depiction of violence. Here too, however, it is made clear that the policies are voluntary and, in the NAB view, must be left so. The policy statement includes a provision that the principles it contains will not be interpreted or enforced by anyone, including the NAB, but that interpretation and application are left solely to the discretion of the broadcast licensee. "Both NAB and the stations it represents respect the individual broadcaster's First Amendment rights to select and present programming according to its individual assessment of the desires and expectations of its audience and of the public interest."[18]

A very different media view has been presented by Ted Turner of Turner Broadcasting. He agrees that television causes violence and maintains that if the industry does not start a rating system, Congress should "ram it down their throats. . . . Unless you keep the gun pointed at their heads, all you'll get is mumbly, mealy-mouthed B.S. . . . They just hope the subject will go away."[19] While most likely not ceding the protection of the First Amendment, he provides insight into the need for whatever regulation the amendment may allow.

Congressional Action and Inaction

While Congress has recognized the problem of media violence, its approach has generally been simply to study the issue or to ask the industry or other governmental bodies to consider the problem. There have now been more than forty years of congressional hearings on violence in the broadcast media. The first such hearings were conducted in 1952 by the House Interstate and Foreign Commerce Subcommittee.[20] Among the most recent were those conducted in 1993 by the Subcommittee on the Constitution and the Subcommittee on Juvenile Justice of the Senate Judiciary Committee.[21] In between, a variety of congressional hearings have occurred, and the issue has been studied by the National Commission on the Causes and Prevention of Violence, the Surgeon General, the National Institute of Mental Health, and the Attorney General's Task Force on Family Violence.[22]

The broadcast media have not been the only media to come under congressional scrutiny. In 1954, Senator Estes Kefauver led a Senate Judiciary Committee Subcommittee to Investigate Juvenile Delinquency inquiry into the relationship between comic books and juvenile delinquency. In the early 1950s there had been a great increase in the number of comic books published and in particular in the publication of crime and horror comics. As the committee report described such comics, they "evidence a common penchant for violent death in every form imaginable. Many . . . dwell in detail on various forms of insanity and stress sadistic degeneracy. Others are devoted to cannibalism with monsters in human form feasting on human bodies, usually the bodies of scantily clad women."[23] The description is not inapt for some of the motion pictures and television of current concern.

While the relationship between televised violence and aggressive behavior is better established today, the subcommittee even then recognized the possibility of a similar connection between comic books and delinquency. The subcommittee concluded that "this country cannot afford the calculated risk involved in feeding its children, through comic books, a concentrated diet of crime, horror, and violence."[24] Despite this conclusion, the subcommittee determined not to regulate comic books but instead to rely on industry self-regulation, even though earlier attempts at self-regulation had failed. This approach, too, was an early parallel to the current congressional approach to media violence.

Congress has begun, once again, to study the issue of violence in media. In recent hearings before the Senate Judiciary Committee's Subcommittees on the Constitution and on Juvenile Justice, the heads of the major television networks were called before the subcommittees to answer for their depictions of murder and mayhem. While some members of Congress have indicated that they will consider some controls on media depictions of violence, if the media themselves do not exercise self-control,[25] thus far Congress has been rather timid in its actions.

There has been some legislation introduced. The Television Program Improvement Act of 1990[26] was enacted, but the act provides only an exemption from antitrust laws for any industry discussion or agreement to limit violent material on television,[27] without requiring any such limits. In a 1993 effort, bills were introduced in both houses of Congress calling for the establishment of a "Television Violence Report Card."[28] These bills would have required only that the Federal Communications Commission evaluate and rate the violence on television programs and rate sponsors on the violence of the programs on which they advertise. While the results would have been published in the *Federal Register*, there was no provision, other than potential public reaction to the reports, for decreasing the violent content of the television fare. Another 1993 bill would have gone somewhat further and would have required that warnings as to the nature of the material about to air accompany any broadcast of violent material.[29] Even that bill would not have limited violence but would, at least, have provided some opportunity for parents to control the exposure of their children to such material.

Still other bills would have demanded more direct action. One would have required the development of "V-chip" technology that would allow television owners to block out violent programming.[30] Televisions would be equipped with an electronic chip able to detect a signal accompanying programs considered violent and, if the owner desired, would not display the program. The approach would benefit parents who do not want their children exposed to violence. It would do nothing to respond to the dangers such children face from the children of other parents who do not have televisions with "V-chips" or do not activate the chips.

Another pair of bills asked the Federal Communications Commission to limit violence in programming during the hours when children are likely to be in the audience.[31] That approach does have the advantage of not requiring the cooperation of parents. It also could have been implemented more quickly, since it would not face the time lag involved in newly equipped televisions replacing those already in use. There may, however, be some question of the FCC's authority to regulate television in this manner.[32] Furthermore, the bill addressed only the broadcast media and would have done nothing to affect the violence available on cable, in the movie theater, or through videotape rentals.

Congress has been reluctant to take direct action to limit depictions of violence in the media. Any direct action that has been contemplated was limited to the broadcast media, as media historically more subject to regulation and to the licensing authority of the FCC. This reticence may be explained by First Amendment concerns. That was clearly the basis for the decision in the 1955 report on comic books to rely on industry self-regulation. The subcommittee rejected any governmental censorship as "totally out of keeping with our basic American concepts of a free press operating in a free land for a free people."[33] This respect for the First Amendment has carried over to the current debate. Even Senator Paul Simon, who has been described as being "on a personal crusade to clean up violence on television,"[34] has expressed First Amendment concerns over colleagues who "want to go much further than is healthy for a free society."[35]

The congressional concern over broadcast media violence has recently been matched by a concern over violent video games. Senator Joseph Lieberman has expressed strong concern over games like *Mortal Kombat*, *Lethal Enforcers*, and *Night Trap* in which the game player participates in violent situations. In *Mortal Kombat* the character representing the player engages in a martial arts competition with another character. The player may "finish" his opponent by, among other options, tearing off his head complete with spinal column, accompanied by a graphic loss of blood. The characters in *Mortal Kombat* are digitized, which provides greater realism than would pure animation. In *Lethal Enforcers* the player uses "The Justifier," a piece of hardware that looks like an oversize handgun. The player uses the gun to participate in the action, killing characters on the screen, complete with splattering blood. *Night Trap* provides greater realism, with interactive video using human actors and actresses. In that game the player participates as a character trying to prevent a group of hooded men from doing violence to a group of sorority women.

The relationship between video game violence and aggressive behavior is not as well established as that between television violence and aggression. It may be postulated that aggression is more likely to follow from the player's direct involvement in the violence of a video game than from the passive observation of televised violence. That conclusion has, however, not been demonstrated. The question has simply received little attention, compared to the effort devoted to the study of the effects of television. Furthermore, what studies have been done were done in a different era. A study that compares the effects of playing *Pac-Man* to the effects of playing *Missile Command*[36] says little with regard to the effects of playing games in virtual reality. As the simulated participation in violence becomes more realistic, whatever effects exist would seem likely to grow, but once again, that hypothesis has not been proven.

Even without proof of the effects, Congress has begun to consider action. In December of 1993 Senator Lieberman and Senator Herb Kohl convened a joint hearing of the Subcommittee on Juvenile Justice of the Senate Judiciary Committee and the Subcommittee on Regulation and Government Information of the Senate Committee on Government Affairs. The hearing was to consider a bill to establish a National Independent Council for Entertainment in Video Devices, an independent agency of the federal government that would oversee the development of voluntary standards to warn parents of the content of video games. The bill would also have provided an exemption from the antitrust laws to allow the industry to develop such standards. The day of the hearings, the industry, in an effort to restrict regulation to self-regulation, announced its intent to create its own rating and warning system. Once again, various segments of the industry raised First Amendment concerns, concerns shared by several members of the subcommittees.

The First Amendment concerns are more complex than they would be in the broadcast arena. Whatever additional powers Congress may gain from the fact that the airways are owned by the public and subject to congressional and administrative regulation are lacking in the video games arena, as they are with motion pictures and videotape rentals.

The lessons the entertainment industry have learned from the long history of congressional inquiry into media violence have not been those that might have been desired. Rather than taking the criticism to heart, most of the media refuses to believe that it plays a role in societal violence. As George Vradenberg, executive vice president of Fox, stated in a 1995 interview on the Public Broadcasting System program *Frontline:* "I think most in the television business do not accept the view that what we put on the television, what is on over the air, is contributing in any significant measure to violence in society."[37]

What it appears has been learned is that Congress will be assuaged by media promises to behave in the future, or at least to provide notice when it does not behave. Congressional action on television violence appears to have been forestalled by a June 1993 pledge on the part of the four broadcast networks to provide warnings when their prime-time programming contains violence. That the success of television in avoiding any mandate was not missed by the video game industry is shown by its interposition of a promise of voluntary labelling on games involving violence. Given the First Amendment concerns of members of Congress, such promises seem to be sufficient to remove the issue from the front burner and to at least delay, if not kill, any legal constraints.

Using Federal Regulatory Power over Broadcast Media

The National Foundation for the Improvement of Television has suggested another possible course of federal action to control one aspect of media violence. The foundation's concern is the quality of television in the United States and it has focused on that medium in its approach to the issue of media violence. Since the broadcast media are subject to federal regulation, the foundation has recognized the possibility of addressing the problem through action before the Federal Communications Commission. To that end, they filed, in March 1993, a *Petition for Rule Making* before the FCC.[38]

The petition proposes a rule denying or withdrawing licenses from television stations and cable operators that have a policy or practice of transmitting excessive dramatized violence between the hours of 6 A.M. and 10 P.M. Excessive violence is defined as an amount inappropriate for minors or exceeding guidelines the FCC would establish under the proposed rule. Violence is also defined as the use or threat of physical force against another and such violence becomes excessive when it portrays homicide, rape, various forms of aggravated assault, or other violent acts that the average person would consider excessive or inappropriate for minors. The proposed rule would also require a violence rating system and warnings of violent content at the beginning of any program with excessively violent content broadcast between 6 A.M. and 10 P.M. Such warning would be repeated at the end of each commercial break.

This is not the first time the Foundation to Improve Television has sought FCC action to control violence in television. The Foundation filed a *Petition for Rulemaking* in 1969 directed toward similar ends.[39] That earlier petition also occurred during a time of increasing concern over television violence, as well as sexually oriented programming. From 1972 to 1974 the volume of complaints over violent or sexually oriented material increased from near 2,000 to more than 25,000. There were petitions filed to deny renewal of broadcast licenses,[40] and in addition to the Foundation to Improve Television's petition for rulemaking, a similar petition from another group.[41] Finally, in 1974, Congress directed the Commission to take "specific positive action . . . to protect children from excessive programming of violence and obscenity."[42] The FCC response was to issue its 1975 *Report on the Broadcast of Violent, Indecent, and Obscene Material*.[43] The Report recognized the need for governmental action concerning obscene and indecent material, noting its recent action against the Pacifica Foundation for the broadcast of indecent material. However, with regard to violent material or non-indecent sexually oriented material and what was appropriate for children, the Commission deferred to the broadcast industry to regulate itself.

The Commission expressed concern that attempts to regulate in this area would be practically difficult to administer and would raise serious statutory and constitutional issues. The statutory concerns centered on the anti censorship provision of the Communications Act, which forbids censorship by the FCC.[44] The Commission was unsure of any regulatory authority over non-indecent sexual depictions in broadcasts. While not directly addressing the authority to regulate violent material, the same concerns would carry over. This is seen in the fact that the only direct authority the Commission found to override the anticensorship provisions was a statutory prohibition and direction to the Commission to enforce a ban on the broadcast of obscene, indecent, or profane language.[45] With regard to constitutional concerns, the Commission noted that attempts to limit the broadcast of non-indecent sexual material or violent material would raise First Amendment problems.

Prior to the report, FCC Chairman Richard Wiley did initiate discussions with executives of the three major television networks. He suggested a commitment to reduce the level and intensity of violent and sexually oriented material, that material not suitable for young children be scheduled after 9 P.M., and that such programs be accompanied by warnings. He also raised the possibility of a rating system. In response, the networks each developed guidelines to govern programming. The National Association of Broadcasters also adopted an amendment to the NAB Television Code similar to the guidelines adopted by the three networks. The guidelines included a family-viewing period in the early evening and advisories or warnings to accompany material in that period that might be unsuitable for young persons and to accompany material broadcast later in the evening that would be disturbing to significant portions of the audience.

The Commission decided that the actions taken by the industry obviated the need for governmental regulation and were a major accomplishment in self-regulation by the industry. Given the statutory and constitutional concerns, the Commission deferred to industry. Rather than enforceable limits, the result was a system of voluntary guidelines.

Even that result was short lived. Shortly after its adoption by the networks and the NAB, a group of television writers and production companies challenged the family-viewing plan in federal court. The court declared the plan unconstitutional in *Writers Guild of America v. Federal Communications Commission.*[46] The court treated the plan as an agreement between the three networks, the National Association of Broadcasters, and the FCC. Moreover, it appeared to the court that the Commission had pressured the networks and the NAB into adopting the policy. Chairman Wiley's discussions were attributed to the Commission, and the adoption of the policy by the networks and NAB, under Commission pressure, was held to be a violation of the First

Amendment. The court would have allowed truly voluntary plans on the part of broadcasters, but the plans adopted had not been voluntary.[47]

The resurgence of concern over media violence shows that the public is not satisfied with any remaining, voluntary industry efforts at self-regulation. At least one recent member of the Federal Communications Commission did seem willing to take action against the rising tide of violence. In 1993, then Chair James Quello suggested that the FCC's approach to the broadcast of indecent material be carried over to violent material.[48] Current Chair Reed Hundt's position is less clear. In his September, 1993, confirmation hearings he did not offer any specifics on how the FCC would deal with television violence.[49] Since then, he has expressed concern over violence on television and has said that he will enforce aggressively any federal law dealing with such depictions.[50] On the other hand, he has said that although there is a need for the industry to recognize the seriousness of the problem, he does not want to see the FCC become the "Federal Censorship Committee."[51] Since the Foundation to Improve Television's petition is still pending before the FCC, Hundt and the other commissioners will have the opportunity to make their views officially known.

State Attempts to Limit Distribution of Violent Material

Several states have also attempted to limit access to materials depicting violence.[52] Those states have limited their attempts to controlling access by minors. Such limitations to minors may be based on a political or philosophical unwillingness to censor materials made available to the adult population, but they may also be based on a belief that a general ban on violent material would be unconstitutional. Such a concern, given the court's treatment even of statutes addressing distribution to minors, would seem reasonable.

Missouri is among the states to impose a ban on distribution to minors. Under the Missouri statute, videos are to be kept in a separate area and are not to be rented or sold to persons under seventeen, if, when taken as a whole and employing contemporary community standards, the video "has a tendency to cater or appeal to morbid interest in violence for persons under the age of seventeen" and "depicts violence in a way which is patently offensive to the average person applying contemporary adult community standards with respect to what is suitable for persons under the age of seventeen." The material must also, taken as a whole, lack "serious literary, artistic, political, or scientific value for persons under the age of seventeen."[53]

The Missouri approach was to mirror the United States Supreme Court's

Miller v. California[54] test for sexual obscenity substituting violence for sex and inserting, where called for, the phrase "under the age of seventeen." Thus, for example, the *Miller* test's requirement that material appeal to the prurient interest became a requirement that the material "appeal to morbid interest in violence for persons under the age of seventeen."[55]

Tennessee and Colorado also adopted statutes restricting the dissemination of violent material to minors. The Tennessee statute includes excessively violent material in with sexually explicit material in banning the dissemination of either to minors. The statute made it unlawful knowingly to sell, rent, exhibit, or make available to a minor any depictions, including videos, films, photos, drawings, etc., of "a person or portion of the human body, which depicts nudity, sexual conduct, excess violence, or sado-masochistic abuse, and which is harmful to minors." Another section of the same statute applied similar restrictions to books and other printed matter and sound recordings containing "explicit and detailed verbal descriptions or narrative accounts of sexual excitement, sexual conduct, excess violence, or sado-masochistic abuse, and which is harmful to minors."[56] Also unlawful was knowingly exhibiting, for monetary purposes, or selling an admission ticket to a minor for the exhibition of a motion picture depicting such material. It was a defense that the minor was accompanied by or had the written permission of parent or guardian.

The Colorado statute,[57] like Missouri's, employed a scheme similar to that of *Miller v. California.* One significant difference between the Missouri and Colorado statutes was that Colorado limited its ban to depictions or descriptions of actual violence resulting in death or great bodily injury. That difference has greatly limited the scope of the statute and probably explains why it is the only one of the three not to have been challenged. Both Missouri and Tennessee's statutes have been declared unconstitutional as violative of the First Amendment. Those decisions will be discussed in Chapter 3, and it is, of course, the thesis of this book that the cases were wrongly decided.

The Inefficacy of Media Self-Regulation and the Recurring Nature of the Debate

The debate over media violence has not been quite as much at the forefront over the past year as it was in prior years. It is not over, however, and is likely soon to reach its earlier levels. The 1994–95 television season did see renewed controversy focused on the children's show *Mighty Morphin Power Rangers.* Again, the reaction in the United States was limited to public debate, led this time by teachers of young children, and the banning of Power Ranger products from some schools. Reactions in other countries were stronger.[58] The Ontario branch of the Canadian Broadcast Standards Council found that the show exceeded standards for violence and that it encouraged children to imitate that violence. The findings led a cable channel to withdraw the program. The show was also banned in New Zealand, over the same concerns. Norway also took the show off the air, but later reinstated it after reconsidering the basis for that decision, the beating death of one child by others, finding no tie between the death and the program.

The rekindling of the debate over media violence is to be expected. The recent debates over the acceptability of violence in television have their precursors in other media. The debate over violence in those media also showed a cycle of public outcry, promises of industry self-regulation, the failure of such regulation, and renewed calls for governmental regulation. That cycle indicates that current promises are also likely to be forgotten, or that at least there will be a lack of agreement as to what was entailed by the promises. Concern over the Power Rangers is the initial chapter in the renewed debate.

The history of crime and horror magazines and comic books provides an illustrative example. In the late 1800s, there was a growth in the existence of magazines devoted to tales of crime and bloodshed. Public concern grew over the effects such publications might have on those who read the material. That concern went beyond suggestions of media self-regulation and led to legal restrictions on violent material.

Statutes addressing the distribution of stories of crime and bloodshed began to appear in 1884. A New York statute, passed that year, barred the distribution of books, pamphlets, magazines, and newspapers devoted to and principally consisting of "criminal news, police reports or accounts of criminal deeds or pictures and stories of deeds of bloodshed, lust or crime."[59] While the 1884 statute was aimed at the protection of minors from such material, it was amended in 1887 to ban the dissemination of such material to anyone.[60] The following year, 1885, saw nine more states pass similar legislation. Six of the states banned only distribution to minors. The remaining three states addressed publication or distribution to adults as well as minors. By 1913 twenty-four states had adopted legislation signifying a concern over such publications.

The statutes survived for quite some time. The New York statute reached the United States Supreme Court in the 1947 term. In *Winters v. New York*,[61] a conviction under that statute was reversed on vagueness grounds. The Court did not, however, preclude the possibility of a state barring the distribution of violent publications under a sufficiently precise statute. Despite the possibility the Court held out that a properly detailed statute could survive challenge, most states did not rise to the challenge to revise their statutes. Without statutory restrictions, the publishers were left to self-regulation and the efficacy of that approach proved to be lacking.

In the middle years of the current century the issue of magazines devoted to violence again came to the front. The years between 1945 and 1954 also saw an increase in the number of crime and horror comics, featuring brutality, violence, and sadism, usually with sexually suggestive illustrations. By mid-1954 there were more than 30 million copies of crime or horror comics printed each month.[62] This growth in crime and horror comics led to renewed legislation regulating such comics, or comics in general, in several states and municipalities. These attempts, too, were regularly found to be unconstitutional, either because of vagueness concerns or over problems with statutory exceptions.

While states and municipalities at least attempted to take action against the growth of crime and horror comics, the federal response was more restrained. Crime and horror comics did attract the attention of Congress. When Senator Estes Kefauver's committee looked into the effects of comic books on youth, the tenor of the descriptions contained in its report, *Comic Books and Juvenile Delinquency*, would seem to have indicated a willingness to take some action against such materials. However, the subcommittee decided not to recommend the regulation of comic books but instead to rely on industry self-regulation.

This willingness to rely on voluntary standards was despite the fact that earlier attempts at self-regulation, by the Association of Comic Magazine Publishers in the late 1940s, had failed. However, once the Senate determined to investigate the area, the comic book publishers promised renewed action to limit violent content. The industry adopted the Comics Code and provided for the printing of a seal indicating approval by the Comics Code Authority on comics meeting code requirements.

The subcommittee, mollified by the industry's assertions that it would improve its comics, determined that it would continue to rely on self-regulation. Any resort to governmental censorship was rejected as counter to the concept of a free press. Industry and public pressure, on the other hand were seen to raise no freedom of the press problems and had the approval of the subcommittee. Industry self-regulation did have the desired effect, at least in the short to intermediate term. Wholesalers refused to distribute comics not having the seal of the Comics Code Authority, and many publishers of crime and horror comics simply went out of business.[63]

The long-term efficacy of self-regulation is more questionable. After about twenty years of limitation, violence began to make a comeback. Some publishers chose not to comply with the code and avoided distribution problems by leaving the wholesaler out of the scheme and shipping directly to comic book specialty stores. Even some of the major publishers in the field began to produce non-code compliant comics in addition to their code-approved wares.

Observers of the comic book industry contend that the level of crime, horror, and violence in present-day comics is as bad as it was when the Senate opted for industry self-regulation. Modern comic heroes are not content to arrest criminals but instead make a practice of breaking their backs or hitting them in the face with a nail-studded board.[64] The *New York Times Magazine*, *Larry King Live*, and *The Today Show* have all noted the resurgence of comic book violence.[65] The complaints may not have the volume of those in the 1950s, but that may not be the result of any lessening in the level of violence. Rather, the availability of violent images in so many other media, media that may even have more impact on children than comics do, may simply make comic book violence seem not so bad.

The development of the Comics Code was similar to the development of rules for industry self-regulation of motion-picture production.[66] As with comic books, self-regulation in film also lost efficacy. Film producers found greater profits in refusing to abide by the industry's rules. In 1968, the film industry abandoned its self-imposed limitations and adopted, in their stead, a rating system.[67] While the levels of sex and violence would not decrease, and indeed would increase, potential audiences, and the parents of potential viewers, would at least be forewarned.

The abandonment of self-regulation in the motion picture industry may not be of quite the same concern as the demise of the Comics Code. Public perception that comic books are aimed at youth leads to greater concern when that medium depicts graphic violence. Motion pictures are seen as aimed at a variety of audiences, and warnings and age limitations on admission policed by theater operators may seem adequate. A perceived lack of policing in the rental of video tapes with violent content and the accessibility of minors to such tapes appears to be behind the state attempts to limit such accessibility.

The recent public outcry over television violence is also not the first such clamor. When the issue arose in the early 1970s, the Federal Communications Commission deferred to the broadcast industry to regulate itself. While the FCC's unwillingness to take action was motivated by statutory and constitutional concerns over its authority to do so, the decision to defer may also have been based on the industry's willingness to regulate itself. FCC Chairman Wiley's discussions did result in an agreement among executives of the three major television networks and the NAB to reduce the level and intensity of violent material. While the agreement was short-lived, due to the decision in *Writers Guild of America v. Federal Communications Commission*,[68] at least the industry was made aware of the seriousness of public and governmental concern. However, whatever self-regulation remained after the court's decision has not been sufficient to reduce violence to levels acceptable to the public or to Congress.

In the current debate, congressional action appears to have been, once again, at least postponed by yet another promise of industry self-regulation. Representatives of the three major television broadcast networks met in 1992 to consider the adoption of guidelines. The summer of 1993 saw a second meeting. The networks did agree to joint standards to limit glamorized or gratuitous violence and to accompany violent programming with content warnings. The Fox Network also agreed to the standards and cable networks announced that they would include warnings.[69]

The weakness of this attempt at voluntary self-regulation is in the fact that each network determines for itself what violence is glamorized or gratuitous or excessive. The networks do not see their offerings as excessively or inappropriately violent. The June 1993 promises of warnings to accompany violent shows were not applied to any network series in the 1993 television season, although the warnings did accompany some television movies. In response to complaints from then Surgeon General Joycelyn Elders that the networks had not done what they promised, the networks all claimed that none of their series were violent. The Foundation to Improve Television expressed both disagreement and disappointment, and suggested that it was economic concerns over lost advertising revenue that led the networks to avoid warnings.[70]

When principles run up against economics, it is questionable whether the guidelines will have any effect. Senator Paul Simon expressed concern that a reduction in violence in the fall of 1993 would be short-lived. As he noted: "If the [ratings] show a violent program doing well, the herd will follow."[71] If that occurs, he threatens renewed efforts at legislation. Attorney General Janet Reno has also called for legislation. Any inclination she may have had toward relying on industry self-regulation appears to have been weakened by a recognition of the number of past unkept promises of media to impose limits on violence.[72]

Here too, self-regulation has not worked, and unless the threat of legislation is seen as real, there is little reason to think that it will work in anything other than the short term. It is possible that the threat will seem credible. Attention may not turn away from televised violence unless, as happened with comic books, a new medium is seen as a greater threat. Video games and online information services could serve that role, but it is unlikely that television's influence will wane in the foreseeable future, and public pressure is likely to remain high. Indeed, the issue has returned to the forefront rather quickly. A bill introduced in 1995 calls for a television rating code, an expanded version of the V-chip technology, and a prohibition on violent television programming between 6 A.M. and 10 P.M.[73] The bill, introduced by Senator Kent Conrad, drew the support of various groups, including the National PTA, the National Association of Elementary School Principals, the National Association of Secondary School Principals, and the American Medical Association.

While industry concerns over attracting audiences that want to view violent material and the revenues that such audiences may attract will lead the media to continue to take actions that will keep the dispute alive, the voices of those who demand a reduction in violence also will not fade. Parental, professional, and governmental concerns in this area are both strong and legitimate. The concerns are probably even more legitimate than concerns over sexual material. It is reasonable to argue that parents might be adequate to control the exposure of their children to sexually oriented material. If parents find certain television programming objectional, they may turn off the television. Parents may also be able to inculcate sufficiently strong religious or ethical values that any potential negative effect from such material may be avoided. While children certainly have to contend with peer pressure, the decision to engage in sexual activities, absent actual force against the child, is still that of each child.

There is a parallel to violent material. Parents may control their children's access to such material by monitoring the television they watch and the videos they rent. Parents may also establish in their children sufficiently strong values that media violence is less likely to make their children violent. While there may also be peer pressure to participate in violent acts, again the decision is the child's.

There is, however, an important difference between peer pressure to participate in either sex or violence and the possibility of becoming a victim of violence. With sexually oriented material the parent's concern is over whether the material might lead his or her child to engage in behavior that is contrary to the parent's values or that may cause psychological, or even physical, damage to the child. Control over the child's exposure to the material or having provided a strong base of values may lessen those concerns. The concern over the effects of violent material is not only a concern over the psychological impact of the material on one's own child. Rather, the concern is over the effect on other parents' children. If those children are exposed to material that leads them to become violent, that violence is not done solely to themselves. No amount of control of one's own child's television exposure insulates that child from the violence done by others whose access was uncontrolled. It is a lack of trust in other parents that leads to calls for governmental action.

If, in fact, televised or other media depictions of violence cause aggression in viewers, parents will be unable to protect their children from those effects, because the effects work not through their own children but through others. The only effective control would be one that limits the access of all viewers, or at least of all children, to media violence. It is primarily that belief that violent depictions cause violence that leads to calls for government control. The next chapter will examine the evidence for such a cause-and-effect relationship.

2 The Social Science Debate on the Causative Effect of Media Violence

It is clear that much of the social concern over media violence, and in particular television violence, is due to a belief that such depictions cause real violence. It is important to understand the variety of causation under consideration. Obviously, to claim that certain depictions cause violence is not to claim that every person exposed to such material commits acts of violence nor that only such people commit such acts. The issue is, instead, one of probability and correlation. The question is whether a population exposed to depictions of violence is more violent than a population without such exposure.[1] There are several important studies and reports that attempt to answer that question.

In 1969, the National Commission on the Causes and Prevention of Violence issued a report claiming to have found a link between television violence and violent behavior in viewers. The staff report to the commission was clear in its conclusions that mass-media portrayal of violence has an effect on society. Among short-term effects, the report concluded that

> [e]xposure to mass medial portrayals of violence stimulates violent behavior when—(a) Subjects are either calm or anxious prior to exposure, but more so when they are frustrated, insulted, or otherwise angered. (b) Aggressive or violent cues are present (e.g., weapons of violence). (c) Subjects are exposed either to justified or unjustified violence, but more so when justified violence is portrayed.[2]

The Report also found the following statements on long-term effects to be consistent with the research findings and the most informed thinking in social science:

> Exposure to mass media portrayals of violence over a long period of time socializes audiences into the norms, attitudes, and values for violence contained in those portrayals . . . [as among other factors t]he primacy of the part played by violence in media presentations increases.

Persons who have been effectively socialized by mass media portrayals of violence will under a broad set of precipitating conditions, behave in accordance with the norms, attitudes, and values for violence contained in medial presentations. Persons who have been effectively socialized into the norms for violence in the television world of violence would behave in the following manner: . . . They would probably resolve conflict by the use of violence[,] use violence as a means to obtain desired ends[,] use a weapon when engaging in violence[, and i]f they were policemen, they would be likely to meet violence with violence, often escalating its level.[3]

Later studies and reports supported that view, but with varying degrees of strength. In 1972 the Surgeon General's report found "a modest association" between television violence and aggression in some children, but suggested that the effect was small, when compared to other possible causes.[4] On the other hand, in 1982, the National Institute of Mental Health examined the research and concluded:

The consensus among most of the research community is that violence on television does lead to aggressive behavior by children and teenagers who watch the programs. This conclusion is based on laboratory experiments and on field studies. Not all children become aggressive, of course, but the correlations between violence and aggression are positive. In magnitude, television violence is as strongly correlated with aggressive behavior as any other behavioral variable that has been measured.[5]

More recently there has been some criticism of the studies on which the earlier findings of causation were based. The critics include not only media executives but scientists who question the methodology of those studies. Some light may be thrown on the issue through an examination of the sorts of studies involved.

Laboratory Studies

Much of the early work on the effect of televised violence consisted of experiments in the controlled environment of the laboratory. The work of Professor Albert Bandura and his associates has become the classic study.[6] Bandura's study involved nursery school children who were individually exposed to aggressive behavior in various contexts. For one group, an adult was observed playing with various toys, including a five-foot inflatable Bobo doll. The adult model punched the doll, hit it in the head with a mallet, tossed it in the air, kicked it around the room, and sat on it, while punching it in the nose repeat-edly. A second group was shown a film of an adult acting toward a Bobo doll in the same manner. A third group viewed similar action in a film designed to resemble a cartoon but actually involving a cartoon-like stage setting and a human actor costumed to look like a cartoon figure.

After observing the model or one of the films, each child was taken to another room containing attractive toys. The child was frustrated by being told that those toys were reserved for other children but that he or she could play with the toys in the next room. Those toys included nonaggressive toys, such as crayons and plastic farm animals, and aggressive toys, including a three-foot Bobo doll and a mallet. The children were observed playing with the toys and their total aggression levels were rated, with subratings for various forms of aggression. The levels of aggression demonstrated by all three groups were significantly higher than the level of aggression for a control group not ex-posed to the films or real-life model, and the aggression was elevated for both boys and girls. The scientists concluded that exposure to filmed aggression in-creases aggression, with those exposed to the films almost twice as aggressive as the control group. Further, they found no evidence that this learned ag-gression is limited to children who are naturally more aggressive than other children or who otherwise deviate from the behavioral norm.

A second group of studies was undertaken by Professor Leonard Berkowitz and his colleagues. One such study demonstrated the importance of the mean-ing found in, or placed on, an observed event as a factor in its causing later aggression in viewers.[7] Several groups of male university students were shown one of three films. Two groups saw a segment of the film *Champion* in which the actor Kirk Douglas is beaten badly in the boxing ring. One of those two groups was told that the film was of two professional athletes not angry at each other but fighting for a purse. The other was told that Douglas's opponent wanted to injure him because Douglas had insulted him. Two other groups saw a highlight film, of the same length, of a football game in which the Baltimore Colts beat the Minnesota Vikings. Again, with one group the professionalism of the athletes was stressed, while the other was told that the Colts wanted to hurt the Vikings because of insulting comments. The last group saw an ex-citing film of a track race, again of a similar length.[8]

Prior to viewing any of the films, each subject was paired with a confeder-ate of the experimenter. Each subject was asked to think of four ways to solve a problem. The proposed solutions were read to the confederate and the con-federate responded by administering a series of one to five electric shocks to the subject. The number of shocks was said to be a rating of the idea but was

in fact prearranged, so that all subjects would have received the same number of shocks. Prior to watching the film, the subjects would have been at least
somewhat angry with their partners. After the film, the roles were reversed.
The confederate offered prearranged solutions to a problem, and the subject
rated the ideas with one to five shocks. The subjects' responses were recorded
both as to number of shocks administered and duration of the shocks.

In the first response to a proposed solution, significantly more shocks were
administered by those who had watched the boxing or football film and had
been told that the winner wanted to injure his or its opponent than by those
who had seen the same film but with a stress on professionalism. For second and third responses, the "aggressive meaning" group administered more
shocks but not at a level of statistical significance. There was also a significant
difference in the total duration of the shocks administered, with the "aggressive meaning" group delivering longer shocks.

In another of Berkowitz's studies, he again used the track film and the segment from *Champion*.[9] This time the partner, again a confederate of the experimenter, was introduced as either Kirk or Bob. The subjects were then
either angered, by receiving seven shocks, or not angered, by receiving one
shock. They were then shown one of the films, with a justification offered
for the aggression in the boxing film. When the subjects were then given the
opportunity to shock their partners, the number of shocks administered was
noted. Those who were angered administered significantly more shocks than
those not angered, whichever film they saw. There were no significant differences among those who were not angered. Most interestingly, the difference
between those who were angered and saw the boxing film and those who were
angered and saw the track film was significant only when the partner had been
introduced as Kirk. The experimenters concluded that observing aggression
does not necessarily lead to aggression against everyone but instead leads to
aggression against those who are identified with the observed victim.

The laboratory studies have had their critics.[10] Perhaps the best criticism is
over whether or not the results in the artificial setting of the laboratory carry
over to the real world. The imitative behavior involving the Bobo doll took
place in a situation in which the behavior of the model or film seemed to provide permission to play in that fashion or even instruction in how to play with
such a toy. Of course, the same could be said for televised violence. It may
be seen as asserting the propriety of such violent behavior against other persons and as providing instruction on social interaction. Indeed, it is this social
learning that was the focus of such studies. However, other social restraints
and training, as well as introspection on how it would feel to be the object of

violent behavior, may allow for skepticism over whether the effect of watching violence against a toy carries over to the effects of watching violence against another person.

Even in an experiment in which subsequent aggression against a person, rather than a Bobo doll, was measured, there is still room to question the applicability to real life. Any aggression would seem to be a measure of the aggression-inducing effects only in the permission-giving situation of the laboratory. Furthermore, it is argued that most experimental subjects beyond early childhood are likely to recognize that the experimenter will not allow any real harm to the target of the aggression and thus may feel more free to respond in an aggressive manner than the subject would in real life.[11] While that may be true in terms of real harm, the subjects in Berkowitz's studies had been shocked before they shocked their partners. They would seem to have believed that, while not causing significant or permanent injury, they were at least causing pain.

There is also a concern that what is measured in the laboratory experiments is not induced aggression but obedience to, or compliance with, the experimenter.[12] If the subject concludes that there is permission to aggress, the conclusion that the experimenter wishes the subject to aggress may be easily drawn. Any resulting aggression would then speak more to compliance than to aggression, and the applicability to the real world of the conclusion that aggression increased would be questionable. Berkowitz attempted to control for this possibility in some of his work. In the study involving the football and boxing films, he also measured subject awareness of the purpose of the study. While the results from those who were clearly aware of the purpose were discarded in analyzing the main study, a comparison showed that being more suspicious of the real purpose of the study did not affect the validity of the results.[13] Berkowitz and Alioto concluded that their results were not due to any demand effect.

Lastly, it is argued that the conclusion that televised violence causes aggression is, in a sense, too narrow.[14] Subjects who have been excited by any stimulus may turn out to be more reactive in all regards. Television violence would then have been unfairly singled out from among a variety of equally stimulating sources. Further, the increase in willingness to aggress would just be one facet of an increase in all responses. Since aggression was the focus of the study, increased aggression was found, but positive aspects of behavior could also have been increased. Nonetheless, increases in negative behavior were found. The children in the Bandura study had the opportunity to play creatively and nonaggressively but imitated the aggressive behavior. Even if television can be used to teach prosocial behavior, and even if television is but one medium for teaching social behavior, it did appear to lead to imitative aggressive behavior.

Field Studies

Field studies attempt to measure the relationship between television violence and aggressive behavior in experiments involving real-world settings. By examining the effects of television outside of the laboratory, the conclusions they draw are more exportable to the real world; they have greater external validity. On the other hand, since the controls that can be imposed in such settings are not as strong as in the laboratory, there is often room to question the internal validity of the results obtained. Furthermore, even the external validity is often affected by the fact that the settings employed may be somewhat artificial. The possibility of attack on two fronts has led to disagreement over what conclusions can be drawn from these studies.

As an example, Professor Jonathan Freedman,[15] a skeptic on the point of television causing violence, and Professors Lynette Friedrich-Cofer and Aletha Huston,[16] seemingly believers in such an effect, have both examined the same series of field experiments. In similar studies in the United States and Belgium,[17] groups of boys, who were institutionalized because of delinquency or neglect, were shown either violent or nonviolent films for a one-week period. Friedrich-Cofer and Huston analyzed the results:

> In the Belgian study, physical aggression increased significantly . . . in both cottages assigned to violent films, but did not increase in the neutral film cottages. Total aggression, including both physical and verbal aggression, increased primarily in the violent film cottage that was initially more aggressive. In two U.S. studies total aggression was significantly higher in two cottages viewing television violence for 5 days than in cottages viewing neutral films.[18]

Freedman finds in the studies "some evidence to support the causal hypothesis."[19] He concludes his analysis of the experiments:

> It does seem that [one of the experiments] found a consistent increase in aggressiveness for one cottage and a short-term increase on one measure for the other, and [a second study] found a greater increase in aggressiveness after violent films than after nonviolent films. The interpretation of the results of [a third] study depends on which analysis one accepts. At most, there is rather weak evidence for a greater increase in aggres-

siveness following violent films; at worst, there are no main effects, but perhaps a differential increase for low-aggressive boys only.[20]

Even these results may be questioned, Freedman says, because the experiments treated all the subjects as being independent. He finds that assumption flawed, since if a film increased aggression in one boy, an increase in the aggressiveness of others may be in response to the first boy rather than to the film.

Looking to the body of field experiments, Freedman finds the results to be inconsistent with the research as a whole offering "only the slightest encouragement for the causal hypothesis" and even questioning that slight support.[21] Friedrich-Cofer and Huston disagree, finding "a moderately consistent pattern suggesting an effect of television violence on aggression and self-control, particularly for subjects with relatively high baseline levels of aggression."[22] Indeed, in their view, if there is any bias at all, it would be in the underestimation of the effects of television violence, in that the presence of adult experimenters would have had an inhibitory effect.[23]

The disagreement as to the message to be drawn from the results of field experiments should probably be expected. Field experiments lack the controls of the laboratory, so there is room to criticize on that ground. They also may depart to some degree from the real world and use populations that are not representative in situations that are uncommon, for example, juvenile delinquents as a group watching nothing but violent programming. Thus, whatever significant results may be obtained may be argued not to carry over to the real world.

Correlational Studies

Correlational studies do not manipulate variables to determine what effects may result. They are even more real-world in that they examine the demographics of populations in search of relations between demographic variables. The time period of the search may range from an analysis of data gathered at a particular time to an analysis of data gathered over an extended period. A second approach is to gather more detailed survey results from a particular population, again ranging from a single survey to a comparison of survey data gathered over a period of time.

One of the studies of the demographic variety was conducted by Dr. Brandon Centerwall.[24] Centerwall noted a relation between the increase in the availability of television and a ten- to fifteen-year later rise in the homicide rate. He explained the delay by suggesting that homicide is an adult behavior and that the effect of television on children would require a ten- to fifteen-year incubation period. Centerwall's comparisons held true for both the United States and Canada. In both countries the curve representing the increase in televisions in the 1950s was roughly parallel to the curve representing the increasing homicide rate in the late 1960s.

As a control, he also graphed the homicide rate among white South Africans, a country in which television was not available until the mid-1970s. That homicide rate did not show the same increase in the 1960s. Dr. Centerwall predicted that, within ten to fifteen years of the introduction of television, the homicide rate among South African whites would show a similar increase. He reports that the homicide rate has begun to rise in accord with his prediction.

Another, earlier study examined a small Canadian town that, because of its isolation, did not have television until 1973.[25] Groups of first- and second-grade students in that town and in two similar towns that already had television were observed over a two-year period. The two towns to which television was not new did not show any significant behavioral changes in the two years. In the town new to television, however, there was a significant increase in the rates of physical aggression, such as hitting, pushing, and biting other children.

While such demographic studies avoid the artificiality of the laboratory studies and measure real violence or aggression in the real world, something is also lost. Laboratory studies are designed to provide controls on variables other than the variable under examination. In the laboratory an effort is made to assure that the test group and the control group are similar in all respects other than in the viewing of, for example, the Bobo doll film. In the demographic examination of the real world, it is more difficult to establish such controls. Particularly when data is gathered over a lengthy time period, there is a likelihood of uncontrolled variables having an effect. Furthermore, the sheer number of variables that may be present over such a time period increases the likelihood of the same sort of problem. The possibility of such a variable affecting the result lessens the surety with which one can conclude that there is a cause and effect relation, rather than merely correlation.

Centerwall's study presents problems both of unidentified variables and the difficulty of establishing controls. First, the increase in the number of televisions was not the only relevant change in the period under study. The population also changed. While the study controlled for a simple increase in the population by using the homicide rate per hundred thousand people, rather than merely the number of homicides, it did not take into account the change in the composition of the population. The years in which the homicide rate increased were the years in which the baby boom population surge passed through their teens and early twenties, the period of life in which a person is most likely to be violent.[26] It is at least possible, then, that the increase in the homicide rate had nothing to do with the increase in televisions. Indeed, it would not even be a case in which both increases were caused by some third factor; it would be purely a coincidental correlation.

The second problem is in using South Africa as a control population. As Marcia Pally has pointed out,[27] there are substantial differences between South Africa on the one hand and the United States and Canada on the other. South Africa was under much tighter governmental control than either other country in the 1970s or compared to itself in later eras. She also suggests that a siege mentality among white South Africans may have led to less homicide within the group and notes that South Africa did not see the level of recession and unemployment that hit the United States and Canada in the 1970s. Any of these factors would serve as an alternate explanation for the difference in levels of homicide, so South Africa may not serve as a particularly good control. With regard to the study of children as television was introduced to a Canadian town, Pally notes the lack of violence in Canadian television at the time and questions the relevance of the study to the question of television violence inducing real-world aggression.[28]

A second variety of correlational study is exemplified by the survey work of Doctors Lefkowitz, Eron, Walder, and Huesmann.[29] Lefkowitz, et al., began their study in 1955 by examining all the children in the third grade in Columbia County, New York. They gathered data on each child from the child's parents and classmates and the child himself or herself. Each child was given an aggressiveness rating based on classmate response as to which children are most likely to disobey the teacher, start fights, push or shove others, take things from other children, etc. Interviews with parents were used to gather data for each child as to television viewing habits. Programs watched were rated for their violent content, and each child received a score based on his or her viewing of violence. The parent interviews also provided data on some forty other variables regarding personality, intelligence, social status and family situation, factors which had to be controlled for in the study. Follow-up surveys were conducted when the third graders reached the eighth grade and again after graduation from high school. Of 875 children in the initial sample, 460 responded to the post-high-school survey.

When the data were compared for aggression at third and thirteenth grades and watching of television violence at those same grades, several statistically significant correlations were found. The strongest correlation was between aggressiveness at the two ages. For both boys and girls, those who were aggressive at third grade were more likely to be aggressive in the thirteenth grade. For the boys, two additional statistically significant correlations were noted. Watching violent television in the third grade was correlated to aggressiveness in the third grade and even more strongly correlated to aggressiveness in the thirteenth grade.

Again, correlation is not causation and it might be suggested that any causation that might explain the correlation could operate in the opposite direction. That is, it might be suggested that those who are prone to aggressiveness chose to watch violent programs as an alternative to the hypothesis that the violent programming causes aggressiveness. Seemingly in response to such a possible criticism, the study compared the two possibilities. As noted, there was a strong correlation between watching violent television in third grade and being aggressive in thirteenth grade. There was no correlation found between aggressiveness in third grade and watching violent television in thirteenth grade. The study concluded that a preference for violent television in the third grade was causally related to aggressiveness ten years later.[30]

Despite the attempts to determine the direction of causation, there may still be room for the skeptic to question the claimed result. While certainly better controlled than a comparison of the growth of the number of televisions and the later homicide rate, it is always possible to question the adequacy of controls. Furthermore, the system of assigning scores for viewing violence may be disputed. In particular, in the Lefkowitz, et al., study, the grouping of the violence in *Gunsmoke* or the *Man from U.N.C.L.E.* with the slapstick of the *Three Stooges* or the comedy of *Get Smart* may be overly broad.[31] Additionally, the general categories of cartoons and soap opera were included in the nonviolent category, despite the fact that cartoons have long been criticized for their violent content.

Despite the criticism suggested, the correlational studies do seem solidly to establish a correlation between television violence and aggressive behavior. This relation is recognized even by a causal skeptic such as Freedman.[32] The skeptic still can argue a lack of causation either by asserting that the causal theorists have the relationship backward or that both aggression and a taste for violent television are co-effects of a third variable. Causal theorists have to admit that it is impossible to rule out all possible third variables, but still argue that the evidence is strong that television violence causes aggression.[33]

Meta-Analysis

One criticism of the scientific data generally is that many of the studies are of limited significance or that while they demonstrate a relationship between violent viewing and aggression, the size of any effect is minor. Another criticism is that the conclusion that there is a causal relation, or even that a correlation exists, is based on only a subset of the studies done. There is a concern that studies that do not establish such a link go unpublished. If such work goes unpublished, it could be due to a bias on the part of journal editors, but it may only be the result of the conclusions that can be drawn from statistical studies. The failure to establish a statistically significant correlation does not establish that the variables are not related. While a study that did establish such a lack of correlation would be of interest, one that simply fails to support any hypothesis may be less likely to be published.

It is not true, however, that all work that fails to find a statistically significant correlation between media violence and real world violence goes unreported. Professors Stanley Milgram and R. Lance Shotland published a book-length work on a series of experiments that did not find such a relationship.[34] The investigators arranged with the CBS network and the producers of *Medical Center* to film several special versions of that program. In the episodes a character in need of money and angry at a physician leading a charity drive broke into a collection box of the charity. Differing versions showed the character either punished, unpunished, or thinking better of breaking into the box and making a donation instead. The versions, and a control episode, were seen by groups solicited as test audiences and promised a gift. When the individual members of the audience later reported back to pick up their gifts, they were frustrated by a sign, in an empty office, indicating that all the gifts had been distributed. There was also a charity donation box in the office, with money showing. The individuals were observed and it was noted whether they broke into the box and took the money, tried to do so, took only a dollar not completely contained in the box or stole another object. No significant differences in this antisocial behavior were found between the four groups. The experiment was repeated in various other formats, and still no significant results were found. Such an experiment not finding a correlation may be as subject to criticism as those finding a correlation,[35] but they are not always unreported.

An approach to addressing the problems of significance and unreported studies may be found in meta-analysis. Meta-analysis is a quantitative review of the studies contained in the scholarly literature, providing an objective synthesis of the research. The method requires an examination of all the available studies, rather than basing its conclusions on certain selected studies. Such an examination provides better evidence as to the size of the effect of any of the variables studied and allows for comparisons of results based on the methods employed in the subject studies. A meta-analysis may also provide for greater certitude in the conclusions drawn. While one may still question the results of a single study, even when the results are statistically significant, an analysis that shows such a result consistently, from study to study and from method to method, would seem more difficult to question.

A 1990 meta-analysis by Professors George Comstock and Haejung Paik examined almost 200 methodologically sound studies on the relationship between violent television programming and aggressive behavior.[36] The study included both published studies and unpublished work, such as dissertations, in an attempt to include all the available data. Their statistical analysis of that large body of data purported to eliminate the likelihood of publication bias. Based on the meta-analysis, the authors concluded that the data gathered in all the studies of the subject shows that television violence increases aggressive behavior. A later and larger sample meta-analysis, by the same researchers, produced similar results.[37]

Even a meta-analysis may, of course, have its critics. Others have examined the studies analyzed by Comstock and Paik and have questioned the relevance of the conclusions drawn.[38] The criticism has not been over the analysis itself, but has concerned the effect sizes in the studies examined. Even if the relationship between viewing television violence and aggressive behavior is statistically significant, and the meta-analysis results were statistically highly significant, if the contribution of television to aggression is minor, and aggressive behavior is largely due to other causes, the effect of television may be seen as not worth addressing.

A response to the criticism that a small effect makes the data less relevant may be offered in looking at levels of aggressiveness of the individuals composing our society. As with other human characteristics, the results would presumably be a bell-shaped curve centered on the mean aggressiveness score stretching out to tails of the least and most aggressive. If some high level of aggressiveness is taken as the point at which a person may be homicidal, only those in the tail past that point would constitute that danger. If the effect of television is to push the mean toward the more aggressive end of the scale, even by only a relatively small amount, a portion of the bell shaped distribution will be pushed beyond the point at which an individual becomes homicidal. Even if televised violence causes only a small increase in aggressiveness, it could still result in an increased homicide rate.

This argument has also been criticized.[39] The approach treats all forms of aggressiveness as commensurate and relies on that presumption when it is suggested that a small increase may push a portion of the curve into the homicidal range. The counterargument is that there is a difference between homicide and other forms of aggression that is not just quantitative but is instead qualitative. If the difference is qualitative, a small effect will not push individuals into a "homicidal tail" of the curve, because there is a break in the distribution, rather than the continuum presumed.

The criticism may, of course, itself be criticized. The critical argument is offered by, and read by, individuals likely to be so far removed from the "homicidal tail" that their own levels of aggressiveness and the aggressiveness of the murderer seem to differ qualitatively. Those whose aggressiveness is already close to the level required for homicide may not see such a bright distinction between their own aggressiveness and that of one who commits homicide, and it is such people who, it is suggested, would be pushed into the homicide portion of the curve by even a small effect size. The difference could well be quantitative, while seeming to be qualitative to the scientist or intellectual.

Cause and Effect

While the combination of results from the various forms of study seem to provide solid evidence for a causal relationship, there are those who would question the existence of such a causal effect in television. Television executives deny any such effect. Even those who do assert such an effect are only willing to conclude that television is *a* cause of violence in society. The questions over effect size indicate that there is more to the issue than television alone. Even throwing in films and video games will not account for all societal violence, but again that is not the claim of those who would impose some control. In the view of those who would regulate, even the effect size that has been established is cause for concern.

What is interesting is the fact that the television executive can argue that there is no causal effect and not seem disingenuous. It is true that all the psychological evidence can establish is a correlation between viewing televised violence and aggressiveness, and correlation is not the same as causation.[40] The two correlated behaviors may both be caused by a third behavior or experience, or the correlation may be coincidental, but this is a possibility made less likely as more evidence is gathered and the statistical significance of the results becomes greater.

This difference between correlation and causation is of interest in areas other than social science and psychology. As the philosopher David Hume pointed out, we can never experience cause and effect. When we look for cause and effect, we instead experience constant conjunction. Even in as common an experience as striking a match on a dry, abrasive surface and observing that each time the match lights, all we have really observed is that, when the first event occurs, the second also occurs. Even despite this inability to experience directly the cause-and-effect relation, we nonetheless seem comfortable in asserting such a relation based on constant, or even almost-constant, conjunction in this sort of case.

The evidence gathered in psychological studies may leave us less comfortable in jumping from correlation to causation. One factor in this reluctance is the fact that the conjunction present in psychology falls far short of constancy. That, however, cannot be the major factor. In the case of cigarettes and lung cancer, there is also a lack of constancy in the conjunction. Yet, the television executive who denies the aggression-causing effect of televised violence does not seem as disingenuous as the tobacco company executive who claims that there is no evidence that cigarettes cause lung cancer. Further, this difference does not seem explainable simply in terms of effect size. Lung cancer may be more likely to follow a life of smoking than homicide is to follow a childhood of viewing televised violence, but all that can be asserted of either cigarettes or television violence is that it is *a* cause. With cigarettes other environmental factors and genetics play a role, and with televised violence it is also clear that environmental factors, such as the child's upbringing, play a strong role.

The real difference between the ability to deny the causative effect of televised violence and the seeming unreasonableness of denying the causative effect of tobacco would seem to be in the ability to propose an explanatory chain of *physical* events. It is relatively simple to understand, at least in lay terms, how the irritation caused by tobacco smoke could cause changes in the lungs leading to cancer. For most people, psychology is simply lacking as a hard science capable of providing such physical explanations. Without such an offer of a physical chain of events, the skeptic seems more reasonable in denying a causal effect. There is now, however, work in brain science that might provide such a physical explanation.

Professor Paul Mandel of the University of Strasbourg and his research group have studied the roles of neurotransmitters in the brains of rats.[41] They focused on serotonin and on gamma-amino-butyric acid, or GABA. The studies involving GABA are particularly interesting in that they show that GABA serves as an inhibitor playing a role in violent behavior.[42] Mandel worked with strains of rats that, through observation, showed to be particularly violent or particularly passive. For example, the Norway rats he used were more than three times more likely to kill than the Wistar rats he also used. When he studied the brains of rats from these various strains, he found that the GABA levels in the olfactory bulbs of the brains of the killer-rat strains were lower than the levels in non–killer-rat strains. He further found that the injection of GABA into the olfactory bulbs suppressed the killing behavior of these killer rats.

Mandel's work establishes a physical basis, at least in rats, for differences in violent behavior. Rats with lower levels of GABA are more violent than rats with higher base levels of GABA, and if rats low in GABA are given GABA injections they become less violent. Of more direct interest to the media-violence issue, it is reported that Professor Mandel also showed that the GABA levels in rats dropped when the rat observed other animals engaged in aggressive activity; that is, when a rat saw another rat kill a mouse, the observer rat's GABA level dropped.[43] Since the drop in GABA level is physically tied to violence, the conclusion is indicated that violence can be contagious and watching violence makes a rat more violent.

While the work described was with rats, and rats differ from humans, the physical basis for the relation between viewing violence and becoming aggressive in rats may make the conclusion that there is cause and effect in humans, rather than only correlation, more compelling. There may still be questions over the degree of correlation and the effect size, but humans have social inhibitors in addition to neurochemical inhibitors, so the regularity and size of the relation should not approach that in rats. Even accepting the rat studies as evidence of human brain activity, causation is not as established to the degree that it is in striking a match. It is, however, a step in establishing causation to the degree that it is established for tobacco and lung cancer.

The evidence seems strong that viewing violent television causes aggression. While it may still be argued that there is room for debate, even in 1981 "the general consensus seem[ed] to be that there is a positive, causal relationship between television violence and subsequent aggressive behavior."[44] Since that time, the evidence for a causal relationship, of some effect size, has not been shaken. As Senator Kent Conrad said in introducing his bill, The Children's Media Protection Act of 1995,[45] "[t]he scientific debate is over. . . . [There is] convincing evidence that the observation of violence as seen in standard, every day television entertainment, does affect the aggressive behavior of the viewer."[46]

While the scientific debate may be over, the public policy debate, as Senator Conrad recognized, is not over.[47] Indeed, it may be the case that the scientific debate itself is over only for scientific purposes but not for First Amendment purposes. As the next chapter will discuss, the requirements to justify a restriction on protected speech or press are difficult to meet. Scientists, in areas such as psychology, deal in probabilities. Most scientists see the probabilities established in this area as sufficient to establish the conclusion that television violence causes aggression. But, if violent material is protected under the First Amendment, the probabilities may not be sufficient to justify an infringement of that protection. Even greater certainty may be required when a constitutional right is involved.

An additional problem, for First Amendment purposes, is presented by the fact that the scientific conclusion addresses all violent material as a class. The amendment does not allow a wide-ranging attack on a class of material, if only a part of the class presents a problem sufficient to justify the attack. Rather, the restrictions must be aimed with particular focus on the problem material. The scientific evidence may well not be sufficient to meet that requirement. Any longitudinal study can only look at the overall effect of a class of material categorized as violent. While it may be theoretically possible to establish controls to test different varieties of material, in the real world subjects will be exposed to a range of materials that may qualify as violent. That range may be great, stretching from *Get Smart* through the *Three Stooges* to crime drama containing varying degrees of violence. Sorting the data to determine the effect of each variety would be difficult to impossible. Even if it could be accomplished, it has not yet been done, so the social science and psychology results may not be sufficient to justify a restriction on protected material.

If, on the other hand, sufficiently offensive and explicit violent material is not protected by the First Amendment, the data is clearly strong enough to justify restrictions on such material. The data certainly provides the required rational basis for a restriction not infringing on a constitutional right. The interplay between the empirical results, and the rational concern they raise over the effects of media violence, and the constitutional demands to be considered next show the importance of the thesis of this work. The ability to respond to the problem indicated in the data will require the recognition that at least certain varieties of violent depiction are without First Amendment protection.

The Obscenity Exception

While the First Amendment states "Congress shall make no law . . . abridging the freedom of speech, or of the press," the amendment is not the absolute that the language might make it appear. The Supreme Court has recognized several categories of speech that are unprotected by the amendment. *Chaplinsky v. New Hampshire*[1] was an early explicit recognition of such an exception. There the Court considered a case in which the defendant had called a city marshal a "God damned racketeer and a damned fascist." The Court held that "fighting words," words the utterance of which inflicts injury or is likely to incite an immediate breach of the peace, are unprotected by the First Amendment.

The Court has also stated that libelous speech falls outside the scope of First Amendment protection. It did so in the context of group libel, statements asserting the depravity or criminality of a racial or other group, in *Beauharnais v. Illinois*.[2] While later cases may lead to the conclusion that *Beauharnais* is no longer the law, interests in the protection of individual reputations still justify state laws allowing civil recovery for defamation. More recent Supreme Court efforts in this area have been devoted to considering the interplay between allowing recovery for libel and protecting political speech. *New York Times v. Sullivan*,[3] for example, established First Amendment limitations on state libel laws, when suit was brought by a public official. Later cases have examined the First Amendment restrictions on libel suits by public figures,[4] and how "public official" and "public figure" are to be defined.

The First Amendment exception central to this work is that for obscene materials, recognized in 1957 in *Roth v. United States*.[5] The *Roth* Court noted earlier decisions that had assumed obscene material was not protected by freedom of speech or freedom of the press,[6] but *Roth* squarely so held. The scope of the obscenity exception, and its relationship to depictions of violence, is the subject of this volume. But, before examining those issues, it is important to set out the law governing the obscenity exception as applied to sexual depictions. Once that body of law is presented, difficulties the courts have faced in applying the law to violence can be appreciated, and the contours of an expanded obscenity exception can be examined.

In *Roth,* the Court, with Justice Brennan writing the opinion, said that the matter of whether the material, based on which the criminal convictions had been obtained, was obscene was not at issue. Rather, the only issue was whether obscene material was protected by the First Amendment. The holding of the case was that such material is not protected, and the Court cited a long history of statutes and cases, and offered policy arguments for that conclusion.[7]

While the obscene nature of the material involved was not an issue, the Court did begin the process of defining "obscene." The Court noted that obscenity and sex are not synonymous. Sex may be dealt with in ways that still merit constitutional protection. Sexual material becomes obscene when it deals with sex in a manner that appeals to the prurient interest. Such material is that which has "a tendency to excite lustful thoughts," and "prurient" was defined as "[i]tching; longing; uneasy with desire or longing; of persons having itching, morbid, or lascivious longings; of desire, curiosity, or propensity, lewd."[8] The Court also stated that it saw "no significant difference" between case law definitions of obscenity and the Model Penal Code definition: "A thing is obscene if, considered as a whole, its predominate appeal is to the prurient interest, i.e., a shameful or morbid interest in nudity, sex, or excretion, and if it goes substantially beyond customary limits of candor in description or representation of such matters."[9] Finally, the Court cited with approval the test adopted by various American courts: "whether to the average person, applying contemporary community standards, the dominant theme of the material taken as a whole appeals to prurient interest."[10]

While *Roth* established an obscenity exception and made some effort to define obscenity, it took quite some time for the Court actually to adopt a test for obscenity. Finally in 1966, the Court seemed to establish a standard. In *A Book Named "John Cleland's Memoirs of a Woman of Pleasure" v. Attorney General of Massachusetts,*[11] the book at issue also being known as *Fanny Hill,* three members of the Court stated a test. Justice Brennan, joined by Chief Justice Warren and Justice Fortas, found three elements in the test that the *Roth* Court had cited with approval. For matter to be obscene it must be shown that "(a) the dominant theme of the material taken as a whole appeals to a prurient interest in sex; (b) the material is patently offensive because it affronts contemporary community standards relating to the description of representation of sexual matters; and (c) the material is utterly without redeeming social value."[12]

While the opinion was only that of three justices, Justice Douglas concurred, though disagreeing with the statement of the test. In Justice Douglas's view, the First Amendment permitted no censorship of expression not tied to illegal action. Furthermore, Justice Black concurred for the reasons stated in his dissent in *Ginzburg v. United States*.[13] That dissent expressed a view akin to that of Justice Douglas, questioning at least the federal government's authority to burden any speech or expression. Since two justices would provide protection to material even when not meeting the plurality test, and the plurality would protect material meeting its test, that test provided at least a working standard, until a majority finally settled on a test in 1973.

The current test for obscenity was adopted in *Miller v. California*.[14] That test asks:

> (a) whether "the average person, applying contemporary community standards" would find that the work, taken as a whole, appeals to the prurient interest; (b) whether the work depicts or describes, in a patently offensive way, sexual conduct specifically defined by the applicable state law; and (c) whether the work, taken as a whole, lacks serious literary, artistic, political, or scientific value.[15]

In addition to finally obtaining a majority, the *Miller* opinion is important in that the test did undergo a change. No longer would some minor social value save a work from being found obscene. Instead of requiring that the material be "utterly without redeeming social value," the work, taken as a whole, had to have serious value. While graphic, offensive sex scenes might have been non-obscene under the *Memoirs* test, if they were preceded by a poetry reading or followed by the recitation of some moral, it is, under the *Miller* test, the value of the entire work that is to be judged.

While *Miller* states the current test, there is an important later case. In *Pope v. Illinois*[16] the issue was the standard against which to measure the third prong of the *Miller* test. Specifically, was the "serious literary, artistic, political, or scientific value" of the work to be judged by community standards? The Court held that the test was not the ordinary member of the community but rather "whether a reasonable person would find such value in the material, taken as a whole."[17] The fact that only a minority of the community found such value in the work did not mean that it lacked sufficient value to deserve protection. Given the argument in Justice Scalia's concurrence that a "reasonable person" standard provides little help in questions of aesthetics, it is not clear that, even with *Pope*, the definition of sexual obscenity is now complete.

It is also interesting to note that some dissatisfaction with the *Miller* test, and in fact with the whole enterprise of government censorship of obscene material, was expressed in concurring and dissenting opinions in *Pope*. Justice Stevens, in a dissenting opinion joined by Justice Marshall, expressed concern over the reasonable-person standard adopted by the Court. In addition, he argued that there was a deeper flaw, expressing a conviction that it was unconstitutional for the government to punish the possession or sale of obscene materials, at least when there was no involvement of minors or nonconsenting adults. Furthermore, the justice whose opinion began the Court's obscenity analysis, Justice Brennan, joined that aspect of Justice Stevens's opinion. Justice Scalia, in a concurrence, also suggested the need to reexamine the *Miller* test, but it would seem unlikely that he was suggesting that *Roth* be overturned.

While several justices indicated that perhaps the obscenity exception should be dropped from First Amendment law, that would appear unlikely to happen. Justices Brennan and Marshall are, of course, no longer on the Court, and Justice Scalia was probably merely suggesting an adjustment in the test. The obscenity exception is still with us, a more finely tuned *Miller* test is still the test, and despite academic criticism,[18] both seem likely to remain so.

Variable Obscenity

There is a refinement necessary in the obscenity exception if it is to take into account variations in the audience exposed to possibly obscene material. This refinement, the concept of variable obscenity, seems to have originated with Professors William Lockhart and Robert McClure.[19] They suggested that the concept would provide a method for addressing concerns over the exposure of adolescents to materials aimed at an adult audience.[20] If such material is not obscene, it is protected when distributed to adults. That does not mean, however, that the distribution to minors must also be protected. Variable obscenity allows consideration of the audience and the circumstances in determining whether material is obscene. Material considered obscene for a particular audience may be barred from distribution to that audience.

The concept of variable obscenity gained support in *Mishkin v. New York*.[21] There the Court held that, for material designed for and distributed primarily to a sexually deviant group, the proper test for the "appeal to the prurient interest" requirement was the prurient interest of the deviant group. Even if the material had no such appeal to the average person, the material could still be obscene as to the intended and likely target group.[22]

Variable obscenity, as applied to youth, was recognized by the Court in *Ginsberg v. New York*.[23] The defendant in that case was convicted of selling magazines containing pictures of female nudity to a sixteen-year-old boy. The sales were determined by the state courts to be in violation of a New York law making it a crime "knowingly to sell . . . to a minor . . . any picture . . . which depicts nudity . . . and which is harmful to minors."[24] The statute provided a definition of "harmful to minors" as material that "(i) predominantly appeals to the prurient, shameful or morbid interest of minors, and (ii) is patently offensive to prevailing standards in the adult community as a whole with respect to what is suitable material for minors, and (iii) is utterly without redeeming social importance for minors."[25]

As the Court defined the issue, the question was the constitutionality of an obscenity statute prohibiting the sale to minors of material meeting a definition of obscenity on the basis of its appeal to minors, whether or not it would be obscene to adults. The Court first noted that the magazines were not obscene for adults and that the appellant did not argue that the magazines did not meet the statutory definition of "harmful to minors." Thus, the only real issue[26] was the availability of a different standard for judging the obscenity of materials when the materials are distributed to minors.

The Court concluded that the statute did not intrude on whatever area of freedom of speech the constitution grants to minors. The state was seen as having the power to regulate for the well-being of its children, both in support of parents in their upbringing of their children and based on the state's own interest in the character of its youth. The only remaining question was, according to the Court, whether or not the legislature could rationally conclude that exposure to the restricted materials would harm youth.

The state legislature had included in the statute a finding that the material condemned by the statute was "a basic factor in impairing the ethical and moral development of our youth and a clear and present danger to the people of the state."[27] While the Court expressed doubt that the legislature's finding was accepted scientific fact, it did not require that the finding be scientifically established. Because obscenity is unprotected by the First Amendment, it can be suppressed without establishing such a scientific basis. The Court only had to determine "it was not irrational for the legislature to find that exposure to material condemned by the statute is harmful to minors."[28] The Court then looked to the scientific studies available and concluded that, while a causal link between obscenity and the impairment of ethical and moral development had not been established, neither had such a link been disproved. Since the materials were unprotected, the Court refused to require "scientifically certain criteria of legislation" and was unwilling to find a rational basis for the conclusion that such materials harm minors was lacking.[29]

The constitutionality of the New York statute, based on a conclusion of rational relationship of the material to harm to minors, required the lack of First Amendment protection for the magazines at issue. Had they been protected, the Constitution would have required that the statute meet a far stricter test.

Limitations on Protected Speech

Even when material is not included in an exception to the First Amendment's protection, limitations may still be constitutional. The recognition that a constitutional right is implicated does not automatically lead to the conclusion that a governmental action is void. Where there is infringement, the government is asked to offer a strong justification. Rather than requiring only that the law be rationally related to some permissible governmental objective, known as the rational basis test, the action must meet strict scrutiny. The government must demonstrate that it was addressing a compelling governmental purpose and that the means chosen were necessary to, or narrowly tailored to, that purpose.

In the context of the First Amendment, the strict scrutiny test has taken on the mantle of the "clear and present danger" test. That test developed in a line of cases growing out of sedition-like charges relating to speech directed against recruitment of soldiers during World War I,[30] passing through the attempts to suppress communism during the Cold War, and reaching its maturity in *Brandenburg v. Ohio.*[31] The speech involved in these cases had a political component but could also be seen as the advocacy of illegal action. The Court attempted to develop, over time, a line at which teaching and indoctrination crossed over to punishable solicitation of criminal acts, a line between advocacy of abstract doctrine and incitement to criminality. The test developed was whether or not the speech presented a clear and present danger of unlawful activity.

While the strict scrutiny test in First Amendment contexts has been recast in "clear and present danger" language, strict scrutiny might be met by other than the immediate incitement to criminality that that test addresses. Some other compelling purpose might justify an infringement on speech, if the infringement was sufficiently closely tailored to the purpose. Indeed, the Court's language made it appear that it was recognizing another such purpose in *New York v. Ferber*.[32] In that case, the Court addressed the question of whether the state could prohibit the dissemination of nonobscene material portraying sexual activities involving children, as a way to prevent the child abuse inherent in producing such material. The Court recognized that the protection of children from abuse and sexual exploitation was "a government objective of surpassing importance." The court also stated that the distribution networks must be closed, if such abuse was to be prevented. That language certainly sounded like the identification of a compelling purpose and the conclusion that the ban on distribution was necessary to that purpose. Rather than stopping there, however, the Court went on to conclude not that such material was protected with an infringement justified under strict scrutiny, but rather that the material was unprotected by the First Amendment.

The approach taken in *Ferber* may indicate a reluctance to allow any infringement on protected speech, even when a good strict scrutiny argument can be offered. That reluctance explains the difficulties that have been faced by attempts to limit access even of minors to media violence. The attempts to tie television violence to actual violence and to treat media violence as a public health problem appear aimed at identifying a compelling interest in the safety of the public and a claim that limiting exposure to violence is necessary to that interest. Such an approach has not met with success, as the state experience with violent video restrictions shows.

State Restrictions on Distribution of Violent Videos to Minors

The state attempts to limit media depictions of violence, even though limited to minors, have not been well received by the courts. The Missouri statute was challenged by a group of video dealers and distributors and by the Motion Picture Association of America in *Video Software Dealers Association v. Webster*.[33] The district court recognized that *Ginsberg* allowed variable standards as to what was acceptable for youth and for adults but found *Ginsberg* limited to obscenity and held that even violent material enjoys First Amendment protection. Any ban would have to meet strict scrutiny by being narrowly tailored to promote a compelling state interest. The court did recognize a compelling interest in protecting the physical and psychological well-being of minors but determined that the statute had not been shown to be narrowly drawn to serve that interest. Because the statute did not state what types of violence are detrimental to minors, the court could not determine if the statute was narrowly drawn to ban only that expression.

While counsel for Missouri argued that the language employed in the statute was similar to that in *Miller*, the court responded by noting that the material in *Miller* was outside the protection of the First Amendment, while the material at issue in the statute was protected. Where material is protected, narrow-tailoring requires greater precision. The lack of definition was also held to make the statute unconstitutionally vague. Lastly, the fact that the statute imposed strict liability, and the chilling effect such liability would have in an area of protected speech, also made the act unconstitutional.

On appeal, the United States Court of Appeals for the Eighth Circuit affirmed on all three grounds.[34] That court, too, was troubled by the statute's lack of definition. It found even the state's brief to be inconsistent in its identification of a target. The state tried to avoid the problem the lack of definition caused in meeting the narrow tailoring requirement by claiming that violent videos are obscene to children. If they were obscene and unprotected, the ban on distribution to minors would not have to be narrowly tailored to a compelling purpose. While the court agreed with the state's reliance on *Ginsberg* for the proposition that material not obscene to adults may be obscene to minors, the court held that violence, without depictions or descriptions of sexual conduct, cannot be obscene.

Missouri attempted to rely on the similarity of its statute to the language in *Miller* to answer the vagueness charge. The court's response was that the statute did not meet the *Miller* requirements. *Miller* requires that the sexual conduct banned as obscene be specifically defined in the statute or in construction by state courts. Missouri's statute provided no definition of the violent material banned, nor did the court find a readily apparent construction of the statute that would avoid the vagueness concern. Lastly, the appellate court found a constitutional flaw in the strict liability aspects of what it saw as at least a "quasi-criminal" statute. The court required an element of knowledge for any statute that chills expression protected by the First Amendment.

The Tennessee statute was also challenged by a group of book sellers and distributors. The part of the statute addressing violent material was declared unconstitutional in *Davis-Kidd Booksellers, Inc. v. McWherter*.[35] The Tennessee Chancery Court looked to the applicable definition of "excess violence" as "the depiction of acts of violence in such a graphic and/or bloody manner as to exceed common limits to custom and candor, or in such a manner that it is apparent that the predominant appeal of the material is portrayal of violence for violence's sake."[36] The court found the definition to be unconstitutionally vague and thus in violation of the First Amendment.

The court did not rule out the inclusion of violent material in the class of obscene material. In fact, the court cited, in support of its conclusion, a Tennessee federal district court ruling that a similar definition of "excess violence" was unconstitutionally vague, because it "constituted an excessively subjective judgment as to what might be deemed '*obscene* to juveniles.'"[37] On the other hand, the court found no constitutional problem in applying to sexually explicit materials the statute's ban on the sale and display of material "harmful to minors."[38] The court cited *Ginsberg* in holding that the seemingly equally vague phrase used in the New York statute met constitutional requirements.

Ginsberg was, as indicated, an obscenity case, or a variable obscenity case, and vagueness appears to be of less concern where such unprotected material is involved. The Supreme Court has examined the question of what scienter requirement the Constitution imposes on obscenity convictions. The Court has determined that the defendant need not have known that the materials were legally obscene. It is sufficient that the defendant be shown to have known the character and nature of the materials involved.[39] The defendant need not have had foreknowledge of the outcome of a potential legal obscenity determination. The defendant need merely to have known of the explicit sexual nature of the material. The difference may be between vagueness and scienter but the two concepts are related. "The Constitution requires proof of scienter to . . . compensate for the ambiguities inherent in the definition of obscenity."[40]

If knowing the sexual nature of material is sufficient scienter for an obscenity conviction, why is more definition required in a conviction for the sale to minors of materials with excess violence? It would appear that scienter of the nature of the material as violent should be sufficient. One response is that for sexual material to be obscene it must first contain material specifically barred by statute. In addition, the treatment of the material must go beyond community standards for candor and lack serious value. The statutory definition addresses any vagueness concerns over the nature of the material covered. The Court's scienter analysis is addressed to the questions of community standards and significant value. Tennessee's statute, on the other hand, had not specifically defined the types of violence covered. It is possible that the Tennessee court relied on that distinction, without so stating. It may also be, however, that the court simply afforded greater protection to violent material than to sexual material on the grounds that the former is nonobscene, while the latter may be obscene.

The Supreme Court of Tennessee affirmed the decision of the Chancellor that the term "excess violence" is unconstitutionally vague and did directly address the possibility that material may be obscene because of the violence it depicts.[41] The court first agreed with the Chancellor that the statutory definition of "excess violence" was vague in that it was insufficient to provide fair notice or guidance to those dealing in visual materials. The court then went on to determine that the vagueness could not be cured by incorporating violence in the definition of obscenity as to minors. Citing the United States Supreme Court's opinion in *Miller,* the Tennessee court held that "[t]he obscenity definition is specifically designed for sexually explicit materials not violent materials."[42]

The Colorado statute appears, thus far, not to have been challenged. Since the statute addresses only depictions or descriptions of actual acts of violence resulting in death or serious bodily injury, it is less vague and of very limited scope. It may, however, still face challenge on the grounds that even that variety of violent material is protected.

The difficulties the state statutes faced in meeting the strict scrutiny test suggest that if media violence is to be controlled, a prerequisite for that control will be the denial that all depictions of violence, at least when lacking other grounds for an exception to the First Amendment, are protected speech. Media violence must be fit within an existing or new exception to the First Amendment, so that when it becomes sufficiently graphic and offensive it falls outside the scope of the amendment. But, before returning to that suggestion, there is one additional possible route for regulation to be examined.

Regulatory Authority over Broadcast Media

Since much of the debate over violence in the media has focused on television, it is important to recognize that there is additional law governing that medium. Even when material is not obscene, but meets some lesser standard of indecency, the fact that the material is broadcast on the over-the-air media has been held to allow the federal government greater control. *Federal Communications Commission v. Pacifica Foundation*[43] grew out of the radio broadcast of satirist/humorist George Carlin's "Filthy Words" monologue. Pacifica's New York radio station broadcast the material as part of a program on contemporary attitudes toward language. Immediately prior to the 2 P.M. broadcast, listeners were advised that some might find the language to be offensive. The monologue asserted that there were seven words that you "definitely wouldn't say, ever" over the air. In the course of the soliloquy, the words were repeated, over and over again, in a variety of colloquial contexts. The FCC received a complaint from an individual objecting to the broadcast, claiming that he and his young son had heard the material over his car radio. The Commission determined that the broadcast was sanctionable, although it chose not to sanction Pacifica and simply "associated" its conclusions with the station's file for consideration if future complaints were received. While the Commission did not agree that you "definitely [c]ouldn't say, ever" the words in question, it did conclude that such material should be channeled into time periods in which children were not likely to be listening.

Pacifica appealed the FCC ruling, and the case eventually made its way to the Supreme Court. The Court first considered whether or not the Commission had the statutory authority to penalize the broadcast of material such as Carlin's monologue. Standing in the way of such a ban was Section 29 of the Radio Act of 1927, which provided that the Act did not give the Commission the power to censor any radio communication and that the Commission did not have the authority to interfere with the right of free speech, even when that speech was broadcast over the radio. On the other hand, the FCC claimed to find authority to regulate speech such as Carlin's in federal law prohibiting the use of "any obscene, indecent, or profane language" in any radio transmission,[44] and in a more general statute requiring the Commission to encourage the use of radio in the public interest.[45]

The Court held that the anticensorship provision was not intended to prohibit the Commission from regulating obscene, indecent, or profane language but then had to consider whether the language at issue came within that category. George Carlin's words had not been held to be obscene, but the Commission did find them to be indecent. Pacifica argued that only obscene words, words with prurient appeal, were indecent. The Court rejected Pacifica's position and concluded that "indecent," as used in the statute, "merely refers to nonconformance with accepted standards of morality."[46]

Having resolved the statutory issue in the Commission's favor, the Court then had to consider the constitutionality of restrictions on the radio broadcast of indecent language. The Court noted that, compared to the other media, the broadcast media enjoyed a lesser level of First Amendment protection. This lesser protection was justified, in part, by the uniquely pervasive presence of the broadcast media in American life. Broadcast of indecent material would confront the individual not only in public, but in the privacy of one's own home. Warnings such as that broadcast do not provide adequate protection to one tuning in after the program has begun, and turning off the program after hearing the language was seen as an inadequate remedy. The Court also pointed to the accessibility of radio broadcasts to children, even children too young to read. While other media might simply be required not to dispense offending material to children, only channeling into hours when children were unlikely to be listening seemed effective in protecting children from the broadcast of indecency.

Application of *Pacifica* to allow regulation of, and limitation on, the broadcast of violent material requires a reexamination of both the statutory and constitutional analysis in that decision. While the FCC, in its 1975 report issued one week after its decision in *Pacifica,* appeared to question its statutory authority to regulate material that was not both sexually oriented and indecent, the *Pacifica* Court's analysis of the anticensorship statute may allow such regulation.

In its examination of the anticensorship provision, the Court stated that the act denied the Commission the authority to edit broadcasts in advance of their airing. But the Court said that the provision did not mean that the Commission did not have the power to review the content of completed broadcasts as a part of the performance of its regulatory duties.[47] Just as the broadcast in *Pacifica* could affect future licensure decisions, the Commission might be able to take into account in its licensure decisions a policy of broadcasting violent material.

The *Pacifica* Court also used the statutory prohibition against the broadcast of obscene, indecent, and profane language as a limitation on the anticensorship provision. The Court rejected the argument that only obscene material is indecent. It interpreted the statutory ban on broadcasting indecent material to preclude material not in conformance with "accepted standards of morality."[48] Given that broad definition of "indecent," it is not clear why material may not fail to conform with accepted standards of morality by being excessively violent, as well as by being excessively sexual. On the other hand, *Pacifica* was concerned with sexual and eliminatory terms, and the definition given to "indecent" in that context may be read so as to require treatment of sexual or eliminatory topics that goes beyond the bounds of "accepted standards of morality." In either case, the statutory issue does not present a serious problem to attempts to control television violence. If the Commission does not already have the statutory authority, Congress may remedy that situation and indeed bills to that effect have been introduced.[49] The more difficult issue is the constitutionality of any such grant of statutory authority to regulate television violence.

Professors Thomas Krattenmaker and L. A. Powe Jr. examined the constitutional basis of *Pacifica* in an article published shortly after that decision.[50] They raise interesting questions over the applicability of the *Pacifica* ruling to violence on television. Their conclusions indicate First Amendment problems with any FCC attempt to regulate violence. The conclusions would seem to carry over to most, or all, of the recent congressional attempts to control televised violence.

Krattenmaker and Powe base their conclusions primarily on *Ginsberg v. New York, Tinker v. Des Moines Independent Community School District*,[51] and *Erznoznik v. City of Jacksonville*.[52] *Ginsberg*, as has been seen, arose from the sale of a magazine to a minor. The magazine was not considered obscene for adults, but the Court held that the magazine was obscene when distributed to minors, because the material's appeal had to be assessed based on the sexual interests of minors. Krattenmaker and Powe find it difficult to discern the *Ginsberg* Court's basis for this variable obscenity standard. They suggest that *Ginsberg*, with its concern that children require special protection, might be interpreted to allow the states to bar distribution to minors of all harmful material, even those protected under the First Amendment. However, *Ginsberg* also based its conclusion on the premise that obscenity is unprotected. An interpretation concentrating on that premise would limit the scope of the case to material that, while not obscene to adults, shares the characteristics of such obscenity. Thus, *Ginsberg* would apply only to the erotic.

The proper interpretation, Krattenmaker and Powe suggest, is indicated by *Tinker*. *Tinker* examined the actions of a school district in barring students from wearing black armbands in protest of the Vietnam war. The Court held that students have First Amendment rights that are not lost when they enter the schoolhouse, although such rights may be limited by sufficiently weighty school interests. This recognition of First Amendment rights in children, in Krattenmaker and Powe's view, leads to the conclusion that *Ginsberg* is based on the obscene nature of the material there involved, and that the special protections the state may enact for children are limited to erotic material.

They find their conclusion strengthened by *Erznoznik*. *Erznoznik* arose from a municipal ordinance against drive-in theaters showing films on screens visible from a public street if the film contained nude buttocks, pubic areas, or female breasts. The city contended its ordinance was a permissible attempt to protect children. The Court responded by noting that the material banned was not obscene, even to children, because it was not erotic. *Ginsberg*, therefore, was not controlling, and the ordinance was unconstitutional.

While Krattenmaker and Powe recognize that *Pacifica*, "on its own terms," justifies the conclusion that violent material could be treated in the same way the Carlin monologue was, they conclude that *Pacifica* ought not to be read in isolation. Unless *Pacifica* is read so as implicitly to overturn several earlier cases, it must be limited to material which, even though not obscene, focuses on sexual or excretory matters. Their conclusions call into question the constitutionality of FCC attempts to limit the broadcast of violent materials, even the modest limitations found in channeling such materials into hours when children are less likely to be in the audience. This is, of course, an FCC disability that enabling legislation would be unable to overcome.

Even if Krattenmaker and Powe's arguments are rejected, FCC regulation may be inadequate to address the public concerns over media violence. *Pacifica* recognized only the FCC's authority to channel sexually indecent material into hours when younger children are unlikely to be watching or listening. A similar authority to channel violent material may not provide an adequate solution. We may not be quite as concerned over the exposure of eighteen-year-olds to nonobscene but indecent sexual material as we are with the exposure of young children. But individuals in their late teens and early twenties may present great concerns with regard to exposure to violent material. While channeling might protect children in their formative years, it would not prevent exposure to young adults, whose appetite for violence may be increased or who may be led to imitate the action.[53] Furthermore, even with the broadcast media channeled, there remain the problems of cable programming, movies, and rental videos.

Denying First Amendment Protection to the Depiction of Violence

Despite the public perception of a need for governmental action to limit media violence, the response has been limited in scope and success. As the limitations on each governmental approach to regulating and limiting violence demonstrate, the key to controlling media violence lies in finding a way to work with and within the First Amendment. In each case, the amendment has placed strong obstacles in the road to governmental regulation. The states have been limited by courts concluding that their attempts to limit access to violent videos violate the First Amendment. The Federal Communications Commission, with its regulatory authority over the broadcast media, might exercise some control, but there too, there are serious concerns over First Amendment protection. Congress appears to have targeted most of its effort on the broadcast media. Given its earlier view that the First Amendment protects violent comic books, the current limitation may be based on the possibility that the Constitution would allow wider latitude in regulating the broadcast media. But, even in the case of the broadcast media, Congress has been slow to take direct action, and that reluctance is probably best explained by First Amendment concerns.

The one route around the First Amendment protections claimed by producers of violent materials that has been recognized by the courts has been unsuccessful. The states have not been able to demonstrate that their attempts at limiting media violence can pass the strict scrutiny test. While research showing that television violence is a causal factor in societal violence is clearly adequate to meet the rational basis required for a law not limiting a constitutional right, the available research may be argued to be inadequate to satisfy a higher level test. The lack of research on the effects of violent video games would certainly make it difficult for regulation of such games to pass strict scrutiny. Furthermore, an additional difficulty is imposed by the requirement that the statutes or regulations be narrowly tailored to the specific types of media violence clearly shown to cause societal violence.

A better approach, one not facing the difficult showings required by strict scrutiny, is a First Amendment exception. If depictions or descriptions of violence were within an exception to the First Amendment, violent material could be banned or controlled without meeting strict scrutiny. One approach would be to create a new exception, but that is a dangerous route. Creating an exception, when unable to demonstrate the necessity to a compelling purpose that would negate the need for an exception, would be a long step down a short road to the destruction of the First Amendment. Respect for First Amendment principles leads to reluctance to find exceptions and an insistence that all exceptions find a strong historical basis.

The better approach is the inclusion of violent material within one of the existing exceptions. This approach too must be pursued with caution. Too great a willingness to expand the recognized exceptions to include new categories of expression would be just as destructive of the First Amendment as would the willingness to create new exceptions. Inclusion should require a close examination of the excepted category to insure that violent expression is properly included. There should also be a historical analysis showing that there is as strong a basis for including violent material as there is for including the material already contained in the excepted category. Lastly, the policies behind the amendment and the exception must be examined to be certain that inclusion within the exception is justified.

Once again, the thesis of this work is that depictions and descriptions of violence may reach such a level as to be considered obscene for First Amendment purposes. Such materials would then be unprotected and could be regulated, controlled or even banned by the federal and state governments.

The inclusion of violence within the category of the obscene does run contrary to Supreme Court case law. The Court has insisted that material must focus on sexual or excretory activity to be obscene. In the foundational *Roth* opinion, the Court defined obscene material as material dealing with sex in a manner that appeals to the prurient interest. Later cases have been consistent in their application of obscenity doctrine only to material with a sexual or excretory focus.[54] The insistence on such content is best seen in *Cohen v. California*.[55] While the four-letter commentary on the draft displayed on Cohen's jacket may have been offensive, the Court said that it could not be obscene because "such [obscene] expression must be, in some significant way, erotic."[56] In *Erznoznik* the Court quoted the *Cohen* language in holding that even the exposing of minors to films depicting nudity was not obscene, unless the nudity also was erotic.[57] The limitation to sexual material is also seen in the current *Miller* test of obscenity.

While it is clear that the current focus of obscenity doctrine is on the depiction of sexual or excretory activities, that focus, to the exclusion of the consideration of violent material, is unwarranted. The insistence by the Supreme Court that for material to be obscene it must be erotic is misguided. There is nothing in the concept of obscenity that requires that it be limited to sexual or excretory activities. Even more importantly, there is nothing in history or case law, during constitutionally relevant periods, that limits obscenity to erotic material. Furthermore, the policy ground used to justify the exclusion of sexually obscene materials from First Amendment protection speak just as well to sufficiently violent material. Sufficiently violent material may be unprotected solely due to its violence, without need for any inquiry into its sexual content.

If material may be sufficiently violent so as to be obscene, various regulatory routes are opened. Most simply, the FCC and Congress may ban it altogether. State efforts at regulation of, and bans on, violent material would also be constitutional. Furthermore, the concepts of indecency and variable obscenity could be expanded to include materials related to those that are obscene because of their violence. Material that contains violence, but not at so excessive a level as to be obscene, could be considered indecent, just as nonobscene sexual material may be indecent. Then even if Krattenmaker and Powe are correct in requiring that indecency be tied to obscenity, violence could still be the basis for holding material indecent. The FCC, under the *Pacifica* rationale, could then channel the broadcast media's use of such material into hours when children are unlikely to be watching. Likewise, state attempts to restrict access of minors to violent material also would be constitutional. Furthermore, the states should not be limited to controlling access by minors. States would have the authority to ban completely the dissemination of excessively violent material and, under the variable obscenity approach, to ban the distribution to minors of material sufficiently violent so as to be obscene to minors, even if not obscene to adults.

The most important benefit derived from the inclusion of excessively violent materials within the obscene is that there would no longer be a need to meet strict scrutiny to justify regulation of such materials. Just as no demonstration that any evil actually flows from sexually obscene materials is required to ban such materials, no such demonstration would be required for violent materials. Any debate over whether a sufficient link has been shown to exist between televised violence and aggression to support a ban on such programming would become legally irrelevant. Furthermore, the lack of research showing such a connection between violent video games and aggression would no longer present a problem. The removal of such materials from the protected class and its requirements for strict scrutiny would also remove the problems with the narrow tailoring requirement courts have found in attempts to ban violent materials.

In their seminal article on the law of obscenity, Professors William Lockhart and Robert McClure found a lack of clarity in the concept: "No one seems to know what obscenity is. Many writers have discussed the obscene, but few can agree upon even its essential nature. . . . [M]ost writers have found the term hopelessly subjective and lacking in any definite or acceptable meaning."[1] They did note that some writers tie obscenity to a sense of shame usually associated with sexual or excremental matters, but suggested that obscenity may be found in other than the sexual or excremental.[2]

Lockhart and McClure wrote prior to the Supreme Court's decision in *Roth v. United States*.[3] In *Roth* the Court provided a definition of obscenity that clearly tied the concept to sex and elimination. However, as Professor Joel Feinberg has pointed out, the meaning the Court imposed on "obscene" is an "artificial one."[4] Feinberg suggests that all the definitions of "obscene" provided by the Court are "approximate renderings of the sense of 'pornographic' as applied to materials and displays deliberately intended to provoke erotic response."[5] But, in Feinberg's view, simply to assert that only pornographic materials may be obscene is to beg an important and controversial question.[6]

The Court may not be attempting to beg the question. *Roth* and the cases that followed involved sex and excretion. The Court attempted to draw lines determining what of that variety of speech is protected and what is unprotected. The Court's definitions are not question-begging, if they are attempts to distinguish between obscene and nonobscene pornography. It is only when they are viewed as drawing distinctions between the obscene as a general category and the nonobscene that they are lacking. Feinberg finds the Court's definition both too broad and too narrow. The overbreadth, the possibility that some nonobscene sexual material may be captured by the Court's definition, is not at issue here. The underbreadth is. The Court's definition, if it is taken to limit obscenity to sexual or eliminatory depictions and descriptions, is too narrow. The concept of obscenity extends to other varieties of materials, and violent depictions may present as central a paradigm of obscenity as sexual materials.

Obscenity as a Philosophical Construct

Professor Feinberg examines the idea of obscenity in volume two of his work *The Moral Limits of the Criminal Law.*[7] He argues that assertions of obscenity differ both from assertions of immorality and from negative aesthetic labels. He instead finds them to be in the class of evaluative judgments labeled by Peter Glassen as "charientic."[8] The ascription of vulgarity is a typical charientic judgment. A person may be vulgar without being immoral, so the charientic ascriptions, within which he includes "uncouth," "boorish," and "tasteless," as well as "refined," "sensitive," "cultivated," and "civilized," differ from moral ascriptions such as "wicked" and "cruel" as well as "righteous" and "honorable." They also differ from aesthetic ascriptions such as "beautiful" and "ugly." The distinction between the moral and charientic judgment is, for Feinberg and Glassen, the distinction between indignation and hostility on the one hand and contempt, derision, and ridicule on the other.

Feinberg ties the concept of obscenity to that of vulgarity. While vulgarity may be a matter of being "in bad form," ungracious, or unseemly, obscenity is "conduct in the worst possible form, *utterly* crude, coarse, and gross."[9] "Obscenity is the outer limit of vulgarity."[10] Obscenity is a matter of offensiveness so extreme that it produces disgust, shock, or repugnance. The difference between offensiveness and obscenity seems to be in the degree of blatancy involved. "Obscene *persons and actions* are those which are coarse and vulgar to an extreme, or those which are brazenly obtrusive violations of any standards of propriety . . . Obscene *created things* are blatantly shocking depictions or unsuitable descriptions of obscene persons, actions, or objects."[11]

While depictions of sexual or excretory activities may fit within Feinberg's obscenity analysis, his concept of obscenity is not so limited. He specifically includes, as a proper use of the term "obscene," the sentence: "The machine gunning of Bonnie and Clyde in the climactic scene of the film may have been morally and dramatically justified, but the blood spurting out of the bullet holes as bullets splattered the bodies was a naturally revolting sight — so offensive and shocking to the senses as to be obscene."[12] The example serves to make two points. It once again shows how a scene may be morally justified as showing the wages of sin and aesthetically justified as making the drama more powerful but nonetheless be considered obscene. It also shows that, for Feinberg, obscenity may be found in a treatment of violence and death, as well as in a treatment of sex or excretion.

For Feinberg, obscene objects are those that "send shudders up our spines and set our teeth on edge."[13] He suggests a plausible psychological origin for such a reaction in the parental implantation in infants of the "Yuk!" reaction. Infants are very willing to place anything that fits into their mouths. When a parent reacts with "No!," "Dirty!," "Nasty!," or "Yuk!," the infant learns that this is unacceptable behavior. It is not morally unacceptable, and it seems to go beyond an aesthetic judgment. The action, in Feinberg's words, "is simply (what better word is there?) *Yukky*."[14] This proposed early implantation of the concept would explain the visceral nature of ascriptions of obscenity. While morality may be learned later and may be the subject of debate, yukkiness, like obscenity, is something we know when we see.

It remains to be explained why Feinberg's "Yuk!" reaction applies to explicit sexual depictions. Indeed, he does not seem to argue that it must, but only that for many it in fact does. He suggests that a scientist may react to a closeup photo of genitalia in a detached manner. Another observer may enjoy the pictures, while others may find them "yukky." This difference in reaction and its gut-level nature may make it difficult to define sexual obscenity. Indeed, a collective sense of offensiveness may be required, and the second prong of the *Miller* test, asking whether the depiction is patently offensive, might be viewed as embodying a community "yukkiness" standard.

The "Yuk!" reaction may apply to violence and death, just as well as it applies to sex and excretion. The reaction to violence will vary from individual to individual and from act of violence to act of violence. But, so do the reactions of individuals to acts of sex or even to acts of excretion. If the community "Yuk!" standard is sufficient to define those sexual depictions that are obscene, it can also serve to define violent obscenity.

David A. J. Richards takes a somewhat different approach to defining obscenity. He suggests that specific instances of obscenity will differ from culture to culture, but the basis for the judgment remains constant across cultures.

> The concept of the obscene is identical with the concept of those actions, representations, works, or states which display an exercise of bodily function, or such an exercise in certain circumstances, which constitutes an abuse of bodily function, as dictated by standards in which one has invested self-esteem, so that the supposed abuse of bodily function is an object of self-contempt and -disgust.[15]

The tie to shame, found in the *Roth* appeal to the prurient or shameful interest requirement, is based in the fact that the failure properly to exercise bodily functions leads to a loss of self-esteem and thus to a sense of shame.

Richards's approach explains the Supreme Court's focus of the obscenity doctrine on excretion and sex. Excretory incompetence is found in the frailest members of society, the senile, and infants. In a society in which frailty and a general decline in control are a cause of anxiety, impropriety in excretory function will be taken as obscene. The abuse of the excretory function found in public defecation touches deep anxieties in the public, and that anxiety leads to a bar on such displays as obscene.

Richards notes that there is no necessary connection between sexual depictions and obscenity. He traces the tie between the two in our culture to St. Augustine's insistence that the proper function of the sexual organs, and the only proper purpose of the sexual act, is the reproduction of the species. Only heterosexual sex within a marriage is proper. Pornographic depictions present sex, rather than reproduction, and are thus depictions of an abuse of bodily function. Further, pornographic material may lead to masturbation and to sex outside of marriage, thereby causing further abuses of bodily function. These violations of minimum levels of competency in exercising bodily function make such material obscene. Richards argues that his approach offers an explanation of the great wave of obscenity legislation in the latter half of the nineteenth century. The Victorian medical theory that masturbation, or any variety of sexual excess, led to insanity made pornography and the sexual activities thought to follow particularly great abuses of bodily function.

Richards's approach would also seem to encompass depictions of violence. While loss of bowel control may be a cause of anxiety, meeting a violent end would seem even more anxiety-laden. If the level of anxiety caused by a public eliminatory act is sufficient to make that act obscene, public displays of violence should be similarly obscene. Furthermore, violence has a better fit with the abuse of bodily function criterion than does elimination. Public elimination does not involve the misuse of the body. The function is normal; it is the place in which the function is exercised that makes the act obscene. With regard to sex, Richards finds the abuse of bodily function in our culture's ideas of sex as procreative and of masturbation as abuse. But, whatever minor abuse of function is to be found in nonprocreative sex or masturbation cannot match the abuse of function represented by the lopping off of a limb or by a disembowelment.

Etymological Considerations

The *Oxford English Dictionary* provides three definitions for "obscene": "1. Offensive to the senses, or to taste or refinement; disgusting, repulsive, filthy, foul, abominable, loathsome. . . . 2. Offensive to modesty or decency; expressing or suggesting unchaste or lustful ideas; impure, indecent, lewd. . . . 3. Ill omened, inauspicious."[16] While the second definition appears to speak most clearly to sexual depictions, the first is much wider in scope. It would include sex and violence, but it would also capture a large variety of other depictions, including some never thought to have lacked First Amendment protection. Dictionaries of an earlier era do not provide any narrower limits. Samuel Johnson defined "obscene" as "Immodest; not agreeable to chastity of mind; causing lewd ideas[;] Offensive; disgusting[;] Inauspicious; ill omened."[17] While "immodest" and "lewd" may point toward sexual material, "offensive" and "disgusting," let alone "inauspicious" and "ill omened," are not so limited.

While the *Oxford English Dictionary* finds the derivation of "obscene" to be obscure, an examination of that derivation may provide some insight into limitations on the use of the word. There appear to be three competing derivations offered by scholars who have examined the issue. One derivation suggested by commentators is from "ob caenum" which would be "on account of filth" or simply "filth."[18] An alternative is from "ab scaena" or "off the stage," which might mean either "not to be openly shown on the stage of life"[19] or alternatively "off the theatrical stage."[20]

"Obscene" as "On Account of Filth"

If the derivation of "obscene" is taken as relating to filth, it is unclear to what the word ought to apply. While some ordinary uses of the word "filth" would justify including depictions of excretory activities within the concept of obscenity, why should depictions of sexual activities be so included? Since the results of excretory activities may qualify as filth, the ban on depictions of such acts might be "on account of filth." Sexual acts are, however, not themselves filth or filthy, so why would depictions of sexual acts be banned "on account of filth"? Furthermore, if the products of one's entrails are filth and depictions of the production may be banned, ought not the entrails themselves be considered filth and depictions of their exposure through a violent attack on the abdomen be banned?

Certainly not all sexual acts are filthy, and a ban on all depictions of sexual acts can not be justified "on account of filth." Professor Sheldon Nahmod has, in fact, suggested an interesting justification for obscenity laws, based not on the filth of sex but on its sacredness. In his view, the obscenity exception is the carving out of an area where the state may protect the sacred aspects of sexuality and prevent its debasement, commercialization, and desecration. This kind obscenity is exempted from First Amendment protection not because it has low value but it has such high value as to be sacred.[21] While the suggested rationale has not been accepted by the courts or other commentators as the justification for a First Amendment exception, the approach is certainly based on a healthier attitude toward sex than are those approaches that would create the exception because of the "filth" which is depicted.

Of course, not all depictions of sexual activity are banned as obscene. Only those appealing to the prurient or shameful interests may be banned. It may be tenable to argue that some sexual activities or aspects of those activities are filthy and an interest in those acts or aspects shameful. If obscenity is to be based on filth, some way of defining which acts or aspects are filthy must be presented.

Professor Harry Clor offers a preliminary definition of "obscenity" that speaks to the idea of filth. He suggests that obscenity is "a degradation of the human dimensions of life to a sub-human or merely physical level."[22] Clor finds some insight in an analysis of a passage from Joseph Heller's Catch 22. In the passage, Yossarian discovers a wounded friend, disemboweled and barely still alive. Seeing the friend's entrails, as life and spirit slip away, Yossarian concludes that "man is garbage."[23] The conclusion seems to be not that the human body contains garbage, physical material that will eventually decompose, but rather that the body viewed as purely physical, as divorced from human spirit, is garbage. This then is, for Clor, the nub of obscenity. "Obscene literature may be defined as that literature which presents, graphically and in detail, a degrading picture of human life and invites the reader or viewer, not to contemplate that picture, but to wallow in it."[24]

Clor's approach seems to mesh well with the genesis of the concept of obscenity in the individual suggested by Joel Feinberg. The development of the "Yuk!" reaction, with regard to both natural objects and to acts, pertains to the concept of filth. If the internalization of the parental response of "Dirty!," "Nasty!," or "Yuk!" to the attempted ingestion of things found under rocks is the psychological basis for the concept of obscenity, that concept would extend to treatments of humans that Clor finds obscene.

Clor's analysis is insightful. It is the depiction of the human spirit that distinguishes a romantic film, even a romantic film depicting explicit sex, from the depictions of explicit sex that might make another film obscene. In the sexually obscene film, man and, more commonly, woman are reduced to the subhuman, merely physical level—reduced to garbage or filth. It is not the sexual act, but rather the focus solely on the physical aspects of that act, that is filth.

The same points may be made of violence. Just as there is a difference between a sexually explicit romance and sexual obscenity, there is a difference between a death scene and violence that may be taken as obscene. Sexual obscenity focuses on the physical aspects of sexuality, while neglecting the aspects reflecting the human spirit. Romance focuses on one of the highest aspects of that spirit. A death scene can certainly focus on the human spirit, personal relationships, the meaning and intransigence of life, or any of a myriad of other facets of the human spirit or experience. On the other hand, such a scene can depict solely the physical side of death. To the degree that the depiction is purely physical, to the degree that the depiction presents the end of a person's life as though it were the end of subhuman life, to the degree that the person is shown as purely physical garbage, to that degree the depiction may be viewed as obscene.[25]

"Obscene" as "Off the Stage [of Life]"

Clor's analysis actually encompasses both the "on account of filth" derivation already discussed and the "off the stage of life" derivation. He offers two preliminary definitions of obscenity. In addition to that already presented, he writes "obscenity consists in making public that which is private; it consists in an intrusion upon intimate physical processes and acts or physical-emotional states."[26] He sees that definition as being related to the definition based on degradation of life in that "when the intimacies of life are exposed to public view their human value may be depreciated."[27]

Portraying the individual as a purely physical entity treats the person as garbage or filth. Professor Clor also suggests that it is the purely physical side of human existence that humans choose to remove from the stage of life. "The element of obscenity . . . consists in one's being 'too close' to other persons performing intimate physical acts."[28] We withhold from the view of others, and wish others to withhold from our view, those acts that are governed by animal urges rather than the human spirit or in which the observer can experience only the subhuman aspects of the act.

> There are certain bodily acts which will tend to arouse disgust in an observer who is not involved in the act and is not, at the time, subject to its urgencies. What the observer sees is a human being governed by physiological urges and functions. Now, to the participants, the act . . . can have important personal and supra-biological meanings. But the outside observer cannot share the experience of these meanings; what he sees is simply the biological process.[29]

This view explains the private nature of sex, as well as the privacy commonly accorded excretory activities. In the nonromantic physical urges of lust and in the need to eliminate, the human being is governed by the same subhuman urges that affect animals. The reduction to subhuman, to garbage, or to filth, causes us to bar such activities from the open stage of life.

What has been said of sex and excretion can also be applied to other physical needs, drives, or inevitabilities. "[T]here can be . . . obscene views of death, of birth, of illness, and of acts such as eating . . . Obscenity makes a public exhibition of these phenomena and does so in a way that their larger human context is lost or depreciated." [30] Obscenity is not limited to sexual or excretory activities. "[O]bscene literature is that literature which invites and stimulates the reader to adopt the obscene posture toward human existence—to engage in the reduction of man's values, functions, and ends to the animal or subhuman level." [31]

Clearly, Clor's analysis shows why, under the "on account of filth" or the "removed from the stage of life" derivation of "obscene," violence may be obscenity. To treat the human body as fodder for a chain saw is to exclude the humanity of the victim of that violence. It is to treat the person as subhuman, as garbage or filth. As such, it is also removed from the stage of life. While a person may wish to die peacefully in the company of loved ones, that desire is based on elements of the human spirit. While presumably preferring to avoid the experience altogether, if a person is to be dismembered or disemboweled, the experience is less likely one the victim would want to share.[32] The first death has its focus in the human spirit; the second is subhuman.

Recognizing that his approach extends to violence, Clor includes violence within his definition of obscenity. An obscene depiction is "one which tends predominantly to . . . [v]isually portray in detail, or graphically describe in lurid detail, the violent physical destruction, torture, or dismemberment of a human being, provided this is done to exploit morbid or shameful interest in these matters and not for genuine scientific, educational, or artistic purposes." [33] He would also include a similarly lurid depiction or description of death or of a dead body.[34]

"Obscene" as "Off the [Theatrical] Stage"
Havelock Ellis seems credited with the position that "obscene" derives from "off the stage" in the sense of the theatrical stage.[35] It has been argued that this derivation is mistaken,[36] but it does have the advantage of making claims that obscene material does not enjoy the protections of freedoms of speech or press almost tautological. If obscene material is that material that has been banned from the stage, then obviously such material has not been protected. If that is the derivation, a look at the materials historically banned from the stage is re-

quired. Even if that is not the derivation, the same examination will provide an important insight into what historically has been considered so offensive as to be unacceptable for public view.

The examination begins with the origins of Western drama in the Greek theater. The Greeks are said to have been quite tolerant of sexual and scatological themes in comedies but intolerant of violence, but the comparison may be flawed. While it may be, as "D. H. Lawrence declared[,] that 'some of Aristophanes shocks everybody today, and didn't galvanize the later Greeks at all,'"[37] the material spoken of is described as "bawdy blasphemy." A toleration for bawdy speech, even when blasphemous, does not necessarily imply a toleration for the explicit acts of modern sexual obscenity.

While the toleration for sexual depictions in drama may not have encompassed the modern variety, it does not require a journey too far into our society's past to find an era in which Aristophanes would have been shocking. In William Arrowsmith's translation of Aristophanes's *The Clouds*, Strepsiades is said at one point to raise his phallus to the ready.[38] Later in the play, the same character is again said to raise his phallus to the ready, as he threatens Amynias: "I'll sunder your rump with my ram!"[39] Both references to a phallus are to a symbolic leather thong worn by the actor. Arrowsmith recognizes that there is dispute over whether the actor actually wore such a thong but argues that the text only makes sense if there was such a prop.[40] Further, the argument against the wearing of the phallus appears to be based on the earlier appearance of Aristophanes as a character in the play.[41] In his monologue, he describes the play: "She's a dainty play. Observe, gentlemen, her natural modesty, the demureness of her dress, with no dangling thong of leather, red and thick at the tip, to make small boys snigger."[42] Even if Arrowsmith is incorrect and the thong was not worn in *The Clouds*, Aristophanes's description of the demureness of the play in comparison of others indicates that the use of a phallus was not unknown to the Greek theater.

Still later in *The Clouds*, characters representing philosophy and sophistry are rolled onto the stage in large gilded cages. Arrowsmith describes them as being human from the shoulders down and fighting cocks from the neck up. Once again, he recognizes some debate over their form, but the debate appears to be whether they had any nonhuman aspects.[43] With regard to the human portions, Philosophy is described as "large, muscular . . . , powerful but not heavy, expressing in his movements that inward harmony and grace and dignity which the Old Education was meant to produce."[44] Sophistry, by contrast, is "comparatively slight, with sloping shoulders, an emaciated pallor, an enormous tongue and a disproportionately large phallus."[45]

Aristophanes's *Lysistrata,* as translated by Douglass Parker,[46] also has a sexual content. The plot concerns a pact by the women of Greece to withhold sexual relations from the men until the men of the various city-states reach a peace agreement. At one point, both the male and female characters remove their tunics.[47] While the characters appear still to have worn undergarments, the lack of a tunic makes it more obvious when Kinesias later staggers on stage "in erection and considerable pain."[48] The male chorus also seems so affected and various characters appear on stage while attempting to conceal their excitation. When a herald from Sparta arrives, his cloak is thrown open and his phallus exposed.[49] The play also portrays Peace as "a beautiful girl without a stitch on" who appears on stage so unclad and contributes further to the condition of the men.[50] The nudity of the character Peace may seem surprising, but it appears that the Greeks "looked on the naked body, including the sexual organs, without the slightest sense of shame."[51]

Robert Henning Webb's translation of *Lysistrata*[52] has the same tone. When a herald from Sparta arrives in Athens, an Athenian official asks him if he is Priapus in the flesh and suggests that the Spartan is hiding a weapon under his cloak. When asked about the state of things in Laconia, the Spartan replies "Shparta iss rampant . . . ja, und her allies . . . Dere iss a gross uprising efery-vere!"[53] Later a group of ambassadors arrives from Sparta. The Chorus inquires into their health, and the Spartans throw open their cloaks and respond "Vy do you esk? Vat need of verds to zay? Your eyess kann tell you how it shtands mit us!"[54] The Athenians then throw open their cloaks revealing that they are in the same state. The goddess also appears in Webb's translation, there called "Appeasement" and described as "clothed in smiles."[55]

Aristophanes's plays do not match the explicit sex of modern obscene productions. However, the sexual content of those plays would have caused them to be obscene in the early to middle parts of this century. The written version of *Lysistrata,* let alone any film version or a performance, was subject to customs seizure during the first thirty years of this century and, as late as 1955, was considered obscene by the United States Post Office.[56] While the sexual content of Greek drama may seem tame by current standards, in the Victorian and post-Victorian climate in which obscenity law focused on the sexual, material the Greeks considered suitable for the stage would have been banned from the stage, that is, would have been obscene.

While the Greeks are said not to have been as tolerant of dramatic violence, they did allow descriptions of violence. Narrative poetry, and drama, contain such oral depictions.[57] In Aeschylus's *Persians,* combat occurs off stage but a narrator describes the battle. Homer's *Iliad* is quite descriptive of the violent deaths that occur.

Even some audience exposure to violence was tolerated. In Sophocles's *Electra*, Clytemnestra is killed by her son Orestes.[58] The murder takes place in a house out of the view of the audience, but her voice is heard. She pleads for her son to take pity but to no avail. The audience hears her say "Oh, I am smitten!" Orestes's sister Electra urges "Smite, if you can, once more!" and Clytemnestra is heard to say "Ah, woe is me again!"[59]

What Greek drama appeared not to accept was the visual depiction of violent death.[60] According to Professor Roy Flickinger, "[t]he Greek theater suffered no scene of bloodshed to be enacted before its audience. When the plot of the play . . . required such an incident, the harrowing details were narrated by a messenger who had witnessed the event."[61] Professor Peter Arnott is in accord: "We are led up to the point where some violent deed is going to take place, given the motives for the deed and the story behind it, but the deed itself takes place off stage."[62]

It has been suggested that the unwillingness to portray violence may have been based on the small number of actors involved in Greek dramas. Since there was no curtain, the actor who died on stage would have to arise at the end of the scene to appear later in another role.[63] An example of the difficulties presented by on-stage violence may be found in Euripides's *The Medea*.[64] Medea murders Creon and his daughter by sending the daughter a dress with a poison in the fabric. The effects of the poison are not seen, but a messenger later reports to Medea that when Creon's daughter put on the dress, the poison caused it to stick to her skin, burned her, and caused her death. It is also reported that when Creon found his daughter, he fell on her corpse, and the dress also stuck to and killed him. Some rewriting might have allowed the beginnings of the daughter's death to have occurred on stage with her leaving the stage in agony to die off stage. However, if Creon's demise is to occur on stage, the daughter's corpse must be there and Creon's and his daughter's bodies must be removed. Further, Creon's daughter appears nowhere in the play, so another actor might be required. The actor playing Creon might also have to appear as another character after Creon's death. The only dialogue after Creon's death is between Jason and Medea, but Jason and Creon seem never to appear on stage together, so one actor could conceivably play both roles.

While problems in staging might lead to less on stage violence, Arnott argues that the convention is based in aesthetics or taste.[65] Flickinger agrees: "It is customary to explain the Greek avoidance of violence on aesthetic grounds; to assert that the susceptibilities of the Greeks were so refined as to have been offended by scenes of bloodshed. That which would be disagreeable or painful to see in real life should never be presented to an audience."[66] Arnott's and Flickinger's position is supported by Euripides's *Hecuba*.[67] The treatment of violence in the play is typical in that it occurs out of the audience's view. The play begins with the ghost of Polydorus, the son of Hecuba, describing his own murder at the hands of Polymestor, so that homicide, which is important in the motivation it later provides Hecuba, does not take place on stage. When the Greeks demand the Trojan Hecuba's daughter Polyxena as a sacrifice on the grave of the slain Achilles, that death too takes place off stage. Polyxena is led away and the news of her death is brought back by a herald. While the death is described in detail, it does not occur within the view of the audience. These deaths might present staging problems, but the play's remaining violence would appear to present no such difficulty.

When Hecuba takes her revenge on Polymestor, that action takes place in a tent. Polymestor's sons are killed and Polymestor is blinded to the accompaniment of screams and battering on the walls of the tent. The signs of violence are strong, but again the action occurs out of the audience's view. What is particularly telling in this scene is that the action could have occurred on stage. Polymestor survives and takes part in later dialogue. The difficulty of removing a body and the actor coming back as another character does not exist. Further, Polymestor's sons' bodies are carried from the tent and placed on stage, where they remain until the end of the play. Again, the fact that the violence occurs off stage cannot be explained by staging difficulties. Intolerance of violence on stage is the better explanation.

There are also those who would question the conclusion that scenes of violent death were confined to the offstage—were obscene. Professor Walton notes that not all violence occurred offstage and that "Greek tragedy does contain scenes of physical assault, suffering, and even death, to be presented in full view of the audience." [68] Walton cites in support of his conclusion Prometheus's death in an earthquake, and the suicides of Ajax and Evadne. [69] However, whatever may have happened to Prometheus says nothing with regard to violence of person against person. Prometheus was himself a Titan, and neither was his tormentor a human. It was Zeus who brought about any violence toward Prometheus. [70] Ajax does indeed commit suicide in Sophocles's *Ajax*. [71] He firmly seats his sword, point up, in the sand at the sea shore and then throws himself on the point. Evadne also commits suicide in Euripides's *The Suppliant Women*. [72] She appears on a cliff above the funeral pyre of her husband, Capaneus, and shortly thereafter throws herself on the pyre.

Walton's examples show that it is not death that was barred from the stage in Greek drama. But that is not the position of those who argue that violence was barred. Even those accepting the rule against violence note an exception for suicide, death as the result of natural events, or at the hands of the gods. [73]

It is homicide that could not be shown. It was the violence of person against person that was obscene.

Walton's examples are also relevant to the alternative explanation offered for the ban on violence. They call into question the claim that any lack of violence and death may have been based on staging problems. If these nonhomicide deaths could be staged, it would seem that homicides would offer little or no increased difficulties in staging. In fact, Ajax's suicide at the sea shore required a scene change to that location, the only scene change in any of Sophocles's still-existing plays.[74] Sophocles was willing to change scenes to include Ajax's suicide on stage; surely the staging of other deaths would not have presented insurmountable difficulty.

If "obscene" means banned from the stage, then at least the classical Greek view of obscenity included violence. Again, despite claims that the Greeks were tolerant of sexual themes, it may be a mistake to conclude that materials obscene under modern law would have been accepted. However, even if such sexually explicit matter would have been considered obscene, so also was violence.

Roman theater appears to have treated sexual themes with at least as much toleration as had the Greeks. Richard Beacham's study of Roman drama[75] considers performances from as early as the fourth century B.C. He finds comparisons between the performances of Etruscan actors in Rome and the *phallica* of Greece, each involving phallic ceremonies and the invocation of the phallus to assure fertility in newly wed couples. He finds even earlier indications of such themes in terra cotta figures with oversized phalluses in those areas of Italy colonized by the Greeks and suggests earlier Roman performances of farces containing suggestive dance of a sort he characterizes as common of "stag-parties" of this era.[76]

The treatment of sex continues into later eras. The titles of the late third century B.C. plays of Naevius, titles such as *Testicularia* and *Triphallus,* indicate enduring themes. Beacham notes that the *Floralia* festival performances, from at least as early as 173 B.C., were noted for their license, merriment, and their naked female performers.[77] Indeed, he suggests that the Roman adaptations of Greek plays, particularly those by Terence and Plautus, display an outlook on sex more free than that of the Greeks.[78]

While the Romans may have shared the Greek tolerance for sexual themes, Beacham suggests that they did not share the Greek intolerance of violence. He finds a common theme in slaves being verbally abused and threatened with great violence.[79] As an example he provides Plautus's play *Casina* in which two slaves exchange insults "underscored by a variety of escalating knock-about abuse; slaps, blows, trips, and the like."[80] He also notes the use of "verbal violence and descriptive gore" in the works of Accius.[81] Beacham suggests that this increase in violence is an increase in dramatization required for a less sophisticated audience accustomed to more lively, less thoughtful, entertainment.[82] Even a contemporary critic, Horace, is said to have criticized mid-first-century B.C. Roman audiences for their preference for spectacle and sensationalism over poetry and drama.[83]

Despite the suggestion that there was an increased toleration for violence in early Roman theater, the violence Beacham cites may not really violate the Greek view of the obscene. He does not cite to homicides or to the actual infliction of physical punishment. There is verbal abuse and "descriptive gore," but the Greeks were not averse to on stage reports of violence.

The same cannot be said of later Roman theater. In an era in which mortal combat became popular entertainment, theater also became more violent. In Catullus's *Laureolus* a robber is crucified and then torn to pieces by wild beasts. There is death on the stage and the victim vomits blood. Beacham cites to claims that in Titus's reign a prisoner was forced to play the role and was actually killed on stage by a bear.[84] Late Roman theater included real battle scenes, and there were barriers erected between the stage and the audience, so that spectators would not be accidently killed.[85] There seems to have been little objection to the sacrifice of the lives of captured slaves in staging spectacular battle scenes, either land battles or sea battles in immense water-filled arenas.

While the concept of the obscene as that which is banned from the stage did not include violence in the later Roman theater, neither did it include sex. The same report of the prisoner torn apart by the bear also reports the "faithful reenactment" of the legend of Pasiphae concealing herself in a false cow so as to be mounted by a bull.[86] Elagabalus is also said to have ordered, in the third century A.D., that sexual scenes in performances not be simulated but be actually enacted.[87] It has been suggested that the same availability of slaves captured in conquest that supplied actors forced to fight to the death provided slaves to engage in the dramatic staging of sexual acts.[88] It cannot be said that obscenity had shifted its focus from violence to sex. Rather, it seems that the concept of obscenity in that era simply lost all extension.

In medieval drama, particularly religious plays portraying the lives of the martyrs, violence also seems common.

> In the name of sacred instruction and secular diversion, the Apostles were graphically stoned, stabbed, blinded, crucified, and flayed. Other holy men and women variously and vigorously had their teeth wrenched out,

their breasts torn off, and their bodies scourged, shot with arrows, baked, grilled, and burned. Audiences were also treated to bestial scenes of infanticide, and to broad comedies about divinely mutilated Jews. No torment was too extreme or too gory for representation, as medieval drama ignored the classical tenet, advanced by Horace, of not bringing upon the stage what should be performed behind the scenes.[89]

The religious lessons of the violent *mysteres* might justify, without really changing the rule, an exception from the classical view of the obscene. Just as death at the hands of the gods was not obscene, death for the cause of God might also be nonobscene.

Another problem is raised, however, by public executions. Executions might be considered irrelevant to a consideration of the "off the [theatrical] stage" derivation of "obscene." Executions are acts of the state in the enforcement of the law. They may be viewed as nonentertainment, even when conducted in public. Certainly the rationale behind public trials, even in an era of televised trials, goes beyond their entertainment value. Public executions might be argued to have had an educational or deterrent value. This justification is somewhat undermined, however, by the fact that the people of Mons once purchased a criminal from a nearby town, so that they could see him executed.[90] That may indicate more of an interest in entertainment.[91] It may simply be that public execution and the "[m]iracle plays and *mysteres* were violent theatre for a violent era"[92] and that the view of obscenity had changed.

It is also the case that the classics of English drama contain violence. Many of Shakespeare's plays were set against a background of violence. It would be impossible to tell the story of the struggles between the Houses of York and Lancaster and between the English and the French, the stories of Bosworth Field and the Battle of Agincourt, without a general atmosphere of violence. As was true of the Greeks, a great deal of the violence remains in the background and is learned of through narration. Audiences are moved from place to place on various battlefields, as reports of casualties flow in. There are also the suicides that were accepted in Greek drama—Romeo and Juliet, and Antony and Cleopatra. Unlike Greek drama, however, armed conflict and death are also presented on the stage. Characters enter and exit fighting, and there are violent deaths.[93] While it may be that, compared to his contemporaries and predecessors, Shakespeare's works contain less violence and less bizarre violence,[94] murder is not uncommon.

Despite the existence of violence, it is important to note that Shakespeare's plays were not as violent as they could have been and that some violence occurs off the stage. In *Titus Andronicus,* a play considered Shakespeare's "grisliest,"[95] the worst of the violence is behind the scenes. Lavinia is raped, and her hands are cut off and her tongue cut out. The violence against her is described and she appears on stage with bleeding mouth and bloody stumps where her hands were, but Shakespeare chose not to show the violence. While the decision not to show the rape may have been based on the combination of violence with sexual content, that would not explain the exclusion of the rest of the violence. Nor can it be explained by staging difficulty. Later in the play Titus Andronicus submits, on stage, to having his hand cut off, believing that it is in exchange for the lives of his sons. If Shakespeare could stage that amputation, the amputation of Lavinia's hands could also have been staged. Furthermore, contemporaries had found ways to stage the biting off of one's own tongue.[96] The step to cutting out the tongue of another could not have been too difficult.

Most of the on-stage violence in Shakespeare involves duels or other individual combat employing swords. In such scenes Shakespeare avoided the currently common theme of the slasher sadistically torturing and murdering a helpless victim. In Shakespeare's swordplay the combatants are of roughly equal age and rank and status, and the typical encounter has been described as having character of "a trial by combat, a feudal contest conducted according to mutually understood rules."[97]

There are also, however, Shakespearean killings where this equality and flavor of trial by combat are lacking. Sometimes, while the killing involves only one attacker, the victim is physically weaker than the killer. The smothering of Desdemona by Othello provides such an example. Professor Barish also notes a category of what he calls "sacrificial" killings in which individuals are set upon by groups.[98] He includes the killing of York in *The Third Part of King Henry the Sixth* in which York is subdued, taunted, and then killed. He also includes the killing of Lady MacDuff and her child by Macbeth's minions.

Another frequently cited example of Shakespearean violence is the blinding of Gloucester in *King Lear.* The act occurs in view of the audience with Gloucester bound and falling far short of an equal combatant. In this regard, Shakespeare stands in contrast to the Greek theater in which blindings occurred off stage, even when self-inflicted as in Sophocles's *Oedipus the King.*[99]

Some of Shakespeare's contemporaries were even more taken with violence. Professor Barish notes the flaying of one character and the killing and cutting out the heart of another, the biting out of a character's own tongue, and the boiling of a character in oil in the works of playwrights more or less contemporary to Shakespeare.[100] Although even such examples may not match the goriness of the medieval era, they do show a greater tolerance for violence than was allowed in Greek drama.

While there may have been an increased tolerance for violence, it also appears that there was, in some venues, a parallel increased tolerance for sexual displays. The psychologists Eberhard and Phyllis Kronhausen, in their study of the history, law, and psychology of pornography, claim that exhibitions of human intercourse for the entertainment of select audiences were not rare in France from the Renaissance through part of the eighteenth century. They further note that exhibitions of copulating animals were customary in that era in various European societies. These forms of entertainment were not hidden away. Animal copulation was exhibited at various festivals, and while the audience for human copulation may have been select, it was before mixed audiences of men and women.[101]

In later continental theater, Flickinger argues that the Greek aesthetic objection to violence carried over to French drama in the early part of the twentieth century.

> This is the French position. . . . "A character in [French] tragedy could be permitted to kill himself, whether he did it by poison or steel: what he was not suffered to do was to kill someone else. And while nothing was to be shown on the stage which could offend the feelings through the medium of the eyes, *equally was nothing to be narrated with the accompaniment of any adjuncts that could possibly arouse disagreeable sensations in the mind.*"[102]

On the other hand, starting in the same era, from 1897 to 1962, and in the same country, the Grand-Guignol Theater in Paris was devoted to horrific drama that both terrorized and amused audiences. "[T]he Guignolers [went] happily, if homicidally, about their business of gouging out one another's eyes, cooking villains in vats of sulphuric acid, hurling vitriol and cutting throats, all to the accompaniment of hysterical laughter and hideous shrieks."[103]

While the classical view may have been that it was violence that was obscene, views of violence as obscene seem to have varied with the times. Of course, the same is true of sexual activities as obscene. As either an aesthetic or moral concept, the focus of obscenity has changed over time. What was acceptable on the stage in one era may be unacceptable in another. What is clear is that "obscene" as "banned from the [theatrical] stage" does not have a sole application to sexual or excretory activities. Such activities may only be talked about in some eras, with more or less explicitness, and shown in others. The same is true of violence: it could only be described in Greek drama but could be shown in gory detail in other eras.

Narrowing the Concept

As has been seen, obscenity is broader than sex and excretion. As Professor Frederick Schauer sums up the general concept, " '[o]bscene' refers to that which is repugnant or disgusting to the senses, or offensive, filthy, foul, repulsive, or loathsome. . . . It is not incorrect to say that war or gory violence is obscene."[104] Nor, it appears, would it be incorrect to say that a great variety of other acts or objects are obscene. But if obscenity is to be a concept useful to the law, it must be narrowed. The broad extension presented in this chapter must be reduced to a core. Otherwise, obscenity would include too much material that has never been excluded from First Amendment protections.

Professor Feinberg criticizes Professor Richards's work on the ground, among others, of its being overly broad.[105] He suggests that the "natural use and function" approach is implicated for a Catholic couple using a condom. Since the natural function of the sex organs is procreation, sex using a condom would be an unnatural use of the sex organs and hence would be obscene. However, while some may view such an act as sinful, the ascription of obscenity seems unwarranted. Feinberg also suggests that, under Richards's analysis, smoking is an obscene act, because it is an unnatural use of the lungs. Furthermore, he notes that Richards's position that obscenity is based on the failure to exercise competently a bodily function would make impotence obscene.

Richards's work may help to explain why cultures find certain acts obscene, but it may not be of much legal use. While it helps in showing that the Supreme Court's definition is narrower than the common usage of the word "obscene," it provides little additional help in the legal arena. There must be, within Richards's broad concept, some way to delineate a subclass of the obscene to which First Amendment protection is denied. Nothing in Richards's work helps to distinguish that subclass.

Feinberg may also be criticized for presenting an overly broad concept of obscenity, at least from a legal point of view. He includes as obscene: "a dank cavernous fungus or a slug . . . [,] bloated profits, cynical irresponsibility . . . [and d]eliberately telling a gross and unvarnished lie clearly to deceive others and to help the speaker gain at their expense."[106] Such uses are by no means poor use of the English language. Phrases such as "obscene profits" are common, but the broad extension of the concept is inadequate to draw the lines required by First Amendment law.

The concept must be reduced to its core if obscenity is to be without constitutional protection. Feinberg does, while denying the identity of obscenity and pornography, appear to find at least some sexual depictions to be at that core. Yet, violence and death are, for him, equally central to the concept. Of the ten sentences he presents as examples of proper, nonsexual, uses of the term, five have to do with death, either by violence or accompanied by exultation.[107] This is not a coincidence. He states that death is

> a subject so liable to obscene treatment, it is a wonder that it has not broken into the Model Penal Code's Unholy Trio [of sex, nudity and excretion] and enlarged it into a quartet. . . . [T]here is nothing more obscene in a perfectly literal, hardcore sense, nothing from which we naturally shrink with greater disgust and horror, than a close-up view of a dead human body with it [sic] protruding eyes and greenish skin. Nor is there any more obscene conduct imaginable than patently inappropriate responses to a dead body—desecration, savage dismemberment, brutal gestures, cannibalism, or necrophiliac embraces.[108]

Presumably, Feinberg would not disagree such desecration or savage dismemberment of a live body would be at least as obscene, as several of his example sentences indicate. Violence, at least violent death, is for Feinberg as central as sex to the concept of obscenity. If it is only that core that is unprotected by the First Amendment, depictions of violence can be sufficiently offensive to be within the exception.

While Feinberg seems to include violence within the core of obscenity and gives it more attention than any other nonsexual topic, that failure to include other varieties of depiction does not necessarily rule out the possibility of extending his approach to other areas. If First Amendment protections are to depend on the sort of analysis under which Feinberg can find violence to be obscene, there may be a danger that the concept can be stretched even further. Having opened the door to include violence with sex, if sufficiently graphic and offensive, as obscene and unprotected, there should be concern over what else comes through that door. The etymological analysis is helpful in that regard.

The definition of "obscene," either in current or seventeenth-century usage, provides little help in assuring that the obscenity exception will not overreach its proper scope. Neither is much aid obtained in the first two of the suggested derivations of "obscene." The suggestion that obscene literature is that which portrays a degrading picture of human life, not for the purpose of contemplation but rather so that the reader or viewer can "wallow" in the graphic, detailed depiction of people as garbage,[109] might also be extended beyond what would be good for the First Amendment. Sex and violence both fit Clor's description, but there is little to no guarantee that some depictions involving other topics might not also be found obscene under this approach. The second derivation of "obscene" as "off the stage of life" suffers from the same possibility of over-extension. If obscene depictions are those which, when made public, intrude on the intimate or which, when exposed to public view, lose their human value,[110] again the scope may be wider than would be best for First Amendment purposes.

While each separate piece of the analysis may not distinguish sex and violence from other potential areas of additional exception from First Amendment protection, in combination they may provide sufficient limitation. Under each approach, violence is as central as sex, and it is difficult to conceive of another area that would also be so central. Nonetheless, even that small likelihood may be cause for concern, in the face of what may appear to be fairly flexible approaches to the concept of the obscene. It is with regard to this concern that the last derivation of "obscene" is so important.

While the derivation of "obscene" from "off the [theatrical] stage" is only one of several suggested derivations, it is important in that it speaks most closely to the issue at hand. If the question is what material is denied First Amendment protection and is to be kept from the stage, and if the answer is "that which is obscene," then an approach to obscenity that focuses on what has been kept from the stage is of particular importance. Such an approach makes the concept of obscenity depend on an examination of the sort of depiction that has, over the ages, been sufficiently offensive so as to be banned from the scene. It is also the approach that makes the most sense of claims that obscene material has never been protected from proscription. If obscene material is that which cannot legally be shown on stage, then such depictions are legally unprotected.

While different eras have tolerated differing degrees of violence and of sex on the stage, the two would appear to be equally at the core of the concept of obscenity. Importantly, this historical approach is less subject to expansion, and any further limitation of the First Amendment, than the other approaches examined. There would appear to be only two other topics that have been similarly barred from the stage at various times in history. In each of those two areas, the Constitution specifically protects the speech involved, leaving only sex and violence within the class of the obscene.

The first potential additional topic is that of political speech critical of the government or of society. The forced suicide of Socrates shows the early danger involved in such speech, although his offense had heretical aspects as well. Professor Beacham reports that, in 206 B.C., the poet/playwright Naevius was imprisoned and later exiled for questioning the abilities of a powerful family of Roman consuls,[111] and that Tiberius ordered the suicide of a playwright who had written verse unflattering of him.[112] Repression of political speech remained common in all ages and in all cultures right up through the *Schenck v. United States*[113] and *Debs v. United States*[114] cases in the World War I era. The prosecutions of communists in the 1950s, at issue in *Dennis v. United States*,[115] *Yates v. United States*,[116] *Scales v. United States*,[117] and *Noto v. United States*,[118] and the whole McCarthy era carried on the tradition. Even as late as the Vietnam era, Dr. Benjamin Spock and the Reverend William Sloane Coffin suffered a conviction for their political speech, before the United States Court of Appeals recognized their right to utter such speech.[119]

Despite the prevalence of prosecutions for political speech, it is undeniable that such speech is at the core of the First Amendment. The Supreme Court, in its examination of criminal convictions based on political speech, has never declared such speech unprotected but has, instead, focused on the dangers necessary to justify a conviction in spite of the conceded First Amendment protection. Whatever history may be presented showing a lack of protection for political speech, the constitutional choice has been made to protect such speech in the United States.

The only other area the history of which can match sex and violence in being barred from the stage is blasphemy and heresy. Socrates's speech had its heretical aspects, and throughout history there are places and eras in which heresy would lead to execution. Professor Beacham writes of the difficulties faced by Roman aediles in planning entertainment that would please a public audience without offending religious interests.[120] The long history of prosecution and punishment for blasphemy, from ancient times to the present, is well documented by Leonard Levy's recent work, *Blasphemy: Verbal Offense Against the Sacred, from Moses to Salman Rushdie.*[121]

Heresy and blasphemy are particularly interesting in that they may be argued also to fit, in a broad sense, within the "people as garbage" approach to obscenity. Those who would be interested in punishing blasphemy and heresy would consider the recognition of a supreme being, in fact a very specific supreme being, as essential to the human spirit. The denial of that supreme being could be viewed as a denial of the human spirit and, for that reason, might be seen as obscene. Despite the fit between heresy and blasphemy and the concept of obscenity, here too the Constitution prevents the expansion of obscenity to that area. The religion clauses of the First Amendment embody the constitutional decision that religious thought and speech are not to be subject to government control. Even if historically obscene, such speech cannot be argued to be legally obscene in our constitutional system.

However one approaches the concept of obscenity, the concept is not limited to sex and excretion. Violence is equally at the core. There may be other topics that are less central, and an expansion of the First Amendment exception to exclude those topics from protection would seriously weaken the First Amendment. But a recognition of what is truly at the core of the concept of obscenity is merely to focus properly the exception rather than to provide a license for expansion. Furthermore, the core is limited to sex and violence and a further refocusing aimed at expansion would appear unwarranted.

The discussion in this chapter has been extralegal. It shows only that the concept of obscenity in ordinary discourse is broader than sex and excretion and properly includes violence. It also demonstrates that the core of the concept, at least as restricted by the Constitution, is limited to those two areas. What is lacking from the discussion, at this point, is a demonstration that the same constitutional restrictions that exclude political and blasphemous speech from the legally obscene do not also exclude depictions of violence. Clearly, any exclusion of violence would be less explicit than the exclusions of political and blasphemous speech. Violence, unlike political speech, is clearly not at the core of First Amendment protections. Neither does violence, unlike blasphemy and heresy, enjoy the specific protection of a clause like the religion clauses. Violence simply does not enjoy the same protected status as politics and religion, and there is no constitutional command to exclude it, for legal purposes, from the core of the concept of obscenity.

The conclusion that there is no constitutional command to protect depictions of violence, even coupled with the conceptual inclusion of violence as at the core of obscenity, does not necessarily lead to the conclusion that violence is unprotected. The Supreme Court, in *Roth*, held that obscenity has been historically without legal protection. If that history has consistently limited the legal use of the term "obscene" and concept of obscenity to the narrower extension of sex and excretion, the more limited concept would control in a legal context. It would be only the sexually obscene, and not violent obscenity, that would have been historically without legal protection, and the Court's limitation of obscenity to sex and excretion would be correct. However, as the next chapter will demonstrate, the history of obscenity law is not so limited, and even in a legal context, depictions of violence may properly be deemed obscene solely by virtue of that violence and without regard to any sexual or excretory content.

5 The History of Obscenity Law and the Development of Its Limitation to Depictions of Sex

Legal history and the light it sheds on the state of law in significant eras provides important insight into the protections afforded by various constitutional guarantees. With regard to the original Constitution and the Bill of Rights, the law of the colonial era and in the early stages of the United States indicates the abuses that provisions such as the Fourth Amendment were designed to address. Additionally, the acceptance of certain practices in that era may provide evidence that a particular guarantee in the Bill of Rights was not intended to bar that practice.

When the interpretation of a constitutional amendment is at issue, the relevant history extends to the time of the adoption of that amendment. This is important in an analysis of the Bill of Rights, because of the necessity of the Fourteenth Amendment to the application of the first eight amendments. The various provisions of the Bill of Rights are, by their terms, directed to the national government and not to the states. It is only through their incorporation in the Due Process Clause of the Fourteenth Amendment that any of the provisions of the Bill of Rights were brought to bear against the states. Any significant change in law between the adoption of the Bill of Rights and the Fourteenth Amendment could lead to the conclusion that a particular protection exists against the federal government but that it was not the intent of the adopters of the Fourteenth Amendment to incorporate that protection against the states.

Changes in law or developments in legal history that occur after the adoption of a particular guarantee or the incorporation of that guarantee in the Fourteenth Amendment are of lesser interest. Such changes do not speak to the intentions of the framers or of the adopters of a particular amendment, although if the intent was to adopt a provision that would change with the times,[1] any changes in the legal climate would be important.

Obscenity Law at the Time of
the Bill of Rights

In determining the scope of various provisions of the Bill of Rights, the Supreme Court has at times examined the state of the law and legal and political practice in the era in which they were adopted. The strongest use of such history is found in *Marsh v. Chambers*.[2] That case involved the Nebraska legislature's practice of engaging in prayer led by a state-paid chaplain. The practice was challenged as violative of the First Amendment prohibition against laws respecting an establishment of religion, as applied to the states under the Fourteenth Amendment. The accepted test for determining Establishment Clause violations would have been found in the three factors derived from *Lemon v. Kurtzman*[3] and known as the *Lemon* test. That test, whether the statute or action has a secular purpose, whether its primary effect is to advance or inhibit religion, and whether there is an excessive entanglement of government with religion, might well have spelled the end of the practice.

The *Marsh v. Chambers* Court chose not to apply the *Lemon* test. Instead, the Court looked to history. While recognizing that historical practices do not justify constitutional violations, such practices could provide an indication of the intent of the framers with regard to that practice. In particular, the Court noted that the First Congress employed a chaplain to lead it in prayer, and that fact was more than mere historical pattern.

> In this context, historical evidence sheds light not only on what the draftsmen intended the Establishment Clause to mean, but also on how they thought that Clause applied to the practice authorized by the First Congress — their actions reveal their intent. . . . It can hardly be thought that in the same week Members of the First Congress voted to appoint and to pay a Chaplain for each House and also voted to approve the draft of the First Amendment for submission to the States, they intended the Establishment Clause of the Amendment to forbid what they had just declared acceptable.[4]

While the history was that of Congress, rather than state legislatures, the Court noted similar historic practice of state legislatures. Moreover, the Court noted that it would be "incongruous" to be more stringent in applying the Clause to the states than in applying it to the federal government.[5]

Any evidence of the intent of the First Congress is especially important in interpreting the provisions of the Bill of Rights, since those amendments were drafted and submitted to the states by that Congress. Furthermore, the special status of the First Congress goes beyond the Bill of Rights. The acts of the First Congress speak to the meaning of provisions within the Constitution. As the Court explained in *Hampton v. United States*,[6]

> In the first Congress sat many members of the Constitutional Convention of 1787. This Court has repeatedly laid down the principle that a contemporaneous legislative exposition of the Constitution when the founders of our government and framers of our Constitution were actively participating in public affairs long acquiesced in fixed the construction to be given its provisions.[7]

The Court's reliance on legal history, however, goes beyond granting special status to the actions of the First Congress. The acts of the Second Congress played a role in *United States v. Watson*.[8] The issue there was whether a warrantless arrest by a postal inspector violated the Fourth Amendment. The government did not rely on any exigent circumstances to justify the lack of a warrant but rather rested on the existence of a statute authorizing such arrests, as long as there was probable cause. The statutory grant was the same as that given to United States Marshals and agents of the Federal Bureau of Investigation, the Drug Enforcement Administration, the Secret Service, and the Customs Service. The Court noted the ancient common-law rule that a law enforcement officer could arrest without a warrant for a misdemeanor committed in his presence or for any felony, so long as there was reasonable ground for the arrest. This formula also was the prevailing rule under state constitutions and statutes in the era of the Constitution and Bill of Rights. Since that rule prevailed in the states, the Court found import in the fact that in 1792 Congress invested United States Marshals and their deputies with the same powers in executing the laws as those possessed by sheriffs and deputies in the states. The fact that the Second Congress saw no inconsistency between the Fourth Amendment and the grant of arrest power to Marshals matching those of local law enforcement officers spoke in favor of the constitutionality of the practice. The legal climate in the constitutional era helped in finding the meaning of a provision of the Bill of Rights.

Even without the official acts of an early Congress, the state of the law in the constitutional era has been found important in various contexts. Justice Black, in his dissent in *Katz v. United States*,[9] noted the existence of the practice of eavesdropping in the colonial era and the failure of the framers of the Fourth Amendment to bar evidence so obtained. For Justice Black, those facts spoke against the exclusion of evidence gathered through warrantless hidden microphones.

In *Gregg v. Georgia*,[10] in considering whether death was inherently cruel and unusual punishment, the plurality opinion noted that death was a common sanction in every state at the time of the adoption of the Eighth Amendment as indication that the framers of the amendment did not intend its abolition. The plurality drew additional strength for its conclusion from the fact that the Fifth Amendment contemplates the continued existence of capital punishment in requiring a grand jury for the prosecution of "a capital, or otherwise infamous crime" and in the double-jeopardy clause protection against being "twice put in jeopardy of life or limb."

More closely related to the First Amendment issue at hand, *Chaplinsky v. New Hampshire*[11] established that "fighting words," those words that cause injury by their very utterance and are likely to cause the person to whom they are addressed to fight, are not protected by the First Amendment. The Court disposed of any First Amendment concerns by noting that the right of free speech is not absolute and that "[t]here are certain well-defined and narrowly limited classes of speech, the prevention and punishment of which has never been thought to raise any Constitutional problem."[12] The Court found fighting words to be within that unprotected class and did so without anywhere near as much history as provided in the obscenity cases.

The Court also relied on the colonial-era legal climate, and was somewhat more forthcoming with its history, in the group libel case *Beauharnais v. Illinois*.[13] The Court noted that libel of an individual was a crime in the colonial era, providing some supporting citations. The only issue for the Court then was whether the colonial-era crime of individual libel could be extended to group libel. While the Court did find some evidence that group libel was a colonial era crime, the Court did not rely on that evidence but instead argued that the extension was a reasonable extension of the colonial-era practice.

The Court, in *Roth v. United States*[14] was, then, following a well-traveled road in considering the regulation of speech in the constitutional era. The *Roth* opinion begins by noting that the freedoms of speech and press were never considered absolute and that at the time of the Bill of Rights libel could be prosecuted.[15] The Court also cited to statutes on blasphemy or profanity from each of the thirteen colonies or states and from Vermont that predate the Bill of Rights[16] and quoted a Massachusetts statute of the era making it criminal to publish " 'any filthy, obscene, or profane song, pamphlet, libel or mock sermon' in imitation or mimicking of religious services."[17] Since the Court was using the historical legal climate to find an exception to the First Amendment guarantees of free speech and press, the contours of the statutory climate are important in determining the scope of the exception. A careful look at the statutes cited, and at other relevant historical material, is required.

Turning to the statutes cited, Connecticut's *Act for the Punishment of Divers Capital and Other Felonies*[18] made it illegal "wilfully to blaspheme the Name of God the Father, Son, or Holy Ghost, either by denying, cursing or reproaching the true God or his Government of the World."[19] The act was a blasphemy statute. It would appear to have little to do with modern obscenity law, but it does establish that in Connecticut there was not an absolute right to free speech.

Delaware's *An Act Against Drunkenness, Blasphemy; and to Prevent the Grevious Sins of Prophane Cursing, Swearing and Blasphemy*[20] might appear from its title's inclusion of profanity to be more on point, but it too was aimed at preserving sanctity, this time of government as well as religion. Section four made it illegal for "any person within this government . . . prophanely [to] swear, by the name of God, Jesus Christ, or the Holy Spirit, or curse himself or any other person."[21] Section five, not so limited to members of the government, punished blasphemy by the pillory, branding on the forehead, and thirty-nine lashes.[22]

Georgia's statute was less specific in the nature of the profanity it barred. Its *An Act to Regulate Taverns, and to Suppress Vice and Immorality*[23] imposed fines against anyone taking a profane oath or trading with slaves without a permit.

The Maryland statute again shows the colonial concern over blasphemy. Illegal under the act were "blaspheming or cursing God, or . . . denying our Saviour Jesus Christ to be the son of God, or denying the Holy Trinity, or the Godhead of any of the Three Persons, or of the Unity of the Godhead, or . . . uttering any profane words concerning the Holy Trinity or any of the persons thereof."[24] Penalties ranged from fine or imprisonment on the first offense, the addition of a forehead brand on the second, to death, without benefit of clergy, on the third offense.[25]

In addition to the Massachusetts law using the word "obscene," the Court cited three other Massachusetts statutes. The first, titled *Blasphemy*, made it illegal to

> blaspheme the holy name of God, Father, Son, or Holy Ghost, with direct, presumptuous, or high handed blasphemy, either by wilful or obstinate denying the true God, or his creation, or government of the world, or . . . curse God in like manner, or reproach the holy religion of God, as if it were but a politick device . . . or . . . utter any other kind of blasphemy of the like nature and degree.[26]

The focus again is clearly on the protection of religious sensibilities. Other sections prohibit idolatry and witchcraft, and the penalty for violation is death. Interestingly, the citations of authority accompanying the various sections are all biblical.[27] Again there is no indication that the statute is aimed at the depiction of sexual acts, the modern focus of obscenity law, but again the statute does show the existence of some limits on speech.

The second statute, titled *An Act Against Blasphemy,*[28] is once again clearly aimed at the protection of religion. The statute does address cursing but only bars cursing God, Jesus Christ, or the Holy Ghost. Further banned is exposing to contempt and ridicule any of the books, all presented by name in the statute, of the Old or New Testament.

The last Massachusetts statute cited would appear from its title, *An Act to Prevent Profane Cursing and Swearing,*[29] to be of more general application and perhaps more closely related to obscenity. However, the act states as its justification that:

> the horrible practice of profane Cursing and Swearing is inconsistent with the dignity & rational cultivation of the human mind, with a due reverence of the Supreme Being and his Providence, & hath a natural tendency to weaken the solemnity and obligation of Oaths lawfully taken in the administration of Justice; to promote falsehood, perjuries, blasphemies, and the dissoluteness of manners, and to loosen the bonds of civil society.[30]

The focus of the statute seems far-removed from modern obscenity and aimed not at swearing and cursing in the modern sense but rather at invoking the name of God in a curse or in an unlawfully taken oath.

Two New Hampshire statutes, adopted within a week of each other in 1791, are cited. The first is titled *An Act for the Punishment of Certain Crimes Not Capital.*[31] The act contains a prohibition on libel and an additional prohibition on denying the existence of God or blaspheming the name of God, Jesus Christ, or the Holy Ghost. It further bars cursing or reproaching the word of God as contained in the Old and New Testaments, once again reciting the names of the books of the Bible.

The second statute, like the third of the Massachusetts statutes, bans profane swearing and cursing.[32] Unlike the Massachusetts statute, however, the explicit focus on using the name of God or unlawfully swearing is not present. The statute simply imposes a fine, imprisonment for one hour, or ten lashes on any person who "shall profanely curse or Swear."[33] The capitalization of "Swear" may indicate a formal oath, but there is no such hint as to a limitation on the meaning of "curse" to religion, unless "profane," and its derivation from "in front of a temple" is taken to provide such a focus.[34]

The aim of the first of the two sections cited from New Jersey's law[35] is unclear. Section eight of the *Act for Suppressing Vice and Immorality* provides a half-dollar fine for anyone profanely swearing or cursing. While supporting the proposition that not all speech was protected at the time of the Bill of Rights, the section certainly does not focus on sexually explicit speech, the focus of *Roth*. The animus behind section nine is more clear. It is designed to protect the dignity of the judicial process by punishing profane swearing or cursing in the presence of a justice of the peace, while in the execution of the office.

Like the first section cited from New Jersey, the New York statute simply imposed a fine, this time of three shillings, on anyone profanely swearing or cursing.[36] *Roth* also cites a New York case in the footnote setting out the statutes. Since the case is post–Bill of Rights, its relevance in the portion of *Roth* in which it appears can only be as an explanation of the pre–Bill of Rights statute cited. *People v. Ruggles*[37] upheld the criminal conviction of an individual, who loudly proclaimed to a large crowd that "Jesus Christ was a bastard, and his mother must be a whore." The charge was blasphemy, and the court determined that the First Amendment, while protecting discussion of religious views, did not protect blasphemy.

The focus of the North Carolina statute is less clearly on the protection of religion. The cited section, section III of *An Act for the Better Observation and Keeping of the Lord's Day, Commonly Called Sunday, and for the More Effectual Suppression of Vice and Immorality*,[38] prohibits profane swearing or cursing, with increased penalties for public officers so doing. In addition to a possible religious connotation to "profane" the previous section of the statute, as indicated in the title, prohibits work on the "Lord's day" so that people can "carefully apply themselves to the Duties of Religion and Piety."[39] Other sections are directed to swearing and cursing in court and to being drunk on Sunday.[40] The focus appears to be on the protection of religious practice or on the maintenance of religious, judicial, and perhaps public, dignity.

Both the Pennsylvania statutes cited are also aimed at the protection of religion. The first, *An Act to Prevent the Grievous Sins of Cursing and Swearing*,[41] punishes by fine or imprisonment "any . . . person [who] shall wilfully, premeditatedly . . . blaspheme, or speak loosely and Profanely of Almighty God, or Christ Jesus, or the Holy Spirit, or the Scriptures of Truth."[42] The second, *An Act for the Prevention of Vice and Immorality*,[43] similarly punishes "any person of the age of sixteen years upwards [who] shall profanely curse or swear by the name of God, Christ Jesus, or the Holy Ghost."[44]

The Rhode Island statutes cited contain a section imposing a penalty of a fine up to one hundred dollars and two-month imprisonment for blasphemy and a section prohibiting profane cursing and swearing upon pain with a fine of fifty cents to one dollar for a first offense.[45] Again the aim of the profane cursing and swearing section is unclear. While it does support the proposition that not all speech was protected, its focus may again be on religion.

The title alone of the South Carolina statute, *An Act for the More Effectual Suppressing of Blasphemy and Prophaneness,*[46] is enough to indicate its purpose. The act recites its concern with those who "openly avowed and published many blasphemous and impious Opinions, contrary to the Doctrines and Principles of the Christian Religion, greatly tending to the Dishonour of Almighty God."[47] The statute makes it illegal to "deny any one of the persons of the Holy Trinity to be God, or . . . assert or maintain that there are more Gods than one, or . . . deny the christian religion to be true, or the Holy Scriptures of the Old and New Testament to be Divine Authority."[48] Interestingly, the statute applied only to those educated in the Christian religion or having professed the Christian religion within South Carolina.

The Court cited two Vermont statutes. The first, *Act, for the Punishment of Certain Capital, and Other High Crimes and Misdemeanors,*[49] made it illegal to "publicly deny the being and existence of God, or of the Supreme Being [or] contumeliously reproach his providence, and government."[50] Here too, the statute was clearly aimed at the protection of religion. The second, *Act, for the Punishment of Certain Inferior Crimes and Misdemeanors,*[51] forbade profane swearing or cursing. Again, a link to religion might be drawn from the use of "profane," but the context of the statute in a collection of sections regarding public disturbances and obstructing public proclamations makes it appear aimed at keeping the public peace.

Lastly, the Virginia statute[52] cited prohibited profane swearing or cursing on pain of an eighty-three-cent fine for each offense or ten lashes, if unable to pay. The statute appears aimed at the general maintenance of public dignity, as shown by the fact that it also prohibited drunkenness, imposing the same penalty.

The only statute actually quoted by the Court was Massachusetts' statute prohibiting " 'any filthy, obscene, or profane song, pamphlet, libel or mock sermon' in imitation or mimicking of religious services."[53] The particular importance found in the wording of that statute appears to be its tie between profanity and obscenity. Since the other statutes cited addressed blasphemy and profanity, a tie between profanity and obscenity would turn the other statutes into obscenity statutes. The difficulty with this approach is that even the Massachusetts statute does not provide adequate support for the general proposition that obscenity and profanity were legally related. The only relationship present in the statute is that neither obscenity nor profanity could be

used in any " 'song, pamphlet, libel or mock sermon' in imitation or mimicking of religious services." [54] A statute criminalizing the use of either in mimicry
of religion does not equate the two and provides less help than it might first
appear in defining the concept of obscenity.

The pre–Bill of Rights statutes cited in the *Roth* opinion do establish that
the freedoms of speech and press were not absolute in that era. In the "off
the stage" sense of "obscene" certain materials or speech could be seen as obscene. To that degree, the cases support the proposition that obscene material
did not enjoy protection in the constitutional era. However, the material subject to prosecution under such obscenity statutes was not the sexually explicit
material that is the focus of modern obscenity law but was instead speech that
was religiously offensive.

It is not surprising that, when the *Roth* Court went in search of early obscenity statutes, it found blasphemy laws. Professor Frederick Schauer notes
that the origins of obscenity law are in the protection of religion.[55] Professors
Morris Ernst and Alan Schwartz agree that the early interest of the censor was
not on sexual material but would extend the focus to political, as well as religious, expression.[56] David Tribe also finds the origins of censorship to be in
the protection of religion.[57]

While the Greeks and Romans may have had what Schauer describes as
"virtually unlimited freedom in dealing with sexual matters," [58] there was less
toleration of religious heresy or of blasphemy. While violence was less tolerated than sex, censorship with regard to religious matters was legally enforced
and could lead to prosecution and even execution. Professor Tribe agrees that
early censorship was aimed at religious ideas and notes religious connotations
to words such as "profane," as meaning in front of a temple, "obscene," as in the
way of a stage for religious rites, and "lewd," as lay or nonclerical.[59] Even at the
end of the Roman era, when the role of censor passed to the church, the focus
remained on the blasphemous and the heretical. Schauer states that only in the
sixteenth century did anything resembling modern obscenity regulation by the
government start to appear.[60] Even then the resemblance is very vague when
compared to the law put forth in *Roth* and its progeny. One must wait until
the late nineteenth century to find any exclusive focus on sexual depictions.

While the development of censorship and of obscenity law out of an interest in the protection of religion explains the result of the *Roth* Court's search
through the colonial-era and early state statutes, the Court could have found
better support had it broadened its search. By the time of the revolution, obscenity law in England had branched out from its exclusive focus on religion.
That development in pre-revolution common law might be seen as having

historical relevance with regard to the question of whether or not the First Amendment protections are absolute. Given the English-common-law heritage of American common law, English law in the colonial era speaks to the legal climate in the colonies at the time of the revolution and informs the view as to the legal climate at the time of the Constitution and Bill of Rights.

Looking to English law, what is generally regarded as the first pure obscenity case[61] is the 1663 case *The King v. Sir Charles Sedley*.[62] In fact, the divorce from the religious basis of censorship in *Sedley* may be viewed as being less than complete. Leonard Levy includes the case in his work on blasphemy and notes that while the reporters did not use the word "blasphemy," Sedley was said to have, along with other actions with a more modern obscenity cast, preached blasphemy, abused the scriptures, and preached a Montebank sermon.[63]

While there may have been some religious overtones, the *Sedley* case is closer to modern obscenity law than its predecessors.[64] Sedley and friends had gotten quite drunk at an inn in London. They went out on the balcony of the inn, and Sedley stripped naked. He assumed a variety of immodest poses and made statements and performed acts which could easily be viewed as sexually indecent. Additionally, however, Sedley urinated in bottles and then poured the bottles down on the crowd that had gathered below the balcony. That act caused a small riot.

While Professor Schauer finds importance in the case in that it was the first in which "offensiveness to decency, apart from religious or political heresy, was an element of an offense against the state,"[65] the nature of the indecency is open to debate. It was not his nakedness and sexual poses alone that led to his conviction. His conviction was "for shewing himself naked in a balcony, and throwing down bottles (pist in) vi & armis among the people in Covent Garden, contra pacem and to the scandal of the Government."[66] The focus may be seen to be as much on an act of violence and the ensuing breach of the peace. While he may have been naked, he seems to have been at least as intent on insulting the crowd as on appealing to their sense of the erotic.

This reading of *Sedley* is supported by *The Queen v. Read*.[67] Professor Leo Alpert calls that 1708 case the first actual prosecution for literary obscenity.[68] While *Read* did address literature rather than incitement to riot, the court rejected the idea of bringing indictments for obscenity. In dismissing the indictment, the court said "[a] crime that shakes religion, as profaneness on the stage, &c. is indictable; but writing an obscene book, as that entitled, *The Fifteen Plagues of a Maidenhead,* is not indictable, but punishable only in the Spiritual Court."[69] The publication of the book was simply not against any law. "[I]t indeed tends to the corruption of good manners, but that is not sufficient . . . to punish."[70] With regard to the Crown's attempt to cite *Sedley* as precedent for a conviction, Justice John Powell found *Sedley* distinguishable by the vi et armis present there. Leonard Levy concludes therefore that Sedley's crime was based on its violence rather than sexual obscenity.[71]

The next English case, in 1727, is said by Schauer finally to establish obscene libel as a common law crime. *Dominus Rex v. Curll*[72] involved a conviction for publishing the book *Venus in the Cloister, or the Nun in Her Smock*. While the content of the book was a dialogue on lesbian love, and therefore sexual, its setting was in a convent, and therefore religious. Schauer suggests that, while the conviction might be seen as having religious overtones, the antireligious elements were anti-Catholic rather than anti–Church of England and therefore seem insignificant.[73] On the other hand, Alpert interprets the case as sustaining the indictment because of its attack on religion and it therefore being triable in the common-law courts.[74] In Alpert's view, even with *Read,* the courts were not concerned with obscene literature but rather with punishing offenses against religion. Professor Leonard Levy further notes that Curll had in some way offended the court.[75] That offense led the court to cancel a scheduled reargument and decide that obscene libel constituted a common-law crime.[76] It could easily have also led the court to overlook the distinction between libels against the Catholic Church and against the Church of England.

In any case, English obscenity law appears to have been relatively dormant throughout the 1700s.[77] Both Schauer and Alpert do note the prosecution of John Wilkes in the 1760s for publishing his *Essay on Woman,*[78] but Schauer dismisses the case as one in which Wilkes's offenses were political and his prosecution politically motivated.[79] Alpert is in accord noting that the incentive to prosecute really sprang from the publication of a satirical work exposing corruption in the government, insinuating that King George III was an imbecile, and suggesting the involvement of the king's mother in an illicit relationship.[80] The *Essay on Woman* was only "an instrument, a stratagem, and an excuse for hostilities in the guise of a crusade."[81]

The state of English obscenity law at the time of the American Revolution, then, was better developed than in its American colonies. While the colonial-era statutes addressed blasphemy and heresy, English law may be seen to have grown to include nonreligious offenses. Had the *Roth* Court taken that English common law background as providing a part of the common law tradition at the time of the Constitution and Bill of Rights, the assertions in *Roth* would have been strengthened. The statutes actually cited establish only that the freedoms of speech and press were not understood as being absolute in the colonial era. They do little or nothing to show that the obscene was outside the scope of the protections. An examination of English common law adds to the *Roth* cites by showing a growing tradition that obscene speech was not afforded protection.

If *Roth*'s conclusions are limited to those that can be drawn based only on the statutes cited, then all that the colonial-era statutes establish is that not all speech was protected. That conclusion does not define the protected and the unprotected classes, other than by the fact that blasphemy was among the forms unprotected. The conclusion certainly fails to distinguish between depictions or descriptions of sex and of violence in providing protection to one and not the other. Furthermore, any reference to extralegal sources to determine the historically disfavored varieties of speech would lead just as surely to violence as they would to sex.

If, on the other hand, guidance can be drawn from the English common law, as well as from the statutes cited in *Roth*, that guidance leads to the same inability to distinguish sex and violence. English common law was in the process of developing a proscription against obscenity, but the cases do not serve to distinguish between sex as obscene and violence as obscene. As Professor Alpert, speaking of the state of English law in 1763, says, "the first hundred years which followed Sedley's cavortings on a Covent Garden balcony yielded scarcely anything conclusive as to literary obscenity. There is no definition of the term. There is no basis of identification. There is no unity in describing what is obscene literature, or in prosecuting it. There is little more than the ability to smell it." [82] Whatever support the law at the time of the Bill of Rights provides for *Roth*'s conclusion that sexually obscene materials are without constitutional protection speaks equally well to a conclusion that sufficiently violent materials are also without the protection of the First Amendment.

Between the Bill of Rights and the Fourteenth Amendment

Legal history in the era between the Bill of Rights and the adoption of the Fourteenth Amendment may be relevant in either of two ways. First, the development of the law in the early part of that era can provide further insight into the status of obscenity at the time of the Bill of Rights. If, at the time of the Bill of Rights there was a trend toward leaving some forms of speech unprotected, it might be argued that the continuation of that development could help define the sort of speech that had been unprotected by the First Amendment.

The second possible relevance is to the interpretation of the Fourteenth Amendment. It is only through the incorporation of the First Amendment protections into the Due Process Clause of the Fourteenth Amendment that the states' authority to limit speech is affected. If there was a clear practice on the part of the states to ban obscene speech and press at the time of the Fourteenth Amendment, that could serve as an indication that the amendment was not intended to bar that practice.

It seems clear that the *Roth* Court's use of history after the adoption of the Bill of Rights was directed toward the first potential relevance. The Court opened its examination of legal history in the era by stating that "[a]t the time of the adoption of the First Amendment, obscenity law was not as fully developed as libel law, but there is sufficiently contemporaneous evidence to show that obscenity, too, was outside the protection intended for speech and press." [83] The language appears to use hindsight from the perspective of the early nineteenth century to help determine what the law was in the late eighteenth century. Furthermore, the Court did not separate its analysis of the companion case *Alberts v. California* from the analysis in *Roth v. United States.* Any use of history in the analysis of Fourteenth Amendment incorporation would speak to the former but not to the latter.

The earliest statute cited is New Jersey's *Act for Suppressing Vice and Immorality.* [84] However, that statute is not aimed at erotic material. Much more broadly, it bans from the "public stage . . . or other place whatever, any interludes, farces or plays of any kind, or any games, tricks, juggling, sleight of hand, or feats of uncommon dexterity and agility of body, or any bear baiting or bull baiting, or any like shews or exhibitions whatsoever." [85] The statute continues the trend of the pre–Bill of Rights statutes in establishing that the First Amendment protections were not absolute. However, the statute again fails to use the word "obscene" or "obscenity." Furthermore, it does not make any reference to material of a sexual nature. The closest it comes to such a reference is in stating the legislature's concerns over the corruption of the morals of youth, along with concerns over bringing together idle persons, impoverishing families, gratifying "useless curiosity," and generally serving "no good or useful purpose in society." [86] The concern over the corruption of youthful morals as one of so many concerns, and the failure to focus on the erotic, but rather to attempt to ban most exhibitions, provides support for the claim that there were contemporaneous obscenity statutes only in the sense that there were performances that were "banned from the theatrical stage." The wide sweep of the ban certainly speaks against the modern Court's insistence that the subject matter of the depictions that may be banned as obscene be limited to the depictions of sexual or excretory acts.

The next earliest statute cited is Connecticut's *Act Concerning Crimes and Punishments.* [87] The statute is, by its own terms, an obscenity statute. It makes it illegal to "print, import, publish, sell, or distribute, any book, pamphlet, ballad, or other printed paper, containing obscene language, prints or descriptions."[88] The statute itself, however, provides no support for the later Court's limitation of obscenity to the erotic or even for the conclusion that obscenity includes the erotic. The term "obscene" is left undefined, and common usage and the development of the law up to the time of the statute do not fill in the definition.

The third statute, from Massachusetts, dates from 1835. The chapter, titled *Of Offences Against Chastity, Morality, and Decency,* contained a section prohibiting the sale, distribution, or publication of "any book, or any pamphlet, ballad, printed paper, or other thing, containing obscene language, or obscene prints, pictures, figures, or descriptions, manifestly tending to the corruption of the morals of youth."[89] Once again, it is not even clear in the statute that the erotic is considered obscene, although the inclusion of "chastity" within the chapter title may be seen as providing weak support for that conclusion. Nonetheless, while the goal of preventing the corruption of youth might be read to include in the ban material exposing youth to the erotic, history and usage of "obscene" provide no reason to limit the materials that might corrupt the morals of youth to the erotic.

The latest of the "sufficiently contemporaneous" statutes cited was from the *Of Offences Against the Police of Towns* chapter of the New Hampshire statutes.[90] The statute dates from 1842 and its relevance to the Bill of Rights is questionable. It does, however, provide some insight into what was obscene in its time. The statute provides that "[n]o person shall sing or repeat, or cause to be sung or repeated any lewd, obscene or profane song, or shall repeat any lewd, obscene or profane words; or write or mark in any manner any obscene or profane word, or obscene or lascivious figure or representation on any building, fence, wall, post or any other thing whatever."[91] The use of "lewd" and "lascivious" in the statute might be taken as a focus on the erotic. It should also be noted, however, that the statute may not provide much support for general bans on the obscene. The chapter containing the section concerned public nuisances, and the section itself addresses public recitation or posting, rather than banning the material itself. Thus, any distinction between sexual depictions and depictions of violence as a principle of general obscenity law is weak.

As with the statutes, the cases cited strengthen in whatever support they may offer for a distinction between sex and violence as obscene only as they become less contemporaneous to the Bill of Rights. The earliest of the cases is *Knowles v. State.*[92] Knowles was convicted of violating Connecticut's restrictions on plays and public performances by displaying a "horrid and unnatural *monster*."[93] The description offered of the monster in question fails to match any contemporary views on obscenity.

> And the head of said *monster,* represented by said picture, resembles that of an *African,* but the features of the face are indistinct: there are apertures for eyes, but no eyes; his chin projects considerably, and the ears are placed unnaturally back, on or near the neck; its fore legs, by said picture, are here represented to lie on its breast, nearly in the manner of human arms; its skin is smooth, without hair, and of dark, tawny, or copper colour.[94]

Knowles's conviction was reversed, with the court holding that his exhibition was not within the scope of the statute.[95] The court did, however, accept the proposition that "[e]very public show and exhibition, which outrages decency, shocks humanity, or is contrary to good morals, is punishable at common law."[96] Even under the common law, the conviction could not stand for failure of the information to "particularly state the circumstances in which the indecency, barbarity or immorality, consists."[97]

The opinion does endorse a concept of obscenity. There was a class of material that could be banned from the stage. The court defined that class of exhibitions in terms of indecency, immorality, barbarity, and being shocking to humanity, again a clear expansion to include more than blasphemy and heresy. While sexual depiction may fall within such a description, there is no reason to limit the class to the sexual or excretory. Violence may also fit the description, particularly given the court's inclusion of barbarity.

What is particularly interesting about the *Knowles* case is that a prosecution was brought at all. The decision to prosecute speaks to the belief of the prosecuting authorities, ratified by the conviction in the lower court, that unprotected speech included far more than sex or excretion. In fact, the concept must have gone beyond violence as well. The prosecution of this case speaks to a broad concept of obscenity, such as that argued by Harry Clor. Professor Clor's suggestion that obscenity is "a degradation of the human dimensions of life to a sub-human or merely physical level,"[98] and that obscene literature is "literature which presents, graphically and in detail, a degrading picture of human life and invites the reader or viewer, not to contemplate that picture, but to wallow in it"[99] are clearly invoked by the treatment of the person put on display.

The second of the cases cited is the Pennsylvania Supreme Court's 1815 decision in *Commonwealth v. Sharpless.*[100] Sharpless was charged with exhibiting "a certain lewd, wicked, scandalous, infamous, and obscene painting, representing a man in an obscene, impudent, and indecent posture with a woman, to the manifest corruption and subversion of youth, and other citizens of the commonwealth, to the evil example of all others in like case offending, and against the peace and dignity of the commonwealth of Pennsylvania."[101] The exhibition was not as public as that in *Knowles*, having occurred inside a house, but it was public in the sense that the painting was shown to a paying public audience.[102] It also appears from the charge that the objection to the material focused on its sexual nature.

Chief Justice Tilghman could find no statute contrary to the defendant's acts, but he opined that acts of public indecency were indictable as corrupting public morality.[103] That which corrupts society was said to be indictable as a breach of the peace.[104] Justice Yeates also stressed that that which leads to the destruction of morality in general is punishable under the common law. "The corruption of the public mind, in general, and debauching the manners of youth, in particular, by lewd and obscene pictures exhibited to view, must necessarily be attended with the most injurious consequences, and in such instances, Courts of Justice are, or ought to be, the schools of morals."[105]

Sharpless does provide support for the proposition that obscenity was punishable in 1815 in Pennsylvania. However, it is unclear that *Sharpless* should be taken as supporting the position that obscenity is limited to sexual or excretory activities. While the painting exhibited by Sharpless may have been sexual in its content, the language of the opinion is broader. That which "corrupt[s] public morality" or "corrupts society" or leads to "[t]he corruption of the public mind" was said to be punishable. While the sexual material at issue was held to fall within that category, the opinion does not state that exhibitions depicting other subjects cannot also come within the category, and the broad language used may be taken to allow a wider scope to obscenity law.

Much of what was said of *Sharpless* may also be said of the last of the cases cited, the 1821 Massachusetts case *Commonwealth v. Holmes*.[106] The *Holmes* case was based on the publication of a "lewd and obscene print" contained in the book *Memoirs of a Woman of Pleasure*. The objections to the book and print appear to arise out of their sexual nature, although the issues on appeal were the jurisdiction of the lower court and the sufficiency of the indictment. The court's opinion rejecting the claims on appeal does seem to assume that sufficiently offending sexual material may be banned as obscene. Once again, however, nothing in the opinion supports a claim that the category of the obscene is so limited to such material.

The *Roth* Court's examination of legal history in the post–Bill of Rights era does establish that some forms of speech other than blasphemy and heresy were viewed as unprotected. What the analysis fails to establish is that the extension of the unprotected class was limited to depictions of sex and excretion. As with the examination of the Court's history of the colonial era, a search beyond the Court's cites may provide further insight.

As in the United States, the early 1800s saw the further development of English obscenity law to include material that was offensive for reasons other than its religious or political content. Much of the growth in prosecutions appears due to the activities of the Society for the Suppression of Vice. The activities of the society led to legislation against obscene materials and the prosecution of about three obscenity cases per year throughout the first half of the nineteenth century.[107] Despite this development, Professor Schauer still notes a lack of definition for obscenity in English law until 1868.[108] In that year, the Queen's Bench decided *Regina v. Hicklin*,[109] providing a definition for English law that would affect later American law. Even then, however, it may not be completely clear that obscenity prosecutions were to be limited to sexual explicitness.

Hicklin concerned the publication of a pamphlet titled *The Confessional Unmasked; Shewing the Depravity of the Roman Priesthood, the Iniquity of the Confessional, and the Questions Put to Females in Confession.* The prosecution could be seen as an extension of the censorship protection given religion, but the fact that the attack was on the Catholic Church would weaken that claim. While the concern with the particular work was over its sexual content, the Lord Chief Justice presented a rather broad definition: "the test of obscenity is this, whether the tendency of the matter charged as obscenity is to deprave and corrupt those whose minds are open to such immoral influences and into whose hands a publication of this sort may fall."[110] While the test is certainly broad enough to go beyond religious or political heresy and encompass sexually explicit materials, it also seems broad enough to include depictions of violence, if such publications can "deprave and corrupt those whose minds are open to such immoral influences."[111]

While the language employed in *Hicklin* might extend to violence, the prosecutions leading up to that case, and *Hicklin* itself, appear to have been centered on sex. Professor Schauer suggests an interest in stemming French postcards, while at the same time stating that the era leading up to *Hicklin* provided no definition of obscenity.

> Works were prosecuted and convicted on the basis of whether or not they were immoral, with little if any concern for precise definition of terms or application of the statutes, or for what constituted the common-law crime of obscene libel. Obscenity was something that all people felt they

could recognize instantly, and there seemed no need for elaborate judicial definitions.[112]

Despite the suggestion that obscenity was undefined until *Hicklin,* it is probably reading too much into the statement to conclude that the modern focus of obscenity on sex had not yet developed. Obscenity may have lacked a definition in the sense of the standard against which sexual depictions were to be measured, but it became clear in the era that the focus was on sex. Even if English law is read to have defined obscenity in terms of sexual depictions in this era, the relevance of any post-revolution English development to American law is limited.

Law in the United States between the Bill of Rights and the Fourteenth Amendment failed to develop the focus that was developing in England. While the cases cited in *Roth* do show that sexual depictions could be prosecuted as obscene, they do not limit prosecution to such depictions. In fact, there appear to be few prosecutions to provide a basis for the development of a definition. Obscenity statutes were enacted in several states in the 1820s and 1830s and in more just prior to the Civil War. The federal government also passed an obscenity statute in 1842, mirroring the English concern in that it was aimed at the importation of French postcards. But even in these years, a broad definition of obscenity is suggested. Under the definition developed in the few pre–Civil War cases, obscene material was "whatever outrages decency and is injurious to public morals."[113] While that test may include sexually obscene material it certainly does not exclude violent material.

Obscenity Law from the Fourteenth Amendment to *Roth*

The *Roth* opinion also cited several Supreme Court opinions that show that the "Court has always assumed that obscenity is not protected by the freedoms of speech and press."[114] The cases date from 1877 to 1953, which fall somewhat short of having "always assumed" obscenity to be unprotected, particularly from the point of view of constitutionally relevant eras. They may add to the earlier state cases and statutory law establishing that not all speech was protected in the colonial era, and that obscenity was outside that protection in the era following the Bill of Rights. The Supreme Court cases are, however, limited in their relevance in that most of the references to obscenity are dicta and none make any effort to define obscenity, particularly with any limitation excluding violence.

Several of the cases concerned regulation of the mails and interstate commerce. *Ex Parte Jackson*[115] held constitutional a federal statute prohibiting using the mails for lottery advertisements, while noting that the act also prohibits mailing obscene materials. *United States v. Chase*[116] again held constitutional the same statute, but excluded private letters in plain envelopes from the definition of obscene writing. *Public Clearing House v. Coyne*[117] again had to do with bans on mailing obscene materials and held that the postmaster's refusal to deliver such materials did not violate due process. *Hoke v. United States*[118] included regulation of obscene materials along with regulation of prostitution as within Congress's power to regulate interstate commerce. *Hannegan v. Esquire, Inc.*[119] again accepted limitations on mailing obscene materials.

Other cases mentioned limitations on obscene materials in arguing for or against other limitations on constitutional rights. *Robertson v. Baldwin*[120] merely mentioned limits on obscene material as an exception to the Bill of Rights in ruling on the constitutionality of involuntarily returning deserting merchant marines to their ships. *Near v. Minnesota*,[121] in disapproving prior restraints on the press, noted that there may be prohibitions on publishing obscene materials. *Chaplinsky v. New Hampshire*,[122] in holding that fighting words were without First Amendment protection, included obscenity and profanity as also unprotected. *Beauharnais v. Illinois*,[123] in its discussion of group libel, said that no one contends that obscene speech can only be punished if it presents a clear and present danger.

Most interesting among the cases cited is *Winters v. New York*.[124] The cite was to a portion of the opinion noting that, while value in speech may not be required for protection, if material is obscene or profane, it may be controlled. However, what makes the cite interesting is that the statute, under which the material at issue was argued to be obscene, focused not on sexual or excretory activities but on crime and violence.

The *Roth* Court also cited its cases reviewing convictions under federal obscenity law.[125] Those cases, dating from 1895 to 1932, all held constitutional prohibitions on the use of the mails for shipping obscene materials. It is in these cases, dating from well after the adoption of the Fourteenth Amendment and more than a century after the Bill of Rights, that a definition of obscenity focusing on sex and excretion begins to develop. Of the cases cited, *Swearingen v. United States*[126] is of particular importance. It is that 1896 case that has been cited as the first American case in which it became clear that obscenity had developed an exclusive focus on sexual activities.

The *Roth* opinion also notes, in support of its conclusion that obscene material merits no First Amendment protection, twenty federal obscenity laws enacted between 1842 and 1956.[127] As with the state statutes and the case law cited, the older the federal statute the less clear the focus. The 1842 enactment barred the importation of "indecent and obscene" prints, paintings, lithographs, engravings, and transparencies.[128] The 1857 statute amended the 1842 statute to include articles, images, figures, daguerreotypes, and photographs.[129] Neither statute defines "obscene" or "indecent." Neither does either establish a basis for distinguishing sexual obscenity from violent obscenity.

The next federal statute was enacted in 1865. It barred from the mails "obscene" books, pamphlets, pictures, and prints, along with other "vulgar and indecent" publications.[130] The 1872 statute added printed or engraved "disloyal devices" and envelopes or postal cards with "scurrilous epithets" to the items not to be mailed.[131] Again no definitions are provided, and the language — "vulgar" and "scurrilous" — may go beyond depictions of sexual activity.

The first federal general criminal statute, going beyond the mails or importation, was enacted in 1873. The statute applied in the District of Columbia, territories, and other areas within the exclusive jurisdiction of the United States. It banned distribution, exhibition, or advertisement of any "obscene book, pamphlet, paper, writing, advertisement, circular, print, picture, drawing or other representation, figure, or image . . . or other article of an immoral nature, or any drug or medicine, or any article whatever, for the prevention of conception, or for causing unlawful abortion." [132] The statute also amended the 1872 statute to bar from the mails the objects banned in federal territories.[133] Again no definition is provided; however, that portion of the statute amending the 1872 statute adds "lewd, or lascivious" to "obscene" as adjectives describing the items banned.[134] That language may indicate the beginning of a focus on sex. Further, the concern over contraception may provide some additional, though weak, evidence for such a focus.

An 1876 statute simply amended the 1872 statute to increase the penalties,[135] and an 1888 statute cited increased the scope of mail bans. It barred misrepresenting the contents of mail and further declared unmailable anything in an envelope or wrapper "upon which indecent, lewd, lascivious, obscene, libelous, scurrilous, or threatening delineations, epithets, terms, or language, or reflecting injuriously upon the character or conduct of another, may be written or printed." [136] A second 1888 statute amended the first 1888 statute and the 1872 statute in minor ways.[137]

An 1890 statute cited again addressed importation, barring the same sorts of objects distribution of which was declared illegal in the 1873 statute.[138] The statute also addressed federal government employees aiding or abetting in violations of federal law prohibiting distribution, advertisement, exhibition or mailing the same sorts of objects.[139] An 1897 statute extended the mail bans to private express companies and common carriers,[140] and a 1905 statute amended the 1897 statute to include a ban on exportation of such materials from the United States, its territories, and the District of Columbia.[141]

A 1909 statute adds "filthy" and "vile" to "obscene, lewd, or lascivious" in describing the materials banned from the mails—materials similar to those in the 1888 and 1890 statutes.[142] The addition of the new adjectives might signal more focus on sexual materials but, depending on the meaning of "filth," need not have that connotation. A second 1909 statute was a minor amendment in the exportation statute,[143] and a 1920 statute reflected technological change in adding "filthy" motion pictures to the banned filthy books, pamphlets, and pictures of several earlier statutes.[144]

The Tariff Act of 1930 added seditious materials and lottery tickets to those that could not be imported, while maintaining the ban on "obscene or immoral" materials.[145] While still providing no definition of "obscene," the statute does begin to reflect the view that even obscene materials may have worth. It provides that "the Secretary of the Treasury may, in his discretion, admit the so-called classics or books of recognized and established literary or scientific merit, but may, in his discretion, admit such classics or books only when imported for noncommercial purposes."[146]

The next two cited statutes, parts of the Communications Act of 1934, also reflect technological innovation, banning "obscene, indecent, or profane language" from the airways[147] and setting penalties for such broadcast.[148]

A 1948 statute is particularly interesting. The statute codified a portion of the 1909 statute discussed above, under the title "Mailing obscene or crime-inciting matter," and added that the term "indecent" includes matter that would tend to incite arson, murder, or assassination.[149] While the section title does distinguish between "obscene" and "crime-inciting," perhaps showing that by the 1940s the two categories were distinct, the inclusion of crime-inciting material as indecent calls into question any sole focus on sex in the earlier statutes.

The three remaining statutes have little to add. A 1950 statute cited adds phonograph records, electrical transcriptions, and other sound recordings to the categories of objects that may be obscene, within the 1948 statute.[150] A second 1950 statute increases the powers of the Postmaster General with regard to mailings of "obscene, lewd, lascivious, indecent, filthy, or vile" materials.[151] Lastly, a 1955 statute amends the 1948 statute in ways that cast no new light on the definition of "obscene."[152] The definition of "indecent" as including material tending to incite arson, murder, or assassination remained, and in fact still remains in the current statute.[153]

The *Roth* Court's reliance on federal statutes does little to provide a definition for obscenity. At best, weak support for a sole focus on sexual depictions is found in the use of terms such as "lewd," "lascivious," "filthy," and "indecent" in some of the statutes. But at least one line of statutes includes crime-inciting material within the indecent. Lacking any statutory definitions of "obscene," the statutes must be interpreted in the context of obscenity cases and the common meaning of the word. The case law cited does show a development in which "obscene" does take on the focus the Court finds, but at a date later than any that would be of constitutional significance. Common usage provides no better basis for the Court's conclusion. Indeed, it is not clear even at present that the use of "obscene" should be so limited.

The last source to which the Court turned in support for its denial of protection to obscene materials was in international sentiment. The Court said that its rejection of protection for obscene materials "is mirrored in the universal judgment that obscenity should be restrained, reflected in the international agreement of over 50 nations."[154] The cite to what the opinion makes appear to be a 1956 treaty would be weak support for the constitutionality of obscenity bans or for a specific definition of the obscene. A 1956 treaty would show only the international climate at the time of *Roth* rather than at any more constitutionally relevant time. The treaty, however, has a longer pedigree, dating from the Agreement for the Repression of the Circulation of Obscene Publications, in force since 1911.[155] Even that earlier date is, of course, after any dates of constitutional importance, and the treaty shows only the modern era's willingness to ban obscene publications.

The relevance of the treaty on sexual obscenity remains unclear. It certainly would appear irrelevant to the Constitution. While the meaning of "obscene" in eras of constitutional relevance is important, any developing consensus in the 1900s is irrelevant. Beyond its irrelevance, the strength of the claim that there was an international concern directed to sexual obscenity may even be questionable. The United States has struggled with what should be considered obscene. Even the general Anglo-American focus of obscenity on sex did not become clear until the late 1800s. The surety with which the conclusion can be drawn that such a focus also existed in other signatory nations at the time of the treaty is diminished by translation difficulties with such a complex concept and the development of a focus in those countries.

While the *Roth* cites do not support a conclusion that obscenity, at the time of the Fourteenth Amendment, was limited to sex and excretion, the legal use of the word did develop that focus in the era that followed. Morris Ernst traces the current widespread bans on sexually obscene materials to the early 1870s and the work of Anthony Comstock, a "neurotic individual" who enjoyed the financial support of J. P. Morgan.[156] The Comstock Act,[157] passed with less than ten minutes of debate, "placed in a separate banned area all material which would excite sexually impure thoughts."[158] The states quickly followed in copying the federal legislation.

Even after the Comstock Act, however, at least one federal court seemed to include nonsexual material within the category of the obscene. In 1889, a person was convicted in federal court for mailing a postcard calling someone a radical, and the same court convicted another defendant for mailing a postcard to a newspaper saying "You can take your paper and Democracy and go to hell with it."[159] Nonetheless, the focus on sex appeared to be developing, and Schauer finds it finally clear with the decision in *Swearingen v. United States*[160] in 1896 that only sexually oriented material could be obscene.[161]

Summary

At the time of the adoption of the First Amendment, obscenity law, as such, had not yet appeared in the United States. There were statutes, however, that show that not all speech was considered protected in the era preceding the Bill of Rights. In particular, blasphemy and heresy were banned. Those bans are indicative of the roots of obscenity law in the protection of religion. If additional guidance is sought in colonial-era English common law, a further development of obscenity law may be found. It is at least arguable that English law had gone beyond requiring a focus on religion. Even then, however, the subject of that expanded scope was unclear.

In the era following the Bill of Rights, obscenity statutes and cases do appear in American law. The definition of obscenity in those cases is, however, unclear. The cases may indicate that the area of unprotected speech had grown in the era of the Bill of Rights, but they do little to establish a definition of obscenity. While English law did develop a focus on sex, by the middle of the nineteenth century the relevance of that law in the then independent United States is limited.

It is really only in the era after the adoption of the Fourteenth Amendment that American law developed the sole focus on sex that the Court announced in *Roth*. The era in which the focus developed is a constitutionally irrelevant era. The period between the Bill of Rights and the 1870s is too long for a development in the 1870s or later to lend an understanding of the First Amendment. A development after the adoption of the Fourteenth amendment also fails to speak to any differences between the protections of speech imposed on the states as opposed to the federal government. There is simply no constitutional basis for the claim that to be obscene material must depict sex or excretion.

Constructing a *Roth*-Style History for
Banning Depictions of Violence

Suppose that the Supreme Court, in 1957, had not been faced with the sexual obscenity convictions considered in the companion cases *Roth v. United States* and *Alberts v. California*.[1] Suppose instead that the Court had faced a case in which individuals had been convicted for violations of federal and state laws against publishing or distributing excessively violent materials. What sort of history could the Court have constructed to show, as *Roth* did for sexual obscenity, that such material was not protected by the First Amendment?

Given the presentation of the preceding chapter, it should not be surprising that a history could be presented that would be quite similar to that in *Roth*. Indeed, many of the Court's *Roth* statements could be statements in the hypothetical opinion. The opinion's historical analysis could begin, as did *Roth*, with a consideration of the freedoms of speech and press in the colonial era. As it did in *Roth*, the Court could state:

> The guaranties of freedom of expression in effect in 10 of the 14 States which by 1792 had ratified the Constitution, gave no absolute protection for every utterance. Thirteen of the 14 States provided for the prosecution of libel, and all of those States made either blasphemy or profanity, or both, statutory crimes. As early as 1712, Massachusetts made it criminal to publish "any filthy, obscene, or profane song, pamphlet, libel or mock sermon" in imitation or mimicking of religious services.[2]

The statutes cited in *Roth* do show that the freedoms of speech and press were not absolute in the era of the Bill of Rights, but that fact does not speak uniquely to sexual obscenity. Just as a lack of absolute protection leaves open the possibility of proscription for sexual obscenity, it leaves open the potential for a ban on other sorts of depiction, including the excessively violent depictions that might be characterized as violent obscenity.

The hypothetical opinion could continue, as the *Roth* opinion did, with: "At the time of the adoption of the First Amendment, obscenity law was not as fully developed as libel law, but there is sufficiently contemporaneous evidence to show that obscenity, too, was outside the protection intended for speech and press."[3] Given the 1957 statutory focus of "obscene" on sex and excretion, the Court would have to explain that in the era contemporaneous to the Bill of Rights the word did not have that focus. The legal use of the term was wider in scope and more closely matched the less limited use of the word in ordinary, nonlegal, language.

The same cases cited for the proposition in *Roth* would provide similar support in the hypothetical opinion. In fact the cite to *Knowles v. State*,[4] at 1808 the earliest of the contemporaneous cases cited, indicated at least some contemporaneous support for the position that the obscene included far more than sex and excretion. That prosecution was based on the display of a "monster," eyeless but with apertures for eyes, having a projecting chin, ears well back on the neck, forelegs on the chest in the manner of arms, with smooth dark skin and no hair.[5] While the state supreme court held the exhibition not to be within the statute, the prosecution and the lower court had no difficulty with a definition of the obscene that included displaying persons as freaks in a sideshow atmosphere. An analysis of the concept of obscenity and the historical treatment of obscenity in drama would be required to flesh out the concept invoked by the cases cited. That analysis would find violence to be as central as sex to the concept of, and the prohibition against, the obscene.

The *Roth* Court also cited to more recent Supreme Court case law, dating from 1877 to 1953, as evidence for the proposition that the "Court has always assumed that obscenity is not protected by the freedoms of speech and press."[6] Federal statutes, dating from 1842 to 1956, were cited in further justification for that assumption.[7] As has been seen, law throughout most of the nineteenth century did often proscribe obscenity, but there was a lack of definition for the word. Any support *Roth* could draw from the law in that era would be available for the hypothetical opinion's conclusion that violent obscenity was unprotected.

The place where *Roth* and the hypothetical opinion would have to diverge in their historical analyses is in the late nineteenth century, after the Civil War Amendments. Only in that era did an exclusive focus on sex in obscenity law develop, and only with the 1896 decision in *Swearingen v. United States*[8] did it become clear that only sexual material would be considered legally obscene.[9]

The concept of obscenity had existed for millennia and had not solely focused on sex. It was finally the Victorian era's obsession with sex and its belief that masturbation led to insanity that led to the capture of the word "obscene" itself by those crusading against sexual material. That fits with Morris Ernst's conclusions that the American antisexual obscenity movement's leader, Anthony Comstock, was a "neurotic individual"[10] who "suffered from extreme feelings of guilt because of a habit of masturbation."[11]

The *Roth* opinion uses late-nineteenth- and twentieth-century statutes to show a continued effort to suppress sexually obscene material. Those statutes, at least those among them in which the focus on sex is clear, would not be usable in the hypothetical opinion. It is worth repeating that those later statutes are constitutionally irrelevant. They indicate the more recent use of the word "obscene," but they say nothing of the use of the word in constitutionally relevant periods of our history. Through the use of the word "obscene" they lay claim to the earlier statutes and cases that addressed obscenity, yet the focus of that earlier law was not solely on sex and excretion. While the hypothetical opinion may not use the later law, it has as good a claim as *Roth* had to the law in the relevant eras. As a result, the hypothetical opinion could simply ignore late-nineteenth- and twentieth-century obscenity law and conclude that law at the time of the Bill of Rights or the Fourteenth Amendment supports a ban on violent obscenity as well as *Roth* found it to support the ban on sexual obscenity.

While the hypothetical opinion could ignore all law after the 1868 date of the adoption of the Fourteenth Amendment, there is law from which the opinion could draw support similar to that found in *Roth*'s use of post–Fourteenth Amendment law. Those interested in limiting depictions of violence did not have the success of the crusading Antony Comstock. Nonetheless, a substantial body of statutory law addressing depictions of violence developed in the same era in which the use of the word "obscene" was being captured by those seeking to limit sexual depictions. Further, while the movement toward statutes banning depictions of violence may have lacked the crusading zeal of Comstock, it is interesting to note that the first of the statutes was enacted due to the efforts of the New York Society for the Suppression of Vice and the New York Society for the Prevention of Cruelty to Children,[12] the organization established by the antiobscenity crusader Anthony Comstock.[13]

The first of the statutes aimed at violence, and serving to limit any effect of a developing focus of the word "obscene" on sex, was passed in New York in 1884. The statute made it illegal to distribute "any book, pamphlet, magazine, newspaper or other printed paper devoted to the publication, and principally made up of criminal news, police reports or accounts of criminal deeds or pictures and stories of deeds of bloodshed, lust or crime."[14] The statute was aimed originally at the protection of minors from such material, but an 1887 amendment extended the ban on the dissemination of such material to adults.[15] Although the statutory language did include the word "lust," which may have a sexual connotation, the focus of the statute was on violence and crime. Despite this focus on violence and crime, the statutory section was titled "Obscene prints and articles," a title it retained until struck down as vague in 1948 in *Winters v. New York*.[16]

The New York legislature's 1884 act was quickly followed by similar enactments in other states. The year 1885 saw nine more states pass bans on depictions of violence. Several of the statutes speak only to distribution to minors. The Massachusetts statute, using language similar to that employed by New York, provided for imprisonment or a fine for anyone who sold, loaned, distributed, or gave to a minor "any book, pamphlet, magazine, newspaper or other printed paper devoted to the publication or principally made up of criminal news, police reports, or accounts of criminal deeds, or pictures and stories of lust or crime."[17] Again, the belief that such publications were obscene is shown by the title of the act—*An Act concerning obscene publications*.

Minnesota and Missouri also limited their prohibitions to distribution to minors. The language was quite similar to that of the New York and Massachusetts statutes. Minnesota's statute addressed the distribution of "any book, pamphlet, magazine, newspaper, or other printed paper, devoted to the publication or largely made up of criminal news, police reports or accounts of criminal deeds, or pictures and stories of deeds of bloodshed, lust, or crime."[18] The title of the chapter—*An act to prevent the sale or otherwise disposing of obscene, immoral, and indecent books, pamphlets, papers, pictures and other objectionable wares*—and of the section caption—*Prohibiting the promulgation of obscene literature*—are again telling. The Missouri statute similarly banned distribution to minors of "any book, pamphlet, magazine, newspaper, story paper or other printed paper devoted to the publication, or principally made up of criminal news, police reports, or accounts of criminal deeds, or pictures and stories of deeds of bloodshed, lust or crime."[19]

The Maine statute, like those in Minnesota, Massachusetts, and Missouri, again addressed only distribution to minors, and it used similar language to describe the publications affected, those "principally made up of criminal news, police reports, or accounts of criminal deeds, or pictures and stories of lust or crime."[20] The section was captioned *Sale, etc., to minor children of criminal news, obscene pictures, etc., punished*. Despite the use of the word "obscene," the Maine statute probably should not be read as an insistence that violent materials are obscene. The title, as well as the structure of the section, probably indicates more a grouping of two sorts of violations rather than an inclusion of depictions of criminality within the obscene.

The Ohio statute does seem to classify violent material as obscene. The Ohio statute again applies only to minors, and the description of the publications barred is again similar to the statutes already cited. The statute affects "any printed paper, illustrated paper, newspaper or periodical devoted to the publication of criminal news or police reports, accounts or stories of deeds of lust, immorality or crime."[21] The section caption was *Penalty for disposing of obscene literature, etc., or advertising same.* While the statute also banned distribution of "obscene, lewd, lascivious or indecent book[s],"[22] the inclusion of crime reports under the section caption may be an indication that these accounts of criminal deeds and crime were considered by Ohio to be obscene. The Oregon statute used similar language and applied only to minors.[23] The statute did group crime literature in with obscene materials but seemed to treat them as two different, if related, classes.

The remaining 1885 statutes applied to adults as well as to minors. While the scope of the statutes expanded, the descriptions of the banned publications remained similar. The Michigan statute again reached "any book, pamphlet, magazine, newspaper, or other printed paper, devoted to the publication or principally made up of criminal news, police reports, or accounts of criminal deeds, or pictures and stories of deeds of bloodshed, lust or crime."[24] The act was titled *An Act to prevent the sale or otherwise disposing of obscene, immoral, and indecent books, pamphlets, papers, prints, pictures, writings, and otherwise objectionable news.* Again, at least a relationship to obscenity is indicated.

The Connecticut statute used almost identical language and also applied to adults.[25] Some relationship of violence and obscenity might be found in the fact that the statute was titled *An Act concerning Obscene and Immoral Publications,* although the ban on violent material was in a separate section from the ban on "obscene or indecent" material. The inclusion would at least seem to show that the violent and the obscene were related and faced similar prohibitions.

The last of the 1885 statutes was enacted by Colorado. The language is somewhat different, but the aim seems to have been the same. The statute included a ban on publishing "by pictures or descriptions, indecent or immoral details of crime, vice or immorality, calculated to corrupt public morals, or to offend common decency, or to make vice and crime, immorality and licentiousness attractive."[26] Also proscribed by the statute were nude pictures, pictures of persons in "indecent attitudes or positions," and drugs and instruments for inducing abortions or preventing conception. The inclusion of materials detailing crime in the statute is again interesting in that such material was subsumed within a section captioned *Penalty for exhibiting or selling obscene books.* The statute provides further support for the proposition that violent depictions were historically not only banned but also were considered obscene.

The following year, 1886, saw Iowa and Kansas enact statutes banning depictions of violence. The Iowa statute used the familiar language in describing the banned material but instead of addressing stories of "bloodshed, lust or crime" the statute applied to stories of "immoral deeds, lust or crime."[27] The statute was limited to distribution and exhibition to minors but again is of interest in that the caption of the section was *Giving or showing to minors, obscene or immoral literature, etc., prohibited.* Further, the chapter title was *Relating to Obscene Literature,* and the act was titled *An Act to Suppress the circulation, advertising, and vending of Obscene and Immoral Literature and articles of Indecent and Immoral use, and to confiscate such property.* At least in Iowa in that era, the word "obscene" would again appear not to be limited to depictions of sexual or excretory activities but would include depictions of crime. The Kansas statute dropped "lust" from the description of banned descriptions of criminality, banning depictions of "bloodshed or crime."[28] The act applied to adults, as well as minors, and again seemed to consider the material obscene, as the chapter was titled *Relating to obscene literature,* and the act was titled *An Act to suppress and prevent the printing, selling . . . indecent or obscene literature, prints or etchings, drawings or papers, or any article or instrument of immoral use, and prescribing the punishment therefore.*

Nebraska and Pennsylvania followed suit in 1887. The Nebraska statute was limited to minors and barred publications "devoted to . . . or principally made up of criminal news, police reports, or accounts of criminal deeds, or pictures and stories of immoral deeds, lust or crime."[29] The Nebraska chapter title was *Obscene Literature;* however, the statute contained one section proscribing obscene literature and another containing the language quoted. The Pennsylvania law also applied only to minors and used the now-familiar language to describe the material banned.[30]

The initial surge in enactments slowed, but two years later, in 1889, Illinois used language nearly identical to that of the New York statute but limited the bans to distribution and exhibition to minors.[31] The act was titled *Obscene and Immoral Newspapers.* In still another two years, in 1891, Montana used similar language in its ban on distribution to minors.[32] The title of the Montana statute *Obscene Literature,* is again of interest, since it appears to include depictions of criminality within the obscene.

The years 1894 to 1895 saw four more states enact similar bans. The Kentucky statute,[33] dating from 1894, used the familiar language in a statute, not limited to minors, captioned *An Act to prevent the printing and distribution of obscene literature, and the sale or exhibition of obscene pictures, and the manufacture or distribution or sale of articles or instruments for immoral use.* The prohibition against crime depiction was in a separate section from bans on obscene and lewd material. The 1894 Maryland statutes addressed only distribution or exhibition to minors and again used the familiar language to describe the banned material.[34]

The 1895 North Dakota statute was contained in a section titled *Obscene Literature.* The section applied to adults, as well as minors, and included a ban on material "devoted principally or wholly to the publication of criminal news, or pictures, or stories of deeds of bloodshed or crime."[35] It is not clear that violent material was to be considered obscene. The statute bars material that is "indecent or obscene . . . or paper devoted . . . to . . . bloodshed or crime."[36] Since violent material is presented as an additional class of banned material, such material may not be included in the indecent or obscene material already mentioned, but again, there does appear to have been a relationship between the two.

The 1895 Indiana statute was not limited to minors and barred the circulation of material characterized by the section title as "pernicious literature." The affected material was defined as "any paper, book, or periodical, the chief feature or characteristic of which is the record of commission of crime, or to display by cut or illustration of crimes committed, or the acts or pictures of criminals, desperadoes, or of men or women in lewd and unbecoming positions or improper dress."[37] While violence might be different from sex, Indiana addressed both in the same section.

All the statutes discussed predated the 1896 decision in *Swearingen v. United States,*[38] the opinion that Professor Schauer takes as the point at which it finally becomes clear that obscenity is limited to sex.[39] In the era in which obscenity law was developing an exclusive focus on sex, the states reacted by enacting new statutes to control the violent literature which was being excluded from the common law and statutory definitions of the obscene. Some of the new statutes seemed to refuse to accept the exclusion of violence and continued to call such depictions obscene. Others did not insist on the obscenity label, but enacted new bans to assure that such material would be barred, despite the emerging restrictive definition.

Even after *Swearingen,* several states joined the effort to include violence in the category of legally unacceptable material. The first, an 1897 Texas statute, may be questionable as to its application to violent material. The statute bars material "devoted mainly to the publications of scandals, whoring, lechery, assignations, intrigues between men and women and immoral conduct of persons."[40] While criminality may be immoral, it is not clear that the aim of the statute is a ban on depictions of crime. While the relevance may be questionable, Justice Frankfurter, in his dissent in *Winters v. New York*,[41] did characterize the Texas statute as being similar to the 1884 New York statute.

The second post-*Swearingen* statute was an 1899 enactment by Wisconsin. The statute, an amendment to the statutory chapter addressing obscene books, papers, and literature, used language like that in New York and applied to any distribution of such materials.[42] The next was enacted ten years later in Washington in 1909. That statute applied to adults as well as minors and was similar in its description of the material affected. Interestingly, despite *Swearingen*, the prohibition on materials "devoted to the publication, or largely made up of criminal news, police reports, accounts of criminal deeds, or pictures of deeds of bloodshed, lust or crime"[43] was contained in a section titled *Obscene literature*.

Lastly, in 1913 South Dakota made it unlawful to present "by or with moving pictures, or in any manner, any stories or scenes illustrating illicit love, infidelity in family relations, murder, striking an officer of the law, which are suggestive of crime and immorality."[44] The statute did not classify such depictions as obscene, but included the prohibition in a section banning indecent exposure and distribution of sexually obscene materials.

The statutes cited provide an insight into the legal climate in the post–Civil War era. Prior to the late 1800s, there were bans on obscene materials, but it was unclear what material was included within the category of the obscene. Again, it is said to be only with the 1896 *Swearingen* decision that it becomes clear that obscenity is limited to sexually oriented material. In that same era, a significant number of states passed statutes banning depictions of criminal acts. Some of those statutes, those using "obscene" in their titles, may be viewed as an insistence that the category of the obscene is not so limited. Other states, by enacting statutes addressed to material no longer covered by obscenity statutes, may be seen as wishing to ban such material without being concerned over the label to be applied.

Given the unwillingness of the states to restrict the term "obscene" to sexual material or to add laws banning violent material without contesting the extension of the term, it would be worth reexamining precisely what it was that *Swearingen* resolved. *Swearingen* was the appeal of a conviction for violating a statutory ban on sending "obscene, lewd or lascivious" material through the mails. While the statute addressed "obscene, lewd or lascivious" material,[45] the indictment had charged mailing a newspaper containing an article that was "obscene, lewd and lascivious."[46] The Court noted that the statutory language might be read to indicate that "obscene," "lewd," and "lascivious" were distinct categories. Under such a reading, however, the indictment for mailing "obscene, lewd and lascivious" material would constitute three charges and would be "bad for duplicity." To avoid having to arrest judgement, the Court concluded that the words "obscene, lewd or lascivious" described one offense.

The Court went on to consider whether the article mailed was "obscene, lewd and lascivious." Having already determined that the three terms together described but one offense, the conclusion that obscenity spoke to what was lewd or lascivious was obvious. The Court held that "[t]he words 'obscene,' 'lewd,' and 'lascivious,' as used in the statute, signify that form of immorality which has relation to sexual impurity, and have the same meaning as is given them at common law in prosecutions for obscene libel."[47] While the language in the article was "exceedingly coarse and vulgar, and, as applied to an individual person, plainly libelous[, the Court could not] perceive in it anything of a lewd, lascivious, and obscene tendency, calculated to corrupt and debauch the minds and morals of those into whose hands it might fall."[48]

Swearingen was an exercise in statutory construction. It certainly resolved an issue over the meaning of "obscene" in the statute under which the charge had been filed. The case might be read as limited to that statute, in which case the claim that with *Swearingen* obscenity law finally became focused on sex would be overly general. It is also true, however, that the opinion adopted a definition that it saw as established in the common law. The opinion then provides the observation of a very important court on the state of the law. It provides only an observation, rather than a holding, and the Court's view was only important, rather than controlling, with regard to the common law, because the Court was interpreting a particular statute, not issuing a constitutional ruling. There is nothing in *Swearingen* that would keep a state legislature or court from continuing to include violence within the concept of obscenity in the state's development of statutory and common law. Even a federal court interpreting a different statute might not limit the concept of obscenity to the degree it was limited in *Swearingen*. Even more clearly, there is nothing in *Swearingen* that establishes a constitutional difference between the legal protections due violent material and those due sexual material. The issue was solely a matter of statutory labels and the states' continued bans on violent literature and the labeling of that literature as obscene did not conflict with *Swearingen*.

Winters v. New York

One of the statutes against the depiction of violence enacted in the late nineteenth and early twentieth centuries reached the United States Supreme Court in the 1947 term. Winters, a New York book dealer, was charged with violating the 1940s version of the New York statute originally enacted in 1884, as amended in 1887. The statute still prohibited distribution of the same materials, publications made up principally of "criminal news, police reports, or accounts of criminal deeds, or pictures, or stories of deeds of bloodshed, lust or crime."[49] Winters had been found in possession of a large number of magazines titled *Headquarters Detective, True Cases from the Police Blotter* and containing what purported to be true cases of crime culled from police records and files. The magazines were described by the Appellate Division of the New York Supreme Court as "a collection of crime stories which portray in vivid fashion tales of vice, murder and intrigue. The stories are embellished with pictures of fiendish and gruesome crimes, and are besprinkled with lurid photographs of victims and perpetrators."[50] While some of the magazine articles had titles such as "Bargains in Bodies," "Girl Slave to a Love Cult," and "Girls' Reformatory,"[51] perhaps suggesting that some of the stories had some sexual flavor, the objections to the magazines were over the focus on crime, rather than sex. The appellate division affirmed the conviction, noting that a similar statute had been upheld by state courts in Connecticut and that Minnesota, Mississippi, Kansas, Missouri, and Kentucky state courts had all upheld statutes barring depictions of various forms of crime.

The court seemed to recognize the possibility of an overbreadth challenge to the statute. In what appears to have been a response to that issue, the court offered a construction limiting the scope of the statute.

> Publications dealing with crime news as an incident to the legitimate purposes of science or literature are not prohibited. Moreover, as the prosecution readily concedes, the statute does not seek to suppress "a large class of recognized literature including practically all detective and western stories and books." It is aimed exclusively at printed matter which presents tales of bloodshed, crime or lust in a manner that would have a tendency to demoralize its readers and would be likely to corrupt the morals of the young and lead them to immoral acts.[52]

Turning to the consideration of constitutional concerns, the court first addressed the New York Bill of Rights, Article I, section 8 of the New York Constitution, which provided: "Every citizen may freely speak, write and publish his sentiments on all subjects, being responsible for the abuse of that right; and no law shall be passed to restrain or abridge the liberty of speech or of the press." In explaining the meaning of that protection of speech and press, the court said: "The constitution does . . . not shield a printed attack on private character. . . . It does not permit the publication of blasphemous or obscene articles. . . . It places no restraint upon the power of the legislature to punish the publication of matter which is injurious to society according to the standard of the common law."[53] What is of interest in this quote is the fact that the court continued to assert the inclusion of a ban on depictions of crime and violence as in keeping with common law standards running alongside laws against libel, obscenity, and blasphemy. If not an assertion that violence can be obscene, at least the bans on sex and on violence were seen as equally well-established.

With regard to the United States Constitution, the court found it well settled the freedoms of speech and press do not deprive the state of the police power. The court had already noted the tendency of publications, such as those banned, to demoralize the minds of impressionable readers and the possibility of inducing the young to commit lawless deeds. Since it viewed the statute in issue as a valid exercise of the state's police power designed to promote general welfare and protect community morality, the statute was upheld.

Winters again appealed, this time to the New York Court of Appeals, where the conviction was again affirmed.[54] The court of appeals noted that the statute in question was found in article 106 of the Penal Law, an article with the caption *Indecency,* and that the title of section 1141 itself was *Obscene prints and articles.* With regard to the inclusion of violence within the categories of the indecent or the obscene, the court noted that the state's statutes dealing with indecency or obscenity have generally been held to speak to sexual depictions. However, the court determined that subsection 1141(2), the relevant section, had to be read to apply to nonsexual, violent, or crime-oriented material to avoid a partial duplication of section 1141(1).

The question then became whether or not such material could properly be considered obscene. In that regard, the court said:

> Indecency or obscenity is an offense against the public order. . . . Collections of pictures or stories of criminal deeds of bloodshed or lust unquestionably can be so massed as to become vehicles for inciting violent and depraved crimes against the person and in that case such publications are indecent or obscene in an admissible sense, though not necessarily in

the sense of being calculated or intended to excite sexual passion. This idea, as it seems to us, was the principal reason for the enactment of the statute.[55]

The court clearly held, some fifty years after *Swearingen* was supposed to have made it clear that obscenity was limited to sex, that depictions could be obscene because of their violence. The court then went on to address the argument that freedom of the press protected even obscene material and rejected that conclusion.

The court also addressed the possible overbreadth of the statute. It rejected the claim that the statute would ban all commentaries on crime from detective stories to scientific treatises. Such an interpretation would, the court said, be such a manifest injustice and absurdity and that it could not have been intended by the legislature. Furthermore, the material on which the conviction was based was seen clearly to be within the scope of the statute. The court left open the question of whether or not the statute applied to material that did not focus on bloodshed or lust, since the material at issue did have such a focus.

The appellant also raised a vagueness issue, arguing that the statute would make the publication of any work on or about crime hazardous. The court was unswayed. It noted that

> [T]here can be no more precise test of written indecency or obscenity than the continuing and changeable experience of the community as to what types of books are likely to bring about the corruption of public morals or other analogous injury to the public order. . . . [W]hen reasonable men may fairly classify a publication as necessarily or naturally indecent or obscene, a mistaken view by the publisher as to its character or tendency is immaterial.[56]

The analysis is strikingly similar to that employed in sexual obscenity cases. Only Chief Justice Lehman dissented, and he dissented only on this last vagueness issue.

The case was appealed once again and was argued three times before the United States Supreme Court. Finally, in *Winters v. New York,*[57] the lower courts were reversed and the conviction set aside. While *Winters* struck down the statute, it did so on vagueness grounds, while seeming to tolerate the inclusion of such material within the category of the indecent and obscene. The Court noted that the statute went beyond punishing the distribution of material that was obscene or indecent "in the usual sense" and also reached magazines that were "indecent and obscene because they 'massed' stories of bloodshed and lust to incite crimes."[58] The Court, showing an institutional memory limited to the twentieth century, also noted that the material at issue was not "indecency or obscenity in any sense heretofore known to the law"[59] and that the material was not "indecent and obscene, as formerly understood."[60] Yet, the Court did not strike the statute down because it categorized nonerotic material as obscene. Rather, the Court warned against the implication that the state could not punish the circulation of objectionable material, within First Amendment limitations, under a sufficiently definite statute[61] and stated that "[n]either the states nor Congress are prevented by the requirement of specificity from carrying out their duty of eliminating evils to which, in their judgment, such publications give rise."[62]

While believing New York's statute employed an expanded definition of "obscene," that increased inclusion is not what caused the statute to be declared unconstitutional. If the court believed that only erotic material could be banned as obscene, the conviction and statute would easily have fallen on that basis. Instead, it was a chilling-effect concern that led to the statute's demise.

[W]e find the specification of publications, prohibited from distribution, too uncertain and indefinite to justify the conviction of this petitioner. Even though all detective tales and treatises on criminology are not forbidden, and though publications made up of criminal deeds not characterized by bloodshed or lust are omitted from the interpretation of the Court of Appeals, we think fair use of collections of pictures and stories would be interdicted because of the utter impossibility of the actor or the trier to know where this new standard of guilt would draw the line between the allowable and the forbidden publications.[63]

It did not seem to the Court that an honest distributor could know when he might have violated the prohibition. It was not sufficiently clear when a collection of stories of war or crime might become so "massed" as to be a "vehicle for inciting violent and depraved crimes."[64]

Had there not been a vagueness problem, it appears that the statute would have been found constitutional. The Court cited two state court cases based on similar statutes. In *Strohm v. Illinois*[65] a conviction for distribution to minors of material similar in character to that distributed by Winters was upheld. The Court in no way criticized that conviction. Instead, it distinguished the case by noting that *Strohm* "did not involve any problem of free speech or denial of due process for uncertainty under the Fourteenth Amendment."[66] Since the statutes were similar in their language, it appears not to be the target of the statute, but rather the focus on the target, that was the problem in *Winters*.

The other cite was to *State v. McKee*,[67] the appeal of a conviction under a Connecticut statute again similar to New York's. The state court there found no free speech difficulties but reversed, because of a failure of the charge to mirror the statute. The Supreme Court again noted that no issue of denial of due process for uncertainty had been raised.

Justice Frankfurter dissented in *Winters* and was joined by Justices Jackson and Burton. In that dissent, he cited nineteen other state statutes nearly identical to that found to be unconstitutionally vague.[68] He cited four others as being substantially similar.[69] Justice Frankfurter continued, "This body of laws represents but one of the many attempts by legislatures to solve what is perhaps the most persistent, intractable, elusive, and demanding of all problems of society—the problem of crime, and more particularly, of its prevention. By this decision, the Court invalidates such legislation of almost half the states of the Union."[70] He recognized the need to avoid vagueness, but considered the construction given the statute by the New York courts adequate.

Given the ability to save statutes by limiting constructions, the outlook for state statutes need not have been as dire as Justice Frankfurter indicated. Nonetheless, most of the statutes he cited are no longer law, although there are a couple of exceptions. Illinois still has a prohibition against distributing to minors "any book, pamphlet, magazine, newspaper, story paper or other printed paper devoted to the publication, or principally made up of criminal news, police reports, or accounts of criminal deeds, or pictures and stories of deeds of bloodshed, lust or crime."[71] Michigan also still retains a similar statute barring the distribution of "any book, pamphlet, magazine, newspaper or other printed paper devoted to the publication or principally made up of criminal news, police reports or accounts of criminal deeds or pictures, stories of deeds of bloodshed, lust or crime."[72]

Horror Comics and *Kingsley Books v. Brown*

The issue of crime publications again came to the fore in the 1950s, this time in the context of comic books. The years following the *Winters* decision saw a great increase in the circulation of comic books. After taking ten years, from 1940 to 1950, to double in the number of titles printed annually, from 150 to about 300, and in annual revenues, from $20 million to an annual income of close to $41 million, both doubled again between 1950 and 1953. In 1953 the comic book industry printed about 650 titles and had sales of about $90 million. In addition to the increase in raw numbers, the years 1945 to 1954 saw an increased number of crime and horror comics. This variety of comic featured brutality, violence, and sadism, along with sexually suggestive illustrations. It was estimated that by mid-1954 there were more than 30 million copies of crime or horror comics printed each month.[73]

These comics had some sexual flavor, but the focus seemed not to be on sex acts but rather on crimes of violence against scantily clad females.[74] When the Senate Committee on the Judiciary examined horror and crime comics, their concern seemed to be with the violence present. The committee's report outlines the plot of several stories, and the summaries do not detail any sexual content but focus exclusively on the violence involved.[75] One of the stories described concerns an alcoholic husband, whose negligence results in the death of his son. His wife then hacks him to pieces with an ax, complete with spurting blood and an expression of agony on the victim's face. The wife then cuts the body into smaller pieces, places the pieces in the bottles of bootleg liquor he has acquired and returns the liquor to the bootlegger. Another concerns an eight- to ten-year-old girl who would prefer to live with her aunt, rather than with her alcoholic and abusive father and her inattentive mother. She shoots and kills her father and frames her mother, who is electrocuted for the crime. The Senate's descriptions show a focus clearly on violence, although other comic books of the era appear to have had a stronger sex content.

While Congress took no action to ban such comics, there was legislation at other levels of government. The strength of state interest in the control of crime comics is shown by the fact that the Council of State Governments included a model statute for the regulation of crime and sex comics in its Suggested State Legislation Program for 1957.[76] The Council did, however, express a preference for the same kind of industry self-regulation on which Congress relied.[77]

During the late 1950s through the 1970s, these statutes were declared unconstitutional by the lower courts. Some of the statutes fell because they suffered flaws similar to those in the statute struck down in *Winters*. For example, Maryland's Crime Comic Books Act[78] was struck down in *Police Commissioner v. Siegel Enterprises*.[79] Section 421 of the act made it unlawful to distribute to minors "any book, pamphlet, magazine or other printed paper principally composed of pictures and specifically including but not limited to comic books, devoted to the publication and exploitation of actual or fictional deeds of violent bloodshed, lust or immorality." The Maryland Court of Appeals found the same vagueness in the Maryland statute as the *Winters* Court had found in the New York statute, and the fact that the Maryland statute was limited to minors had no effect on that determination.

The Maryland statute also suffered from another constitutional infirmity.

The statute contained an exception for accounts of crime contained in news publications appearing at least weekly, even when drawings or photographs were used to illustrate the news stories.[80] The court found the exception to be a violation of equal protection. The court found it difficult to see how material would be less likely to incite crime, avoidance of which was the legislature's stated purpose for the statute, when it appeared in a newspaper, rather than in a comic book. The exception was seen as particularly unreasonable, since newspapers often contain comic pages or weekly comic sections. While the comic material in the two media might be exactly the same, the comics were not barred by the statute, if the major portion of the publication was non-comic. The court saw this as discrimination based not on what was published but on what was not published.

The state of Washington also passed a Comic Book Act in 1955.[81] In *Adams v. Hinkle*,[82] in an en banc decision by the state supreme court, it too was struck down. The act contained a section defining comic books as "any book, magazine or pamphlet . . . a major part of which consists of drawings depicting or telling a story of a real or fanciful event or series of events, with a substantial number of said drawings setting forth the spoken words of the characters with pointers, or brackets, or enclosures, or by such other means as will plainly indicate the character speaking such words." A license was required for anyone selling comic books, but there was an exemption from the statutory requirements for comic sections of regularly published daily or weekly newspapers.

The court held that the licensing requirement was unconstitutional, as a prior restraint. While *Kingsley Books v. Brown*[83] had held prior restraints on the dissemination of obscene material constitutional, the licensing requirement reached all comic books, whether obscene or not. Further, while the statute stated that crime comic books contribute to juvenile delinquency and were a source of crime, as justification for the act, the legislation was not restricted to crime comic books. A license was required for the sale of any comic, harmful or not. Further, the court found the statute lacking in the provision of standards for the issuance of a license.

The court expressed additional concern over the fact that the statute applied to sales of comics to adults, as well as minors, even though the rationale offered was the contribution of crime comics to juvenile crime. The court also found the same flaws the Maryland court found in its statute. The prohibition against the distribution of "any comic book . . . devoted to the publication or exploitation of fictional or actual deeds of violent bloodshed, lust, crime or immorality by characters depicted either as real or fanciful, human or inhuman, so massed as reasonably to tend to incite minors to violence or depraved or immoral acts against the person" faced the same vagueness problems found fatal in *Winters*. Furthermore, the exemption for the comic sections of newspapers was held to be prohibited by the federal and state equal-protection clauses.

One of the more interesting legislative responses, because of the insight it provides into the problem of drafting such legislation, was a Los Angeles County ordinance struck down by the Supreme Court of California in *Katzev v. County of Los Angeles*.[84] The ordinance stated that the distribution of crime comics to minors posed a clear and present danger of inciting children to commit crimes. It was made a misdemeanor to distribute crime comics to minors, and the statute went to great lengths to define crime comic books, and crimes, in an attempt to avoid the sort of vagueness that had caused the demise of the *Winters* statute.

Crime comic books were defined as:

> Any book, magazine, or pamphlet in which an account of crime is set forth by means of a series of five (5) or more drawings or photographs, in sequence, which are accompanied by either narrative writing or words represented as being spoken by a pictured character, whether such narrative or words appear in "balloons," captions or on or immediately adjacent to the photograph or drawing.[85]

The ordinance also attempted to define "crime" for purposes of the statute. "Crime" was defined as:

> The commission or attempted commission of an act of arson, burglary, kidnapping, mayhem, murder, rape, robbery, theft, trainwrecking, or voluntary manslaughter; or the commission of an act of assault with caustic chemicals or assault with a deadly weapon[,] includ[ing] but . . . not limited to, acts by human beings, and further includ[ing] acts by animals or any non-human, part human, or imaginary beings, which if performed by a human would constitute any of the crimes named.[86]

The last portion of this definition appears addressed to a concern over violence involving cartoon characters and the effect that might have on young children.

The court read *Winters* as holding that publications containing criminal news, accounts of criminal deeds, or pictures and stories of bloodshed, lust, or crime are as entitled to First Amendment protection as other literature. The court also failed to find a clear and present danger to overcome that protection, because the record did not disclose a close, causal connection between juvenile delinquency and the circulation of crime comic books in general.[87] Specifically, the ordinance was too broad in that it applied to all fictional crime, excepting only true stories and stories of crime in religious works. That over-breadth made the statute unconstitutional.

The court also found that the exemptions in the statute for true stories and religious works were a denial of equal protection, under both federal and state law. The court found no reason to believe comic books presenting disgustingly detailed exploits of Murder, Incorporated, John Dillinger, or Jesse James would have less harmful effect than stories of Popeye, Tom Mix, or fictionalized accounts of law enforcement officers. The rational line would not have been between the fictional and the true but would instead be based on the way in which crime was depicted. The exemption for depictions of crime derived from religious writings and for newspapers were held to raise the same objections.

Even with the expanded definitions, the ordinance did not escape criticism for vagueness. The court noted that many children's books of fairy tales and folk tales contained illustrations, some of which would fit the parameters of the ordinance. Banning such books seemed outside the intent of the ordinance, yet if they were not to be included, standards on where the line was to be drawn were seen as lacking. Further vagueness was found in what constituted an account of crime. One last, and interesting, objection had to do with the inclusion of "acts by animals . . . which if performed by a human would constitute any of the crimes named." As the court pointed out, this would seem to include a shark biting off a person's arm, since a similar attack by a person would constitute mayhem or cannibalism. Similarly, the court said a dog shown eating food left on a porch would be barred, since it would constitute theft, if done by a human.

One case involving horror and crime comics made it to the United States Supreme Court. In fact, the case, *Kingsley Books v. Brown*,[88] was handed down the same day *Roth* established an exception for, and began to define, obscenity. *Kingsley Books* held that injunctions may issue against the sale and distribution of obscene material. The obscenity of the material against which the injunction was sought in *Kingsley Books* was not on appeal, and the sole question was the propriety of issuing an injunction. The injunction had issued under statutory authority to enjoin materials that were in violation of section 1141 of the New York Penal Code, the same section that had been at issue in *Winters*. In the period between when *Winters* found the language in that section dealing with reports of crime and violence unconstitutionally vague and the *Kingsley Books* prosecution, that portion of the statute had been repealed.[89] The statute still contained a ban on the distribution of materials that were "obscene, lewd, lascivious, filthy, indecent or disgusting"[90] and the trial court found the publications in issue to be of such character.

The publication giving rise to *Kingsley Books* was a series of "paper-covered *obscene* booklets"[91] published under the title *Nights of Horror*. While the New York state trial court had also labeled the material "obscene" and "pornographic," the description and objections presented by that court focused strongly on the material's violent aspects.[92] That is not to say that the lower court considered the material to be without sexual content. The court noted that, while sexual relationships can be beautiful and healthy, the publications in question did not reflect such beauty. Citing Judge Learned Hand's view that "the word 'obscene' should 'be allowed to indicate the present critical point in the compromise between candor and shame,' "[93] the court had no trouble finding that

> "Nights of Horror" will be found resting at the foot of the scale, clearly marked "shame". No matter how strict the test or how broad the criteria, these volumes will readily measure up to and even surpass the most generous standard. The booklets in evidence offer naught but glorified concepts of lustful and vicious concupiscence, and by their tenor deride love and virtue, invite crime and voluptuousness, and excite lecherous desires. . . . There is no true dissemination of lawful ideas — rather is there a direct incitement to sex crimes and the sordid excitement of brutality.[94]

The court also stated that the material would affect the libido of the normal, healthy person and that the effect on the abnormal person could be disastrous to the individual and others.[95]

The court also went to some length to state its view that the materials were not literature but pornography, lacking plot and style and failing to meet any literary standards.[96] The covers included sexually suggestive drawings, and the volume of misspelled words, poor grammar, and printing errors showed no "genuine literary intent."[97] The only contribution to literature was, in the court's view, as a glossary of terms of sexual anatomy and practices.[98]

While the court did label the material pornographic, the major focus of its objection was on the publications' depictions of violence.

> "Nights of Horror" is no haphazard title. Perverted sexual acts and macabre tortures of the human body are repeatedly depicted. The books contain numbers of acts of male torturing female and some vice versa — by most ingenious means. These gruesome acts included such horrors as cauterizing a woman's breast with a hot iron, placing hot coals against a woman's breasts, tearing breasts off, placing hot irons against a female's armpits, pulling off a girl's fingernails with white-hot pincers, completely

singeing away the body hairs, working a female's skin away from her flesh with a knife, gouging and burning eyes out of their sockets, ringing the nipples of the breast with needles. Hanging by the thumbs, hair pulling, skin burning, putting on bone-compressing iron boots, were usual. The torture rack abounded. Self-torture was frequent. Sucking a victim's blood was pictured; and so was pouring molten lead into a girl's mouth and ears; and putting honey on a girl's breasts, vagina and buttocks — and then putting hundreds of great red ants on the honey.[99]

Certainly, portions of the violence depicted did involve sex-specific anatomical structures. However, the general tenor of the material appears to have been the description of the infliction of pain on every conceivable sensitive area of the body. Genitals and breasts provided such sensitive areas, but so did armpits, the eyes, fingernails, thumbs, and skin and bones generally.

While the court noted the expression of a belief in male power over females and of older males over youth and also the depiction of sodomy, rape, lesbianism, and seduction,[100] these subjects alone would not make the material obscene. A work is not obscene because it discusses an objectional subject or argues for an objectional thesis.[101] Obscenity is instead based in the material used to discuss that subject or argue for the thesis. Such material must include objectional depictions of acts. While those acts have most commonly been sexual or excretory, the objections to *Nights of Horror* appear primarily to be over its depiction of violence. In fact, the complaint on which the prosecution proceeded was filed in September of 1954,[102] just one month after

New Yorkers were stunned to learn of the wanton savagery of four Brooklyn teen-agers who horsewhipped, beat, kicked, and burned their several victims, ultimately drowning one of them — all for amusement. The eighteen-year-old leader . . . boasted of having read every volume in the *Nights of Horror* series. A psychiatrist who examined him found "the parallelism is complete" between *Nights of Horror* texts and pictures and the methods used by the youthful killers.[103]

The impetus for prosecution appears to have been over violence rather than eroticism.

Violence and Obscenity Since *Roth*

While the Supreme Court has never directly held that extremely violent material may not, for that reason only, be banned, lower courts have found

Supreme Court opinions that they believe imply that conclusion. The courts that struck down the bans on distributing violent videos to minors provide examples. The federal district court in *Video Software Dealers Assoc. v. Webster*[104] declared Missouri's bar unconstitutional. While the statute presented vagueness problems, the court did not base its decision solely on that ground. Rather, the court went on to note that the Supreme Court had never held that violent speech is unprotected. From that fact, employing a bit of faulty logic, the court seemed to conclude that such material was protected. While one can argue for that conclusion, the simple fact that it has not been found unprotected does not show that it is protected.

When the federal appellate court affirmed,[105] it agreed with the district court that violent material is protected by the First Amendment. The appellate court provided greater depth in its analysis of the issue of the protection of violent material. The court noted that, at oral argument, the state had conceded that the First Amendment generally protects violent videos. To back up that, perhaps unwise, concession, the court added cites to several lower federal court opinions and to the Supreme Court's opinion in *Winters v. New York*,[106] which the court indicated held that the "First Amendment protects pictures and stories of 'deeds of bloodshed, lust or crime.' "[107] That, however, was not the holding of *Winters*. *Winters* was resolved on vagueness grounds, and the Court did not criticize what it recognized as a different use of the word "obscene." To the contrary, the *Winters* Court warned against concluding that states could not punish the circulation of objectionable material, under a sufficiently definite statute.[108]

The state had also contended that the violent videos addressed by the statute are "obscene" for children and, thus, unprotected. The court responded by citing *Miller v. California*,[109] *Roth*,[110] and *Erznoznik v. Jacksonville*,[111] for the conclusion that "[o]bscenity, however, encompasses only expression that 'depict[s] or describe[s] sexual conduct.' "[112] The court went on to say that "[m]aterial that contains violence but not depictions or descriptions of sexual conduct cannot be obscene. . . . Thus, videos depicting only violence do not fall within the legal definition of obscenity for either minors or adults."[113] Since the material was protected, the court agreed with the district court in its analysis of vagueness and its effect on meeting the strict liability test.

When the Tennessee Supreme Court, in *Davis-Kidd Booksellers, Inc. v. McWherter*,[114] overturned the Tennessee ban on distribution to minors of videos harmful to minors, it too considered the definition of obscenity. The court found vagueness problems, and citing *Miller*, went on to say that the vagueness could not be cured by declaring violence to be obscene as to minors, because the United States Supreme Court had limited obscenity to sexual depictions or description and had not included violent materials.

A Tennessee city had, in fact, earlier experienced difficulties with a similar definition in a city ordinance. *Allied Artists Pictures Corporation v. Alford*[115] considered a Memphis ordinance that prohibited the dissemination to juveniles of material that was "obscene to juveniles." The ordinance defined "obscene to juveniles" as "any description or representation in whatever form, of nudity, sexual conduct, sexual excitement, excess violence, of sadomasochistic abuse" meeting certain other requirements regarding offensiveness.[116] With regard to "excess violence," the ordinance provided a definition identical to that at issue in *McWherter*.[117]

The federal district court found the statute vague, but it is unclear what its position on violence as obscenity was. The court considered the claim that the review system included in the Memphis ordinance operated as a prior restraint and concluded that, as administered, it might be. The court also noted that obscenity is an exception to the prohibition against prior restraints and that the ordinance was then not unconstitutional on its face as a prior restraint.[118] That might be taken as an indication that the inclusion of violence was not seen as a flaw.

The violence section was, however, found to be unconstitutionally vague. The court seemed disturbed by the conclusion it felt it had to draw and opined that a carefully drawn ordinance could be constitutional.

> [S]ociety and parents are to be commended for current concern about the extraordinary portrayals of violent conduct on movie (as well as television) screens. If carefully drawn, under obscenity standards, such portrayals might be subject to permissible criminal standards. The Court reaches this conclusion with particular regret as to excision of two sections of the ordinance, recognizing the difficulty confronting legislatures and councils under Supreme Court standards and recognizing the laudable intent of the drafters of this section dealing with undoubted pernicious effects of excessive violence portrayed in the communicative arts upon youth (as well as adults). . . . Violence in the form of sadism or in relation to prurient acts may properly be considered in determining obscenity, or may be taken into account as an important factor in defining obscenity.[119]

Despite the fact that the *McWherter* court claimed support from *Allied Artists,* that support may be limited to the vagueness of the statutory terms. The *Allied Artists* court seemed willing to base obscenity on violence, and it was certainly clear that violence could at least play a role in such a determination.

The last lower court case of interest here is *Sovereign News Co. v. Falke*.[120] That case, which was very complex procedurally and in the number of issues raised, concerned an Ohio statute against pandering obscenity.[121] The section containing the statute also provided a definition of "obscene":

> When considered as a whole, and judged with reference to ordinary adults or, if it is designed for sexual deviates or other specially susceptible group, judged with reference to that group, any material or performance is "obscene" if any of the following apply: . . .
> (3) Its dominant tendency is to arouse lust by displaying or depicting bestiality or extreme or bizarre violence, cruelty, or brutality; . . .[122]

Despite the fact that the inclusion of violence in the definition of obscenity was limited to violence that tended to arouse lust, the court held that the inclusion of violence within the category of the obscene made the statute unconstitutional.

> Section 2907.01(F)(3) unconstitutionally restricts the display or depiction of extreme or bizarre violence, cruelty or brutality. It is an express holding of *Miller* that only material depicting or describing sexual conduct may be barred as being obscene. . . . Therefore, the restrictions placed on the description or depiction of extreme violence unconstitutionally restrains free expression, and the statute is therefore overbroad.[123]

The lower courts to have held that violence is not protected by the First Amendment have been guided by the definition of "obscene" provided in *Miller* and an implication that anything not within that definition is protected. The *Miller* definition of "obscene" built on the definition, provided by *Roth,* that obscene material is material dealing with sex in a manner that appeals to the prurient interest. The *Miller* Court recognized that the *Roth* definition was more limited than that in common usage and that the material it was discussing was "more accurately defined as 'pornography' or 'pornographic material.' "[124] "Pornographic material which is obscene forms a subgroup of all 'obscene' expression, but not the whole, at least as the word 'obscene' is now used in our language. We note, therefore, that the words 'obscene material,' as used in this case, have a specific judicial meaning which derives from the *Roth* case, i.e., obscene material 'which deals with sex.' "[125] The Court went on to note that it was settled that obscene material was unprotected, but because of the dangers inherent in regulating expression, statutes addressing obscenity had to be carefully limited. The Court then stated the current test for obscenity with its language that focuses on sex. If it was not already clear from *Roth,* it was certainly clear in *Miller* that the Court had limited obscenity, and with it the scope of the obscenity exception, to sexually oriented material. Further strengthening that view is the insistence in *Erznoznik* and *Cohen v. California*[126] that to be obscene a depiction must be erotic, and hence sexual.

These two opinions add weight to the conclusion that obscenity has been limited to the erotic and so to the sexual. However, the recognition that violence can be banned, either as a variety of obscenity or as a separate exception, would not require the overruling of *Erznoznik* or *Cohen*. The depictions that made the material on the drive-in screen objectionable was sexual in nature. The word that led the state to object to Cohen's jacket was one associated with sex. The direct language of *Erznoznik* and *Cohen* could, given the focus of the cases, simply be a reminder to the states that not all sexual depictions or references are obscene. For a sexual depiction or reference to be obscene, it must be erotic. That conclusion would not speak to the propriety of a ban on violence.

The cases that then stand in the way of recognizing violence as obscenity are *Roth* and *Miller*. However, even those cases did not consider the issue of the First Amendment status of depictions of violence. The court could decide that, while the test of what sexual material is obscene is properly stated in those cases, the cases say nothing about the inclusion of violence within the obscene. To the degree that the cases hold that only the sexual can be obscene, they are simply incorrect and should be disavowed. Historically, in common usage and in both statutory and cases law in all constitutionally relevant eras, obscenity has not been limited to sex and excretion and speaks just as clearly to violence. To set the historical record straight, the Court should recognize that violence can be obscene, or if it wishes to restrict the word "obscene" to its modern legal usage, recognize extreme violence, properly defined, as a parallel First Amendment exception.

The examination thus far has been into the extralegal history of the concept of obscenity and into the history of obscenity in the law. While that examination has shown that there is no adequate basis to distinguish sufficiently explicit and offensive sexual depictions from similarly explicit and offensive depictions of violence for purposes of First Amendment protections, that is not all there is to the question. The First Amendment has been argued to embody particular policy judgements. If the policies that underlie the First Amendment speak differently with regard to sex than they do with regard to violence, that would serve to distinguish the two and leave one unprotected while still protecting the other.

The *Roth* Court and various commentators have presented policy reasons for denying First Amendment protection to obscene materials. Much of the policy analysis has been in the context of considering limitations on depictions of sexual activity, but the policy reasons will be seen to carry over with equal weight to violence as obscenity.

The First Amendment and Self-Government

The policy reasons for denying First Amendment protection to obscene material, as presented by the *Roth* opinion, had a historical flavor. Policy concerns expressed by the framers have extremely strong standing as explanations for the scope of the protections enacted in response to those concerns. In its search for policy, the Court said that the First Amendment speech and press protections were "fashioned to assure unfettered interchange of ideas for the bringing about of political and social changes desired by the people."[1] As evidence for that proposition, the opinion quotes a 1774 letter from the Continental Congress to the people of Quebec:

> The last right we shall mention, regards the freedom of the press. The importance of this consists, besides the advancement of truth, science,

morality, and arts in general, in its diffusion of liberal sentiments on the administration of Government, its ready communication of thoughts between subjects, and its consequential promotion of union among them, whereby oppressive officers are shamed or intimidated, into more honourable and just modes of conducting affairs.[2]

Since the *Roth* Court's focus was on the role of the freedom of speech in the process of self-government, that would be a good starting point for an analysis of First Amendment policy.

Meiklejohn and the People as Rulers

This focus on the First Amendment as protective of the role of the people in political and social change and in the administration of government occupies a central place in the work of Alexander Meiklejohn. His book *Free Speech and Its Relation to Self-Government* finds the basis for the First Amendment to be the same as the basis for the Constitution as a whole. Both rest on, and are justified by, the proposition that the people are both the rulers and the governed. He notes that, while some abridging of speech must be allowed, *the freedom of speech* must not be abridged. His explanation of the difference is provided in the context of describing the business of a town meeting.[3] Some speech must be abridged so that the meeting can be conducted in an orderly fashion. There must be rules governing the recognition of speakers, remarks being proper or out of order, and even limitations on repetition of comments already made. On the other hand, *the freedom of speech,* that cannot be abridged, denies the authority to limit speech because of the views expressed. While a speaker who chooses to address a topic not on the floor may be out of order, a speaker cannot be ruled out of order because of the views he or she wishes to express with regard to a topic that is on the floor.

The use of a town meeting as a model for his explanation of the freedom of speech is telling for Meiklejohn, because it clearly shows the active role he saw the ordinary citizen playing in government. This role comes through strongly in his discussion of whether the freedom of speech can be abridged, when speech presents a clear and present danger to the general welfare. His answer that it cannot rests on an analysis of the protection of speech accorded the branches of the government.[4] He notes that the Speech and Debate Clause of Article One of the Constitution protects the speech of members of the Congress. They shall not be called to answer in any other place for any speech or debate in either house. That protection is granted members, even when their speeches pose a threat to the general welfare.[5] The same is true for the courts.

Meiklejohn says that the opinions of dissenting justices of the Supreme Court present a clear and present danger to the acceptance and effectiveness of majority opinions, yet they too are protected. The opinions of legislators and judges are protected, because the freedom of such officials to engage in debate is essential to good government. The role of the people in government requires that same protection for speech by individuals. If the people truly govern themselves, the speech of any individual should be afforded the same protections as the speech of a member of Congress. In fact, for Meiklejohn, the protection provided members of Congress is derivative from the protection provided the governing people.

While Meiklejohn's analysis of the role of the people in government provides for a strong First Amendment, it also suggests limitations on the speech and printed material protected by the amendment. The freedom of speech protected by the First Amendment is limited to speech relevant to self-government. It is that speech that he sees as absolutely protected. He does, however, find another constitutional source for the protection of other varieties of speech.[6] The Fifth Amendment protection against the deprivation of life, liberty, or property without due process of law is seen as protecting a *liberty of speech*. That protection, however, is not absolute. Speech protected by the Fifth Amendment, and that would appear to be all speech not relevant to self-government, is subject to limitation, so long as the limitation is not "imposed unnecessarily or unequally."[7]

Blasi's Checking Value
Meiklejohn's rationale appears similar to that offered by Vincent Blasi in his article "The Checking Value in First Amendment Theory." The "checking value" of the First Amendment is the role that "free speech, a free press, and free assembly can serve in checking the abuse of power by public officials."[8] Professor Blasi notes great emphasis in eighteenth-century free-speech theory on the role of free speech in preventing officials from breaching the public trust. In fact, he states that "if one had to identify the single value that was uppermost in the minds of the persons who drafted and ratified the First Amendment, this checking value would be the most likely candidate."[9]

Blasi does appear to recognize other values behind the First Amendment protections of speech and press. In looking at current understandings of the First Amendment, he finds three general categories of values in addition to his proposed checking value. He recognizes a value of individual autonomy that finds free speech important because of the role it plays in allowing individuals to make choices and to be autonomous individuals. Rather than dismiss this value, he is content to explain how his checking value's basis in consequences differs from the individual autonomy value's emphasis on process. He does not mean to displace the individual autonomy value or any other justifying bases, but states that "the checking value . . . should be viewed as potentially a vital additional component in that constellation of interdependent values."[10]

A second current value Blasi identifies is that of diversity. Diversity is the value behind the marketplace of ideas metaphor in which the competition among ideas leads to the truth, or at least the best approximation of the truth. Again, he does not seek to displace diversity as a value but shows how it differs from the checking value. While both are based on consequences, as opposed to the process value of the individual-autonomy approach, he does suggest that the consequential basis for the checking value is sounder and more timeless than that for the diversity approach.[11]

The third value or theory addressed is that of self-governance, the theory for which Meiklejohn was the most influential spokesperson. Self-governance is the value most similar to that offered by Blasi, so Blasi spends more time addressing it than he did with the other two. The major difference between Blasi's and Meiklejohn's theories seems to be Meiklejohn's more regular active role of the citizen, compared to the exceptional role played by Blasi's citizen. Both are based on consequences; indeed, both are based on political consequences. Yet, the scope of the protections offered by Meiklejohn is broader than that offered by Blasi. If the citizen is to play an active role in self-governance, a wider range of communication dealing with that day-to-day role will be protected. If the citizen's role is only to protest misconduct, the protected communications may not be as wide in scope. While Blasi is offering a value to stand alongside, rather than to displace, other First Amendment values, he does suggest that his value presents a more realistic view of what the framers expected from the people and of the way in which the people actually participate in government.[12]

While the "checking value" theory does identify an important area that must lie at the core of any First Amendment protections, the argument that the protection of the Amendment must be limited to that area is more difficult to make. In fact, Blasi, in his "Checking Value" article indicates that he is "not purport[ing] to offer a comprehensive ordering of First Amendment values or . . . suggest[ing] that the checking value should form the cornerstone of all First Amendment analysis."[13] Rather, he states a purpose of "further[ing] the understanding of one basic value which has been underemphasized in this century and which . . . should be a significant component in any general theory of the First Amendment."[14]

While stating that he does not seek to displace other values, Professor Blasi does offer an inkling of concern with the effect those other values might have on the strength of the First Amendment. He notes that the commitment to diversity has implications with regard to erotic and violent entertainment, as well as commercial speech and gossip sheets, that a checking-value basis does not have. He suggests not that those other areas are undeserving of any First Amendment protection but that perhaps speech aimed at governmental abuse may deserve greater protection. He suggests that the checking value leads to a more discriminating First Amendment. The resulting narrower scope of the checking value "would have special appeal to persons who believe that the noble eighteenth-century ideal of freedom of speech is somehow tarnished when it serves as the basis for resolving controversies over girlie magazines and gossip columns."[15]

The hint Blasi offers that looking to the checking value as the basis for the First Amendment might limit, rather than expand, the scope of the amendment's protections comes to the fore in his later article "The Pathological Perspective and the First Amendment."[16] There he suggests that courts should adopt a "pathological perspective" toward the First Amendment. It should be interpreted so as to provide maximum protection in periods of intolerance and should be targeted for the worst of times.[17]

This approach has its effect on the scope of First Amendment protection. Blasi recognizes that one possible strategy to prepare for pathological periods would be the extension of First Amendment protection to as wide an arena as possible so that retrenchment would be difficult and the reductions that might occur in a pathological period would affect only "doctrinal fat."[18] He also suggests that expansion might improve the "muscle tone" of the First Amendment, since a rarely used amendment will lack the doctrinal refinements and the specialized bar that may be required to protect it in a pathological period.[19] Blasi, however, rejects the expansive approach and adopts a position that "[b]etter equipped for the storms of pathology might be a lean, trim first amendment that covered only activities most people would recognize as serious, time-honored forms of communication."[20] He notes a "close correlation between the ambit of coverage and the ability of courts to keep doctrine simple, informed by tradition, and dominated by principle. The wider the reach of first amendment coverage, the greater seems to be the judicial affinity for instrumental reasoning, balancing tests, differential levels of scrutiny, and pragmatic judgements."[21]

Blasi's "pathological perspective" approach has a counterpart in Meiklejohn's analysis. Meiklejohn criticized the work of his era's other leading First Amendment scholar, Zechariah Chafee. In Chafee's view, the Constitution provided a wider scope for the protection of free speech. Chafee's First Amendment protected two types of free speech interest. He included the public, governmental interest espoused by Meiklejohn, but he also included a private interest in self-expression.[22] Meiklejohn argued that Chafee's inclusion of both interests as First Amendment interests has the same effect as making both interests Fifth Amendment interests.[23] While Chafee may have hoped to see the individual interest granted greater protection, Meiklejohn expressed concern that the effect would be to see the self-government interest granted less protection.[24] The point seems similar to Blasi's in that the inclusion of more speech under the First Amendment protection leads to a weaker First Amendment.

Self-Governance and Obscenity

If Professor Blasi's checking-value approach to the First Amendment sets out the limits of the protection afforded by the amendment, sufficiently violent material, like sexually obscene material, would be unprotected. Neither is commonly directed at curbing governmental abuse of power or in the interchange of ideas necessary in governing.[25] Even if the checking value does not set such limits, its use in free speech analysis may provide an indication of how to delineate the wider protection afforded by the amendment.

While the Court has not limited First Amendment protections to checking-value speech, speech in that area has been recognized as having special status. In *Butterworth v. Smith*[26] a reporter had testified before a grand jury, the term of which had then concluded. The reporter wished to disclose his own testimony and challenged a Florida law against ever disclosing testimony given before a grand jury, even one's own testimony and even after the grand jury proceedings had concluded. The Court declared the statute, at least as applied, unconstitutional. In doing so, the Court noted that "Florida seeks to punish the publication of information relating to alleged governmental misconduct — speech which has traditionally been recognized as lying at the core of the First Amendment."[27]

The Court has come to a similar conclusion in other cases. *Gentile v. State Bar of Nevada*[28] presents a recent example. There the Court reversed a state supreme court determination that a lawyer, who had made extrajudicial statements to the press, knowing that the statements were substantially likely to prejudice a judicial proceeding, should be disciplined. The Court's opinion was written in part by Justice Kennedy and in part by Chief Justice Rehnquist. In that part of the opinion written by Justice Kennedy, he stated:

> There is no question that speech critical of the exercise of the State's power lies at the very center of the First Amendment. Nevada seeks to

punish the dissemination of information relating to alleged governmental misconduct, which only last Term we described as "speech which has traditionally been recognized as lying at the core of the First Amendment." [29]

While Professor Blasi's "checking value" speech may not be the only speech protected by the First Amendment, it certainly has been found to be at the core of the amendment's protection.

There are, however, cases that indicate that more than "checking value" speech may be found at the core of the First Amendment. In *Texas v. Johnson*,[30] the flag-burning case, the Court reversed a conviction for flag desecration as an act of protest. The Court noted that "Johnson was not . . . prosecuted for the expression of just any idea; he was prosecuted for his expression of dissatisfaction with the policies of this country, expression situated at the core of our First Amendment values." [31] Johnson's speech may be seen as other than "checking value" speech. The Court characterized him as protesting government policy, and this may differ from checking the abuse of governmental power. While the use of the law against Johnson's protest may be an abuse of power, the original protest against policy seems different from the *Butterworth* and *Gentile* protests over the abuse of process by the government. If this is accepted as a sufficient difference, the core of the First Amendment would appear to extend beyond the checking value and reach Meiklejohn's speech regarding self-government.

The Court has used this expanded view of the core of the First Amendment in other cases. In *Pickering v. Board of Education*[32] a teacher had been dismissed for speaking out against the Board of Education's funding judgments. The Court held that issues of school funding were matters of legitimate public concern and that teachers, as those most likely to be informed on the issues, must be free to offer their views without fear of retaliation. In so holding, the court was intent on protecting "[t]he public interest in having free and unhindered debate on matters of public importance — the core value of the Free Speech Clause of the First Amendment." [33] The Court noted that that interest was so great that it justified the ruling in *New York Times v. Sullivan*[34] that a public official cannot recover for defamation without showing knowledge of falsity or reckless disregard as to truth or falsity. The core First Amendment interest in free and uninhibited debate was not to be defeated by the fact that the speaker was a public employee critical of his or her superior.[35]

Similarly, in *Frisby v. Schultz*,[36] the Court found at the core of the First Amendment the individual's interest in presenting his or her views on issues of public concern. In that case, the Court considered an ordinance against picketing the residence of an individual. While upholding the ordinance, the Court said: "The antipicketing ordinance operates at the core of the First Amendment by prohibiting appellees from engaging in picketing on an issue of public concern. Because of the importance of 'uninhibited, robust, and wide-open' debate on public issues, . . . we have traditionally subjected restrictions on public issue picketing to careful scrutiny."[37]

The Court came to the same conclusion as to the First Amendment core status of political boycotts in *National Ass'n for the Advancement of Colored People v. Claiborne Hardware Co.*[38] The boycott at issue there was intended to lead to the elimination of racial discrimination. That aim was held to differentiate the boycott at issue from the more common economic boycott, because "speech to protest racial discrimination is essential political speech lying at the core of the First Amendment."[39] Campaign spending limits were also found, in *Buckley v. Valeo*,[40] to violate values at the core of the First Amendment. In invalidating such limits, the Court said: "It is clear that a primary effect of these expenditure limitations is to restrict the quantity of campaign speech by individuals, groups, and candidates. The restrictions, while neutral as to the ideas expressed, limit political expression 'at the core of our electoral process and of the First Amendment freedoms.' "[41]

Despite this central concern with core values, it is clear that First Amendment protections do go beyond those emphasized by Blasi and Meiklejohn. In *Winters v. New York*,[42] a case growing out of attempts to regulate violence, the Court specifically held that First Amendment protections extend beyond protecting the citizen's role in government and the exposition of ideas necessary to that role. The amendment also protects entertainment. The Court found the line between informing and entertaining elusive, noting that fiction may be used to teach doctrine.[43]

While the core of the First Amendment seems to include speech that is a part of self-governance, the amendment's protection extends beyond that core, and the cases defining the core do little to set out the limits of First Amendment protection. The Court's conclusion with regard to sexually obscene materials was not that such materials are not at the core of the First Amendment but that they are outside the scope of the amendment. If violent obscenity is also to be outside the protection of the amendment, it is the limits and not only the core that must be delineated.

The Court, in addition to noting areas that are at the core of the First Amendment, has found certain areas to be other than at the core. In *Federal Communications Commission v. Pacifica Foundation*,[44] the George Carlin "seven dirty words" case, the Court addressed the concern that FCC regulations restricting the hours for the broadcast of indecent speech would have a chilling effect on the broadcast of protected speech. The Court did not share the concern.

> It is true that the Commission's order may lead some broadcasters to censor themselves. At most, however, the Commission's definition of indecency will deter only the broadcasting of patently offensive references to excretory and sexual organs and activities. . . . While some of these references may be protected, they surely lie at the periphery of First Amendment concern.[45]

Indecent language, unlike "checking value" speech, or political speech generally, is far from the core of the First Amendment.

The Court has also recently found nude barroom dancing to be similarly removed from the core. In *Barnes v. Glen Theatre, Inc.*[46] the Court upheld a public indecency statute against the claim that nude dancing was protected expression. The court of appeals had found support for the proposition that such dancing was within the scope of the First Amendment. The Court admitted that there was a basis for such a conclusion and said that nude dancing is expressive conduct "within the outer perimeters of the First Amendment, though . . . only marginally so."[47] Being so far removed from the core, the Court found it easy to justify the state's prohibition on the expression.

Even these cases do not really explain the limits of free speech protections. The statements that indecent speech and nude dancing are at the periphery of the amendment must be read in the context of the cases explaining what is at the core. It would appear to be the distance between indecency and nude dancing on the one hand and speech regarding governmental abuse of power or self-governance on the other that puts the former at the outer perimeter of the amendment's protection.

It is the cases that go beyond setting out the periphery and find speech to be beyond the perimeter that solidify this point. The Court, in *Miller v. California*,[48] helped define the limits by its determination that even expression that would otherwise be considered sexually obscene is unprotected only if "the work, taken as a whole, lacks serious literary, artistic, political, or scientific value."[49] In addition to the political value that might speak to checking value or self-government, literature, art, and science enjoy protection, even in the context of sexual explicitness.

The *Roth* Court itself recognized that First Amendment protections extend beyond purely political speech. "All ideas having even the slightest redeeming social importance—unorthodox ideas, controversial ideas, even ideas hateful to the prevailing climate of opinion—have the full protection of the guaranties, unless excludable because they encroach upon the limited area of more important interests."[50] Nonetheless, the Court determined that obscenity is "utterly without redeeming social importance"[51] and as such is undeserving of the protections of the First Amendment.

The *Roth* Court also quoted its opinion in *Chaplinsky v. New Hampshire*,[52] which had denied constitutional protection for fighting words. The *Roth* Court quoted dicta from *Chaplinsky* to the effect that:

> There are certain well-defined and narrowly limited classes of speech, the prevention and punishment of which have never been thought to raise any Constitutional problem. These include the lewd and obscene. . . . *It has been well observed that such utterances are no essential part of any exposition of ideas, and are of such slight social value as a step to truth that any benefit that may be derived from them is clearly outweighed by the social interest in order and morality.*[53]

It may be difficult to determine the social value or importance of varying forms of speech or message. While the distinction between political speech and nonpolitical speech may be difficult only at the border, with some speech clearly political and some clearly nonpolitical, it would appear to be more difficult to distinguish differing types of entertainment. Nonetheless, to the degree that the entertainment departs from core protected speech, it appears to merit less protection.

The "checking value" or self-governance view of the scope of First-Amendment protection, if interpreted strongly so as to limit protection to the area of checking or governance-related speech, would deny such protection to sexual obscenity, as the *Roth* Court holds. While pornography may be used as a medium for political expression, obscenity in the *Roth* definition was limited to material totally lacking in social (which would include political) importance. Even under the *Miller* definition, pornography is only obscene if it lacks serious value. If material is sexually obscene, it is not seriously political pornography and would not enjoy protection.

The important point here is that just as sexual obscenity lacks protection under the "checking value" or self-governance theories, so also does violent obscenity, if properly defined. If the *Miller* definition is adapted to allow a ban on explicit depictions of violence only when such depictions lack serious value, any work considered violent obscenity would by definition not have serious political value. Just as sexually obscene works, since they are without serious political value, are unprotected under the "checking value" limitation, violently obscene works, also lacking serious political value, are similarly unprotected.

Even without limiting the protection of the First Amendment in the way that Meiklejohn's or Blasi's work would indicate, their theories are important in distinguishing the core, the periphery, and the areas beyond the limits of the amendment. Sexual obscenity is outside that protection because it plays no essential role in the exposition of ideas and serves no useful social purpose. Whatever may be said of sexually explicit material in this regard may also be said of graphically violent material. Unless the violence is in a context that has serious value, in which case it would not be considered obscene under a definition analogous to the *Miller* definition, that material also plays no essential role in the exposition of ideas and serves no socially useful purpose.

Schauer's Free Speech Principle

Frederick Schauer, in his book *Free Speech: A Philosophical Enquiry,*[54] finds several possible sources for what he labels a "Free Speech Principle." Such a principle might be rooted in arguments based on democracy, such as Blasi's and Meiklejohn's, on the need for open debate as the best path to follow in the search for truth, on other utilitarian grounds, or on principles of autonomy or individuality. While the source of the principle will affect the scope of the protection afforded, Professor Schauer does not see a need to identify a single basis, since he recognizes a difference between the coverage of a principle and the protection afforded by the principle. The fact that some form of communication is protected on free speech grounds does not mean it is absolutely protected. All that is meant by a right is that greater justification is required for restricting the act protected by the right than would be required absent the right.[55] How great a justification is required for a particular variety of speech may depend on the source of the right protecting that speech. For example, arguments based on democracy may be added to arguments based on autonomy when addressing political speech. The protection given such speech may then be stronger, and restrictions require greater justification, than for speech protected only because of the value placed on autonomy.

The determination not to insist on a single source for the Free Speech Principle could lead to a right of almost unlimited scope. That problem would be lessened by the fact that the protection need not be absolute. As the scope of a principle becomes less and less limited, the focus and strength of the principle are likely to become more and more weak. Professor Schauer does offer some limitation on the scope of his principle. He refuses to include all acts as speech acts protected by his Free Speech Principle. To come within the category of speech, he requires that the act be communicative. As he notes, any of the justifications for a principle of free speech rest on the communicative aspects of speech.[56] Arguments such as Blasi's and Meiklejohn's are based on the individual communicating with others about governmental abuse of power or on issues of self-governance. The argument from truth and the idea of a marketplace of ideas depend on the communication of those ideas. Even arguments based on autonomy and individuality, if they are to protect more than simply holding beliefs or thoughts, must address the communication of those beliefs or thoughts.

The question then becomes one of what is to count as communication. He includes most instances of the use of language and its equivalents, such as Morse code, Braille, a Bronx cheer, or the wearing of black armbands. However, he suggests that some uses of language, such as meaningless noise to drown out the voice of another, are not communicative. The key appears to be the intent to convey a message. While "messages" may be received where none were intended to be sent, Schauer does not accept these situations as communication. Communicative intent is necessary for an act to be considered speech for purposes of the Free Speech Principle.[57] Even with this restriction, the range of speech protected by principles of free speech would be rather broad.

Schauer directly addresses the issue of the inclusion of the arts as speech for purposes of his Free Speech Principle. He has no difficulty with some works of art, defined broadly to include music, films, poetry, drama, and literature. He finds clear communicative intent in some art, even explicit and intentional political communication. As examples, he cites Picasso's *Guernica,* the film *Z,* and even some of Shostakovich's symphonies.[58] Such instances that are intended to convey political messages and do convey such messages to viewers or listeners he finds central to the Free Speech Principle.

He sees a problem, however, where art is seen as being something other than communication. If art is seen as self-expression, or if there is always a gap between what the artist intends and what the viewer perceives, he suggests that art does not fit neatly into the justifications for the Free Speech Principle.[59] If Schauer is correct here, then art, literature, or film containing violence would be no more protected than other art and could be controlled. However, it is not clear that he should allow the exclusion of art, at least on the bases he suggests. Even if art is self-expression, some speech is also self-expression. It communicates the speaker's or the artist's beliefs or attitudes, and as Schauer seems to recognize,[60] the expression of agreement or disagreement may be relevant to deliberation, whether it be in the area of government or in the marketplace of ideas. Furthermore, even if it is accepted that there is necessarily a gap between the artist's intended message and the viewer's received message, the same may again be said of language of all varieties and when addressing any subject.

When Schauer turns to a consideration of sexual obscenity, he argues that such expression departs completely from the sphere of protected speech, that it is in fact nonspeech. He discusses what he admits is "a hypothetical extreme example of what is commonly referred to as 'hard core pornography.'"[61] The hypothetical ten-minute film is nothing but a close up of sexual organs engaged in intercourse, with "no variety, no dialogue, no music, no attempt at artistic depiction, and not even any view of the faces of the participants."[62] The audience is assumed to be engaged in masturbation.

Schauer argues that:

> [A]ny definition of "speech" (or any definition of the coverage of the concept of freedom of speech) that included this film in this setting is being bizarrely literal or formalistic. Here the vendor is selling a product for the purpose of inducing immediate sexual stimulation. There are virtually no differences in intent and effect from the sale of a plastic or vibrating sex aid, the sale of a body through prostitution, or the sex act itself. At its most extreme, hard core pornography is a sex aid, no more and no less, and the fact that there is no physical contact is only fortuitous.[63]

If pornography is simply a sex aid, it deserves, in Schauer's view, no protection. It is to be treated the same as any physical device designed to stimulate. "The mere fact that in pornography the stimulating experience is initiated by visual rather than tactile means is irrelevant if every other aspect of the experience is the same. Neither involves communication in the way that language or pictures do."[64] The analysis is similar to the conclusion of Havelock Ellis that the "stupid form of obscenity called pornography . . . is a substitute for the brothel and of the same coarse texture."[65]

Schauer recognizes that serious literature can also evoke a physical response, as may art or music.[66] Nonetheless, he says that this "misconceives the issue."[67]

> It is not the presence of a physical effect that triggers the exclusion from coverage of that which would otherwise be covered by the principle of free speech. Rather, it is that some pornographic items contain *none* of the elements that would cause them to be covered in the first instance. The basis of the exclusion of hard core pornography from the coverage of the Free Speech Principle is not that it has a physical effect, *but that it has nothing else.*[68]

Professor Schauer does acknowledge that the brain plays a role in physical sensations, including sexual arousal, but the simple existence of a brain event does not make for a communicative act. Professor Schauer is certainly correct in noting that there is a mental element to pornography-caused sexual arousal. While the final physical effect may be hormonal, the visual images must be processed by the brain before that effect can result. While a physical stimulator does not require any higher-level mental information-processing for its effects, the mental element to pornography-based arousal is not sufficiently distinguishing. The objection to including sexually obscene materials within the protections of freedom of speech appears to be that the brain is not its direct audience or even a coequal audience.

Schauer's position appears to be in accord with psycho-physiological theory. According to the James-Lange theory,[69] stimuli that produce emotions do so without the initial input of the more evolved portions of the brain. Certainly, a visual image that leads to sexual stimulation involves the optic regions of the brain. The image must be recognized. The route to stimulation, however, is through the limbic regions and particularly the amygdala. In an emotional reaction, the limbic system sets in motion a set of physiological responses, which include muscular, nervous system, and hormonal reactions. These responses occur at a level below the conscious. The individual so stimulated recognizes the stimulation through feedback from the systems engaged in the physiological responses. The brain recognizes an increased heart rate and a surge in sex hormones. The James-Lange theory holds that it is the brain's experience of the physiological responses that constitutes our feelings of emotions. The experience at the conscious level, then, is secondary. It in fact occurs only as the chain of events set off by the stimulation passes through the brain for the second time.[70] The target for sexually stimulating images is not the intellect or even the conscious brain. The primary target is the gonads, even though the reaction of the gonads may lead the higher brain to experience some enjoyment. While music, art, and romantic literature may stimulate, they also communicate other messages aimed at the intellect. The brain is at least a coequal audience.

Visual stimuli that cause emotional reactions of fear, horror, or anger proceed along the same route. The optical stimulus requires processing to be recognized, but the direct effect will then be in the limbic system. The physiological result will be an increased heart rate and higher hormone levels. It is the recognition of the heart rate and the reaction to the hormones that constitutes the experience of fear or anger. There are, of course, other situations, more directly involving the higher-order regions of the brain, that may produce fear or anger. It may be that only by thinking about the consequences of received information that fear or anger is aroused. Whatever the role of the limbic and endocrine system in such a reaction, the higher-order brain played an initial role, as well as its role in recognizing the resultant fear or anger. The same is true, however, of sexual arousal. In sexual arousal brought on by feelings of love, there will be a limbic and endocrine system role, but the higher brain will have played an initial role, in addition to its role in recognizing the sexual response. Schauer appears to be addressing the stimulus that simply bypasses the initial role of the higher brain and proceeds directly to a limbic and hormonal reaction. For Schauer that stimulus is more akin to a mechanical sex aid than it is to speech. The response to Schauer needs then only to address similar stimuli of fear, horror, or anger, the visual image that causes a visceral reaction. That stimulus is also less akin to speech than it would be to a mechanical fear- or anger-inducing aid, such as a roller coaster ride or a punch in the nose.

Schauer's position that the brain is a superior audience to the genitals seems reasonable.[71] It also seems reasonable, however, to conclude that the brain is a superior audience to the adrenals, and there is no reason to prefer either the genitals or the adrenals over the other. If material is violent enough to have a hormonal effect, Schauer's arguments would seem to carry over to exclude such material from the protections of the freedom of speech.

Schauer disagrees with this conclusion. He recognizes that violence might be considered obscene[72] but states:

> [T]he arguments that relate to the exclusion of pornography from the coverage of the Free Speech Principle are inapplicable to violence as such. The sex-aid approach to hard core pornography that shows such pornography to be scarcely communicative at all does not appear relevant to the depiction of violence. Although it is possible that a refined categorization approach to freedom of speech might grant publications featuring violence for its own sake (such as a martial arts movie) less protection than would be granted to, say, political speech, this would create problems because of frequent use of violence to emphasize a moral or political argument, as, for example, with the use of vivid depictions of violent death in a motion picture intended to point out the horrors of war.[73]

But, his comparison is not fairly made.

In considering hard core pornography, Schauer hypothesized a film with absolutely no content other than close-ups of sexual intercourse. There was no dialogue, no music, no artistic expression, and for Schauer, no communication. Yet, when he turns to a consideration of violence, he notes violent depictions can be used to make political or moral points. Just as violent material can be so used, so can pornographic material.

It is because Schauer eliminated the possibility of any political or moral message from the film in his hypothetical that the argument has power. An equivalent hypothetical of a film consisting of nothing but a person being carved up with a chain saw, unaccompanied by music, dialogue, or artistic expression would be just as lacking in political, moral, or any other, message. It would serve only to stimulate a visceral reaction. The brain would not be the audience, and the material should not come within the scope of Schauer's Free Speech Principle. Just as pornographic material begins to enjoy protection as it departs from the hypothetical genre and starts to contain a message aimed at the intellect, so too might violent material enjoy the protections of the First Amendment to the degree that it departs from the hypothetical and contains political, moral, or other messages aimed at the intellect.

Before leaving Schauer and in particular the discussion of the James-Lange theory, it should be noted that that theory offers a response to the puzzlement expressed by some as to how the *Miller* test can make sense of the requirements that to be obscene material must be both sexually stimulating and offensive.[74] If the sexual stimulation resulting from a visual image occurs through the limbic system, the higher-order brain can be left free both to recognize that stimulation and to experience disgust with either the image or the limbic reaction to the image. Even if it should prove that some reactions of disgust are based in similar limbic responses, it seems less odd that the higher-order brain would be capable of recognizing two bodily responses than that the higher-order brain would hold two conflicting attitudes.

Sunstein and the Two-Tiered First Amendment

Cass Sunstein has offered an additional general theory of the First Amendment.[75] He suggests a two-tiered First Amendment with a distinction between high-value speech and low-value speech. His suggestion is not simply that the amendment should have two tiers but rather that that is the best understanding of the Court's treatment of the First Amendment.[76] He finds evidence for such a hierarchy in, for example, the treatment of libel law. Speech regarding a public figure enjoys strong protection. Such an official may recover damages for defamation only if it can be demonstrated that the libelous article was published with knowledge of its falsity or with reckless disregard for the truth or falsity of the allegations it contained. When a nonpublic figure is defamed, only negligence must be shown. Speech regarding public figures is high-value; speech defaming private persons is low-value. Speech with political content is likely to be high-value. On the other hand, examples of low-value speech include threats, bribes, perjury, harassing speech, and criminal solicitation.

Professor Sunstein admits that the Court has not provided a clear theory or principle that would unify the classes of speech it has treated as low-value and high-value, but he offers to fill that gap. He suggests that, while there are other free speech values, the emphasis of the First Amendment is on political speech, and such speech must be considered high-value. He also tells us the speech should be considered political "when it is both intended and received as a contribution to public deliberation about some issue."[77] Political speech for Sunstein would appear more inclusive than the speech Vincent Blasi places at the core of the First Amendment and would seem to go beyond Meiklejohn as well.

Sunstein's category of high-value speech appears to encompass more than political speech. He tells us that most art is in the upper tier of high-value speech, and he does not appear to limit that status to art that is explicitly political.[78] Hence, additional guidance in drawing lines is required. In earlier work Professor Sunstein set out factors that may be used to classify speech as "low value" and thus less entitled to protection:

> First, the speech must be far afield from the central concern of the first amendment, which, broadly speaking, is effective popular control of public affairs. . . . Second, a distinction is drawn between cognitive and non-cognitive aspects of speech. Speech that has purely noncognitive appeal will be entitled to less constitutional protection. Third, the purpose of the speaker is relevant: if a speaker is seeking to communicate a message, he will be treated more favorably than if he is not. Fourth, the various classes of low-value speech reflect judgements that in certain areas, government is unlikely to be acting for constitutionally impermissible reasons or producing constitutionally troublesome harms.[79]

While these additional factors may not present a solution in every situation, they do lend some further guidance.

It remains to be seen what implications Sunstein's approach has for sexually explicit speech and for depictions of violence. For Sunstein, pornography, let alone sexual obscenity, would appear to be low-value because it fails to express a position relevant to the popular control of government, the first factor, and the government is, as a result, less likely to have acted for impermissible reasons or to cause a constitutionally troublesome harm, the fourth factor.[80] These two factors appear similar to the concern that speech relevant to self-governance should have the highest value.

The second and third factors also dictate less protection for pornography. They seem somewhat akin to Professor Schauer's position that sexual obscenity is nonspeech. If material contains no message and is intended to contain no message, it might be viewed as noncommunicative. The scope of Sunstein's factors, however, may be wider than the areas falling outside of the protected areas under Schauer's analysis.

In his comments on Sunstein's factors, Professor Larry Alexander indicates that all nonpropositional expression is unprotected and expresses concern that such a distinction leaves unprotected a Diego Rivera mural, literature, art, movies, and dance.[81] He claims that, although such material may convey ideas that could be presented as propositions, taken as a whole they are nonpropositional.[82] Even if one would want to consider art and music that conveys ideas that could be expressed as propositional to itself be propositional, that would still leave nonrepresentational art and music unprotected.

If Alexander's view is the proper reading of Sunstein, more material may be unprotected than would be under Schauer's analysis. Music and nonrepresentational art communicate emotive messages, even if they are nonpropositional. This affective communication is noncognitive and fails to meet Sunstein's second factor. It is not as clear that it fails Schauer's test. For Schauer, obscenity is unprotected because it has nothing other than a physical effect; the brain is not the audience. For music and art, the brain is the audience, even if the message is emotive. On the other hand, it may be going too far to say that such speech is unprotected in Sunstein's scheme.

For Sunstein, the inclusion of speech in the low-value category does not leave it completely unprotected. While high-value speech may require a strong showing of harm before regulation is allowed, government is not completely free to regulate low-value speech. The government's reason for regulation must be legitimate.

> In general, government cannot regulate speech of any sort on the basis of (1) its own disagreement with the ideas that have been expressed, (2) its perception of the government's (as opposed to the public's) self-interest, (3) its fear that people will be persuaded or influenced by ideas, and (4) its desire to insure that people are not offended by the ideas that speech contains.[83]

Thus, all speech enjoys at least some protection.

In his most recent work in the area, Professor Sunstein appears to question the current legal treatment of sexual obscenity. While he suggests that the standards set out in the *Miller* test are fairly protective, he concludes that "it is unclear whether the justifications for regulating obscenity are consistent with a proper interpretation of the First Amendment."[84] Offensiveness plays a major role in the *Miller* test, yet in Sunstein's view government is not supposed to regulate speech simply because people are offended by the ideas contained in that speech. While it may be argued that obscenity regulation is aimed not at ideas but at the way in which the ideas are presented, Sunstein finds this a difficult line to draw.[85] He finds it plausible that the justification for obscenity bans is essentially a justification for banning ideas and is unacceptable under the First Amendment.

If Sunstein is correct in what appears to be his conclusion that the government may not ban sexual obscenity, that position might have an impact on the position that violent obscenity may be regulated. The approach taken throughout has been that there are equal or better reasons for allowing bans on representations of violence than for allowing bans on sexually explicit depictions. If, however, bans on sexual obscenity are inconsistent with the First Amendment, then regulating violent obscenity might also be unconstitutional. There are two ways around this problem. First, it must be noted that Sunstein's position is itself inconsistent with current law. His argument is prescriptive rather than descriptive. Bans on sufficiently violent depictions may still be consistent with the First Amendment, as interpreted by the Court (ignoring whatever impact *Roth* and *Miller* may have), and only be inconsistent with the direction Professor Sunstein suggests the First Amendment should take.

The second approach to Sunstein's challenge is to accept his position with regard to sexual obscenity and still argue that the better arguments ("as good" will now not do) allow for such bans of violence. Sunstein, in fact, takes a position not too far from that suggested. Despite his view on the protection afforded sexually obscene materials, he would allow restrictions on materials that combine sex, perhaps even nonobscene sex, with violence, at least to the degree of allowing civil suits by those harmed by either the production or the use of the material.[86] He notes that such a combination of sex and violence, for which he reserves the label "pornography," is far from central to First Amendment concerns. Furthermore, he argues that such material causes harm and is thus not being regulated because of its offensiveness.

Just as I have argued that the arguments for regulating depictions of violence are at least as powerful as those for regulating sexual depictions, Sunstein concludes that "the argument for regulation of materials that combine sex with violence or coercion is more powerful than the corresponding argument for regulating obscenity."[87] Thus, if Sunstein's theory is to be fatal to that offered here, it must be shown why sex is necessary before violence may be regulated.

One way to make that showing would be to demonstrate that sex with violence causes violence, while violence without sex does not. That topic will be discussed in the next chapter, but the short answer is that it is the violence in a depiction that causes violence. Sexual depictions, while they may increase the effect, are not necessary to that effect. If the aim is to protect against harm resulting from the production or viewing of media, regulation should be aimed at the factor that causes the harm, and that factor is violence. Far from defeating the position argued for here, Sunstein's work, particularly his allowance of regulation based on harm, would appear to support bans on sufficiently graphic depictions of violence.

The First Amendment and Toleration

Lee Bollinger offers a different approach to the search for First Amendment values. Rather than confining his examination to the values that led to the adoption of the amendment, he considers the values that explain current free speech law and particularly the protection given extremist speech. It may be that, as Justice Holmes said, "when men have realized that time has upset many fighting faiths, they may come to believe . . . that the ultimate good desired is better reached by free trade in ideas—that the best test of truth is the power of thought to get itself accepted in the competition of the market."[88] Nonetheless, most of us would feel secure in concluding that the Nazis or the Klan have little to nothing to offer to the marketplace of ideas' development of the truth. While there may be line-drawing problems closer to the center, speech on the extremes may be argued to lack sufficient value to explain its protection.

The line-drawing problem is an aspect of the usual negative justification for the freedom of speech. A negative justification focuses on the evil that could result if there were not a broad First Amendment and government were allowed to regulate speech that is now free. Professor Bollinger, instead, attempts to justify First Amendment law through a positive approach. While it may be difficult to justify the protection of extremist speech as part of the path to the truth or as essential to the democratic process, he finds positive value in protecting speech which in itself has little or no value.

Professor Bollinger's theory is based on his observation that people generally are intolerant of differences. It is a struggle for the individual to tolerate people who act differently, who hold different views, or who are different in almost any other way. It is concern over this intolerance that leads to the free speech principle.

[I]t would be better if we described the purpose of the principle not as that of protecting speech but rather as that of dealing with the phenomenon of what we have called the "impulse to excessive intolerance" generally, though we do that by insisting on an extraordinary degree of toleration only in the limited context of speech activity. The role of free speech is directed at developing a capacity of far greater moment than that of just regulating the appropriate level of legal restraints on speech activity. . . . Law . . . is being used . . . as a major project concerned with nothing less than helping to shape the intellectual character of the society.[89]

We develop an ethic of tolerating even extremist speech, because that attitude of toleration will carry over to other areas in which we might tend toward intolerance.

When Bollinger turns to an analysis of obscene speech, he finds it necessary to distinguish the intolerance felt toward such speech from the intolerance felt toward other varieties of speech society might wish to regulate but does not in the name of free speech. That distinction is necessary if his theory is to serve as an explanation of current First Amendment law. The distinction he draws is based on the psychological observation that the problem with pornography, and so with sexual obscenity, is in its attraction. While there may be disgust, there is also desire. In relation to his main theme, he says: "The real social difficulty posed by obscene material . . . may lie in the potential for confusion about what toleration would mean."[90] The context of the statement, in a discussion of the effect of pornography on violence and discrimination against women, indicates that he is addressing a concern that sexually obscene material will lead to intolerant attitudes toward women, with additional ensuing harm. If that is the concern, there should be an equal concern over violent obscenity. Violence against a person is the very antithesis of toleration. Material that portrays excessive violence may well defeat the tolerance-producing value that toleration of extreme speech is supposed to foster.

Professor Bollinger's concern over the intolerance produced by pornography also seems to rest on a premise that sexual instincts are "not easily estimated" and are at the core of the identity of the individual and the community.[91] He suggests that the central role sexual instincts play in the personality may be the best explanation for the denial of First Amendment protection to sexual obscenity. Much the same could be said for the fear or rage that violent depictions may evoke. The stimuli of rage and fear are also not easily estimated. Furthermore, while sexual instincts may be at the core of personality, so are one's fears and the stimuli that enrage. It would seem fear and rage are more incompatible with tolerance than sexual instincts would be. Lastly, as with sexual obscenity, the mix of interest and disgust is also present with violent death, as the gawking of passersby at an accident readily demonstrates.

First Amendment Absolutism

One theory of the First Amendment that would certainly run counter to the claim that depictions of sufficiently graphic violence can be regulated consistently with the amendment is an absolutist approach. The amendment does state that "Congress shall make no law . . . abridging the freedom of speech, or of the press." "No law" might be read to mean "*no* law," and abridgment would seem to include any kind of regulation. Under such a reading, there could be no restrictions on any variety of speech or press. While such a strict reading of the First Amendment would not necessarily be the reading incorporated against the states through the Fourteenth Amendment, a true absolutist could argue that the states are similarly restricted in their regulation of speech.

Justice Black is sometimes thought to have been a spokesperson for this position. The assignment seems to result from his dissent in *Konigsberg v. State Bar*,[92] a challenge to the refusal to admit to the bar an applicant who refused to answer questions about affiliation with the Communist party. Justice Black, joined by Chief Justice Warren and Justice Douglas, rejected the balancing test applied by the majority in upholding the state's refusal to admit Konigsberg. In doing so, Justice Black wrote:

> I believe that the First Amendment's unequivocal command that there shall be no abridgment of the rights of free speech and assembly shows that the men who drafted our Bill of Rights did all the "balancing" that was to be done in this field. . . .[T]he very object of adopting the First Amendment, as well as the other provisions of the Bill of Rights, was to put the freedoms protected there completely out of the area of any congressional control that may be attempted through the exercise of precisely those powers that are now being used to "balance" the Bill of Rights out of existence.[93]

Despite this language, Justice Black was not taking a truly absolute position. He rejected the majority's claim that his position would invalidate many widely accepted laws and asserted that where speech was an integral part of unlawful conduct, it could be punished.[94] He did agree that his view would invalidate any abridgment of the right to discuss religion and matters of public interest. While he did not limit the scope of First-Amendment protection to such considerations, that is far from taking an absolutist approach.

Justice Black's real concern was with the majority's conclusion that there are no absolutes under the First Amendment. He took that position as leading to a conclusion that even speech that is protected by the First Amendment is subject to balancing and that the freedom of speech is only a conditional freedom. Carried to what he saw as its logical conclusion, the Court's position led to a regime in which candidates would not have an absolute right to state their positions and newspapers would have no absolute right to state their opinions on public affairs.[95]

Justice Black's position was that speech that is protected is absolutely protected. He did not assert that absolutely all speech is protected. He recognized that excepting libel, obscenity, and fighting words from the protection of the amendment was not at issue, although he also did not assert agreement with the exceptions. The issue was instead the level of protection to be afforded speech that was clearly protected, however narrowly one might limit the scope of the amendment.[96]

Professor Meiklejohn also might be thought to be an absolutist with regard to the First Amendment, given the title of his article *The First Amendment Is an Absolute*.[97] However, given his criticism of Zechariah Chafee's inclusion of a variety of forms or topics of speech as constitutionally protected, Meiklejohn cannot be read to include all speech within the protection of the First Amendment. Rather, he limited the scope of the First Amendment to speech aimed at self-government and granted other speech the limited protection of the Fifth Amendment only. Meiklejohn's concern was the use of the "clear and present danger" test to allow the government to abridge speech within the protection of the First Amendment. The claim that the First Amendment is an absolute was, as for Justice Black, an expression of the strength of the protection that should be accorded that class of speech that is protected, not a claim that all speech is protected.

While an absolutist reading would bar regulation of media violence, no one really seems to hold such a position. Sunstein argues that such a position cannot be seriously maintained, since it would prevent the government from regulating perjury, bribery, threats, false advertising, and the provision of unlicensed medical or legal advice.[98] Sunstein suggests that there are two alternatives to this untenable absolutist approach. The first is to treat all speech equally by providing the same level of nonabsolute protection to all speech. The government would be allowed to regulate speech, but only when it could demonstrate that harm flowed from the speech. He argues that this approach is unacceptable.[99] If the protection currently afforded political speech were to remain the same, the burden of demonstrating harm would have to be set at a high level. That high level, when carried over to libel, bribery, and misleading advertising, would remove the ability to regulate in those areas. The alternative, regulating political speech based on the lesser showing required for the regulation of commercial speech or libel of private individuals, would be even more disastrous to a democratic society.

Sunstein's other alternative to the nonabsolutist approach is to recognize the role that value must play in determining the level of protection to be afforded different varieties of speech. That is the position at which all First Amendment theorists eventually arrive. The content of speech is relevant to the protection it is granted. While viewpoint discrimination should not be allowed, the variety of speech involved does determine whether speech is at the core, the periphery, or outside of First Amendment protection. Whatever other speech may be protected, political speech is at the core of the amendment. Other speech enjoys lesser protection commensurate with its lesser value.

Autonomy and Self-Expression

There are positions short of absolutism that would protect sexually obscene depictions. While rejecting the absolutist position that bribery, threats, and other criminal speech directly causing harm must be protected, it still may be argued that there is value in protecting the obscene. One such approach is based on the effect that bans on obscenity may have on nonobscene speech. Professor Edward de Grazia has cataloged the effects of obscenity law on the work of James Joyce, D. H. Lawrence and other serious and respected literary figures,[100] and that history is troubling. However, it is not clear how the excesses of early efforts at limiting obscenity speak to the effect of modern law. There are still segments of the public that would ban nonobscene pornography, as there are those who object to even mild violence. However, the *Miller* test and any parallel test for violent obscenity protect literature of the quality written by Joyce, Lawrence, and even lesser lights.

It is, of course, true that even the modern test may have a chilling effect on nonobscene speech. When lines are drawn, it is always possible that those who would fall on the legal side of the line may be led to restrain their speech or conduct out of fear that they will be found to be on the illegal side. While a chilling effect on nonobscene speech is troubling, the Court has not been so concerned about such an effect as to abandon the obscenity exception. As has been seen, even in *Pacifica,* which concerned nonobscene speech, the Court's response to similar concerns was to note that only speech at the periphery of the First Amendment would be chilled.

While the "chilling effect" argument rests on a concern for nonobscene speech, there are also arguments that obscene speech, even if there were no effect on the nonobscene, should be protected. Perhaps the most noted advocate for such a position has been Professor Edwin Baker.[101] Professor Baker argues that there are two fundamental purposes behind the First Amendment, the participation values recognized by Meiklejohn and Blasi and the fostering of "individual self-fulfillment." While the obscenity exception may be justified if the freedom of speech is aimed at the protection of participation in government, a freedom of speech directed at protecting self-fulfillment would have wider scope and might not admit an obscenity exception.

Baker's argument is that our system of government recognizes the equality and autonomy of the individual. The individual has a right to self-realization and self-determination, and part of defining oneself is tied to the freedom to express even obscene thoughts. While such a claim of protection for self-definition would reach a variety of nonspeech acts, such as homosexual activity, that have not been protected, there is something special about speech that distinguishes it from the instances in which the courts have refused to accept claims of autonomy. The difference, for Baker, is in the fact that speech cannot cause harm in the way the other varieties of conduct can. Speech only harms through its influence on the mind and emotions of a hearer, while other self-expressive activity may cause more direct harm. He sees this more direct harm as necessary for government intervention.

The speech that Professor Baker would protect does not require the communication of the speaker's ideas. He would include the telling of a story purely for entertainment and singing purely to demonstrate the accomplishment of the singer.[102] It would appear that, if these self-expressive activities are protected, an obscene film loop that did nothing more than demonstrate the sexual accomplishment of the participants would also demand protection.

While engaging in obscene activity and producing, distributing, or viewing obscene films may be aspects of self-fulfillment, they simply have not been seen by the Court as having constitutionally protected status. The Court's view of the First Amendment is less inclusive than Baker's. While autonomy arguments may have strong philosophical or policy foundations, when they reach the point of protecting obscenity, they are not the law. If Baker, or a successor, some day convinces the Court that obscene material should enjoy constitutional protection, then a First Amendment exception for violent obscenity may fall along with the demise of the exception for sexual obscenity.[103] Until that day, an argument for a First Amendment exception for violent obscenity may be built on the foundations of the sexual-obscenity exception.

Summary

The theories that have been subjected to the greatest analysis here have been the theories that justify a First Amendment exception for sexual obscenity. Theories against such an exception do not explain the law as it is but instead argue for a change at least as great as that argued for here. The theories that do justify the sexual-obscenity exception have been examined to determine whether or not the justification offered is limited to sexual obscenity or might be equally well applied to violent obscenity.

All of the theories examined find low, or no, value in sexually obscene speech, if such speech is accorded the status of speech at all; and, with little to no value, sexual obscenity may be regulated. For each such theory, the reasons for according sexual obscenity such low value were matched by arguments for according violent obscenity equally low, or lower, value. For each theory that attempts to capture current law in which sexual obscenity is unprotected, the theory offers at least as strong a basis for leaving violent obscenity unprotected by the First Amendment. Hence, not only do philosophical analysis and cultural and legal history lead to the conclusion that violence can be regulated, whatever policy is seen as underlying the First Amendment obscenity exception is in accord.

8 Violence and the Feminist Concern with Pornography

The Feminist Definition of and Attack on Pornography

Feminist legal scholars have recently offered an attack on pornography that differs from that historically employed. Traditionally, pornography has encompassed all sexually explicit speech, both obscene and nonobscene. The basis for disparaging such speech has been a view that exposure of the human body and the frank or explicit discussion of sexuality are unacceptable. While that view with regard to sexuality seems to have come and gone, we are still living with the effects of the Victorian-era concern that excessive sexual activity, including masturbation, could lead to insanity. That view has led to attempts to suppress the sorts of materials that might arouse sexual desire.

The feminists' approach is not based on this same theory of morality. The concern is not directed at the repression of sexual knowledge or of sexual freedom. Rather, the concern is directed at the ways in which sexuality is depicted and the effect that those depictions have on the lives of women.[1] Since the concerns are different, it is not surprising that the definition employed to delineate the sort of material under attack is also different. Rather than addressing all sexually explicit material, feminists are concerned with materials that cause harm to women. The feminists' definition of "pornography" focuses on material that makes the domination or submission of women erotic or that degrades women by treating women as objects to be sexually exploited. Under this approach sexual explicitness is not central. If a portrayal maintains the dignity of all the participants, it is not pornographic, even if it is sexually explicit.[2] The requirement of erotic context may be a concession to the traditional definition of "pornography," but it may also be based on a conclusion that erotic material has a sufficiently visceral impact that it may lead to harmful views toward women without the intermediation of the higher-order brain.

Pornography, as so defined, is seen as being the cause of a variety of evils.

Whereas the historical criticism of pornography addressed the harm such materials could cause men, as consumers, or society in its effect on public morality, the feminist concern is the harm pornography causes women.[3] Pornography is seen as a symptom of sexual inequality and patriarchy, as well as a cause of both. In fact, the effect is seen as so pervasive that it defines reality. Pornography "institutionalizes the sexuality of male supremacy, fusing the erotization of dominance and submission with the social construction of male and female. . . . Men treat women as who they see women as being. Pornography constructs who that is."[4]

It is this view of pornography's effects on the construction of reality that concerns feminists. Pornography is not seen as simply another moral issue. It is a civil rights issue. Pornography is seen as affecting all aspects of women's lives by perpetuating patterns of discrimination. In the workplace, pornography is seen as trivializing the contributions of women and encouraging sexual harassment.[5] But the effects go beyond the workplace and affect all aspects of women's lives.

Pornography is a form of speech, but as with sexual harassment, it is also seen as an act. Pornography is said to be both a discriminatory practice and a defamatory ideology, holding that women are "a lower form of human life defined by their availability for sexual use."[6] Between the two, Professor Catharine MacKinnon sees pornography as better addressed as discrimination, rather than defamation.[7] Her focus is on effects, and the effects seem so direct as to make pornography a discriminatory act rather than a defamatory statement with only secondary effects. She argues that pornography leads to an increase in aggressive behavior and other discrimination against women.[8] When explicit sex is combined with violence, thus meeting one way of making the sexual depiction pornographic, she notes evidence that violence against women increases.[9] But even without violence, she argues that the degrading and dehumanizing image of women found in pornography results in discrimination. Even without violence, such material is said to decrease inhibitions on, and increase acceptance of, aggression against women, reduce the desire of both males and females to have female children, and foster a belief in male domination.[10]

It should again be stressed that MacKinnon's conclusion speaks to materials that degrade and dehumanize women. It is not sexual images alone, erotica, that lead to these negative results. Again, to be pornographic, in the feminist sense, sex must be combined with violence or a demeaning view of women.

While this section has purported to present the feminists' view of pornography, Professor Nadine Strossen has pointed out that not all feminists share the belief that pornography should be banned.[11] She offers counterarguments to those presented by MacKinnon and others, and she does so not on First Amendment grounds but with an argument she sees as grounded in the principles and concerns of feminism.[12] Since she is responding to feminists' arguments, she accepts the definition of "pornography" as limited to sexually explicit materials that subordinate women. She considers herself a feminist and objects to what she calls the "widespread misperception that if you are a feminist — or a woman — you must view 'pornography' as misogynistic and 'detrimental' to women. And you must favor censoring it."[13]

Strossen does not stand alone in this view. The Feminists Anti-Censorship Taskforce and Feminists for Free Expression have both opposed legislative efforts to enact the sort of censorship advocated in MacKinnon's and other feminists' attacks on pornography. Strossen's feminist arguments against censoring pornography include concerns that censorship would affect works that are important to women, particularly to feminists and lesbians, and it would perpetuate stereotypes of women as victims for whom sex is necessarily bad, harming women's efforts to develop their sexuality and strengthening patriarchy.[14] MacKinnon has, of course, not missed the existence of these arguments but, based on what she sees as the overwhelmingly negative effect of pornography on women, comes to a different conclusion.

By labeling the arguments of MacKinnon, and others who agree with her to at least some extent, as "the feminist position," I do not mean to ignore the arguments of Strossen and feminists who would agree with Strossen. Nor do I mean to take either side on the feminist aspects of the debate. The label of "feminist" is employed not to indicate that all feminists must agree with the MacKinnon position but to recognize that her arguments present a uniquely feminist perspective. Rather than take sides, I will present the courts' reactions to the MacKinnon approach. I will also indicate how the recognition of violence as obscenity will provide some of what the MacKinnon camp of feminists is seeking, although certainly not all that they wish.

Antipornography Ordinances and Hate Speech Limits

The feminist concerns over pornography, as distinguished from erotica, gave rise to attempts to pass ordinances regulating such material in Minneapolis, Los Angeles, Cambridge, and other cities. The cities of Indianapolis and Bellingham, Washington, passed antipornography ordinances, and the Indianapolis ordinance became the focus of a legal contest over the constitutionality of such restrictions. The United States Court of Appeals for the Seventh Circuit declared the ordinance unconstitutional in *American Booksellers Association v. Hudnut*,[15] and the Supreme Court affirmed without issuing an opinion.[16]

The Indianapolis ordinance defined "pornography" as:

> the graphic sexually explicit subordination of women, whether in pictures or in words, that also includes one or more of the following:
>
> (1) Women are presented as sexual objects who enjoy pain or humiliation; or
>
> (2) Women are presented as sexual objects who experience sexual pleasure in being raped; or
>
> (3) Women are presented as sexual objects tied up or cut up or mutilated or bruised or physically hurt, or as dismembered or truncated or fragmented or severed into body parts; or
>
> (4) Women are presented as being penetrated by objects or animals; or
>
> (5) Women are presented in scenarios of degradation, injury, abasement, torture, shown as filthy or inferior, bleeding, bruised, or hurt in a context that makes these conditions sexual; or
>
> (6) Women are presented as sexual objects for domination, conquest, violation, exploitation, possession, or use, or through postures or positions of servility or submission or display.[17]

While the original ordinance had provided a definition of "sexually explicit," a later amendment left the ordinance with no definition for that term.

The ordinance contained various prohibitions. It became illegal to traffic in pornography, to coerce others into performing in pornographic works, or to force pornography on anyone. A cause of action against the producer or distributor of pornography was provided to anyone injured by someone who had seen or read pornography.[18] The ordinance also prohibited assault on or injury to any person in a way directly caused by specific pornography.[19] Any woman aggrieved by trafficking in pornography was given the right to file a complaint with the city's equal-opportunity office "as a woman acting against the subordination of women," and men who could "prove injury in the same way that a woman is injured" could do the same.[20] Also provided was an individual cause of action by any person claiming to be aggrieved by the trafficking, coercion, or assault addressed in the ordinance.

The court noted the difference between the pornography defined by the ordinance as "a practice that discriminates against women,"[21] and the obscenity that is unprotected by the First Amendment. The ordinance made no reference to prurient interests or community standards and addressed particular depictions rather than judging the work as a whole and protecting it if it had serious value. It appears not to have been an accident that such protection was omitted. The court noted that the supporters of the ordinance maintain that "pornography influences attitudes, and the statute is a way to alter the socialization of men and women rather than to vindicate community standards of offensiveness." [22] The court also cited Professor MacKinnon, one of the principal drafters of the ordinance, as maintaining "if a woman is subjected, why should it matter that the work has other value?" [23]

The court found fault with the ordinance in that it discriminated on the basis of the content of speech. "Speech treating women in the approved way—in sexual encounters 'premised on equality' . . . —is lawful no matter how sexually explicit. Speech treating women in the disapproved way—as submissive in matters sexual or as enjoying humiliation—is unlawful no matter how significant the literary, artistic, or political qualities of the work taken as a whole." [24] Such viewpoint discrimination was held to be unconstitutional. The court said that it is not the province of the state, but is instead the province of the people individually, to evaluate ideas.

The court's position was that, just as the First Amendment protects speech by Nazis and the Klan, it protects the use of nonobscene sexual images by those expressing a view not shared by feminists. The ordinance defined sexually explicit materials to be pornography or not based on the perspective presented in the materials. If such material subordinates women and depicts women as enjoying pain, humiliation, or rape, or in a position of servility or submission, it is pornographic and restricted, regardless of the overall value of the material. On the other hand, material portraying women as equals is unrestricted, however graphic the sexual content of the material, so long as it did not violate any relevant obscenity statute. But, as the court said: "This is thought control. It establishes an 'approved' view of women, of how they may react to sexual encounters, of how the sexes may relate to each other. Those who espouse the approved view may use sexual images; those who do not, may not." [25]

The court recognized the feminist argument that pornography may change people and may contribute to the perpetuation of the subordination of women, with all the negative effects that accompany that subordination. Nonetheless, the court said:

[T]his simply demonstrates the power of pornography as speech. All of these unhappy effects depend on mental intermediation. Pornography affects how people see the world, their fellows, and social relations. If pornography is what pornography does, so is other speech. Hitler's orations affected how some Germans saw Jews. Communism is a world view, not simply a Manifesto by Marx and Engels or a set of speeches.[26]

The court also addressed the argument that pornography is "unanswerable" and that, for that reason, the "marketplace of ideas" metaphor does not apply and First Amendment protection is thus lost. The response was to note that the likelihood of truth winning out is not a necessary condition for First Amendment protection. In fact, the court said, "A power to limit speech on the ground that truth has not yet prevailed and is not likely to prevail implies the power to declare truth. At some point the government must be able to say (as Indianapolis has said): 'We know what the truth is, yet a free exchange of speech has not driven out falsity, so that we must now prohibit falsity.' "[27] The state, however, must not be allowed to determine the truth and suppress the expression of those who disagree. This is so, the court said, even for varieties of speech that are "effectively unanswerable."[28]

Lastly, the court addressed the argument that pornography is "low value" speech and sufficiently like obscenity to be prohibited. While recognizing that distinctions have been drawn between the political speech at the core of the First Amendment and speech of lesser value, the court noted that none of those cases sustained viewpoint discrimination.[29] It is the topic that determines the position of speech as in the core or the distance of that speech from the core. The position expressed on the topic is not relevant to core status. Furthermore, "pornography," as defined by the ordinance, was not low-value speech. Indeed, the city's motivation in restricting such materials was the influence it has on political and social relations. That influence is indicative of core speech rather than low-value speech.[30]

While the Supreme Court affirmed *Hudnut* without opinion, its later analysis of hate-speech legislation, in *R.A.V. v. St. Paul*,[31] would seem to support the Seventh Circuit's *Hudnut* analysis. *R.A.V.* arose from the actions of several teenagers who burned a cross in the fenced-in yard of a black family. R.A.V. was charged under the City of St. Paul's Bias-Motivated Crime Ordinance, which provided:

> Whoever places on public or private property a symbol, object, appellation, characterization or graffiti, including, but not limited to, a burning cross or Nazi swastika, which one knows or has reasonable grounds to know arouses anger, alarm or resentment in others on the basis of race,

color, creed, religion or gender commits disorderly conduct and shall be guilty of a misdemeanor.[32]

The trial court dismissed the charges, holding the ordinance to be overly broad and finding content discrimination violating the First Amendment. The Minnesota Supreme Court reversed[33] and in so doing construed the ordinance language "arouses anger, alarm or resentment in others" to limit the scope of the ordinance to the sort of fighting words recognized as unprotected by the First Amendment in *Chaplinsky v. New Hampshire*.[34] The Minnesota court also concluded that any content discrimination was not unconstitutional, because the ordinance was narrowly tailored to the compelling governmental interest in protecting the community from bias-motivated threats to public safety.[35]

The Supreme Court of the United States accepted as authoritative the state court's construction, limiting the scope of the statute to fighting words. Nonetheless, the Court found the ordinance unconstitutional. The Court recognized that the general rule against government proscription of speech does contain several exceptions, and that fighting words are among the exceptions. However, the claim that such speech is unprotected was seen as an overstatement that was not quite true. The statement that fighting words and obscenity are unprotected means that these categories of speech may be regulated because of their content, "not that they are categories of speech entirely invisible to the Constitution, so that they may be made the vehicles for content discrimination unrelated to their distinctively proscribable content."[36]

Government is not unrestricted in its regulation of even these "unprotected" categories. As the Court noted, a city would be free to ban obscenity completely, but it cannot ban obscene productions critical of government while allowing obscene productions that include an endorsement of city government. While material may be proscribable on one basis, such as its obscenity or as fighting words, that does not make the material proscribable on other bases, such as political viewpoint.

The Court, recognizing that fighting words also convey expression, characterized the exclusion of such words from First Amendment protection as a finding that "the unprotected features of the words are, despite their verbal character, essentially a 'nonspeech' element of communication."[37] Fighting words were seen as analogous to a noisy sound truck; both are modes of speech. While either mode may be regulated, each does convey ideas and government cannot choose to regulate based not on hostility to the mode but on hostility to the ideas conveyed using the mode.

Turning to the St. Paul ordinance, the Court found it violative of the proscription against content-based regulation. Even as construed by the state court, it was seen as "clear that the ordinance applies only to 'fighting words' that insult, or provoke violence, 'on the basis of race, color, creed, religion or gender.'"[38] Other uses of fighting words to express hostility toward union members, members of a political party, or homosexuals were not proscribed. And that was true no matter how insulting or vicious the words may be. This violated the First Amendment by imposing special prohibitions on speakers expressing views on disfavored subjects.[39]

In addition to subject-matter discrimination, the Court noted that the ordinance went so far as to be discriminatory based on viewpoint. While the ordinance banned the use of racial epithets by both sides of a debate, fighting words not involving race, color, creed, religion, or gender could be employed by those arguing for racial or gender equality but not by those arguing against. As the Court said: "St. Paul has no such authority to license one side of a debate to fight freestyle, while requiring the other to follow Marquis of Queensbury Rules."[40]

The Court could find no justification for this discrimination. It recognized that content-based discrimination within a proscribed category might be allowed, when the basis for the discrimination is the same as the basis for the exception itself. For example, obscenity legislation might be written to address only the most extreme forms of obscenity. The St. Paul ordinance, however, could not be saved by this exception. The First-Amendment exception for fighting words exists, because such speech is "a particularly intolerable (and socially unnecessary) mode of expressing whatever idea the speaker wishes to convey."[41] Had St. Paul singled out a category of fighting words to which this justification applied with particular strength, such as words that are threatening as well as obnoxious, the Court would have allowed the discrimination. But instead, St. Paul addressed fighting words that communicate particular ideas of intolerance with regard to race, religion, or gender. That sort of handicapping of one side of a debate was held to be unconstitutional.

The city also attempted to argue that any content discrimination in its ordinance was justified because it was aimed at the secondary effects of the speech involved. The Court had earlier held content discrimination on such a basis constitutional in *Renton v. Playtime Theatres, Inc.*[42] That case addressed a zoning ordinance that restricted adult-entertainment businesses, without affecting other entertainment. The Court upheld the ordinance as aimed at controlling the secondary effects, such as street crime and prostitution, surrounding such adult entertainment businesses. In an attempt to fit within that exception, St.

Paul claimed not to be attempting to restrict free expression but to be protecting from victimization a particularly vulnerable group, a group historically subjected to discrimination. The Court responded that secondary effects cannot include the reactions of those hearing speech or the emotive impact of speech. A regulation based on such concerns would be a regulation aimed at speech and not at secondary effects.

Lastly, the city argued that even if the ordinance was content-based discrimination, it was constitutional because it could pass the strict-scrutiny requirements of narrow tailoring to a compelling governmental interest. The interest asserted was ensuring the rights of groups historically subjected to discrimination to live in peace. The Court was willing to concede that such an interest is compelling and that the ordinance would promote the interest, but said that the dispositive question was whether content discrimination was reasonably necessary to achieve that compelling interest. The answer was that it is not, because there were nondiscriminatory alternatives available:

> An ordinance not limited to the favored topics, for example, would have precisely the same beneficial effect. In fact the only interest distinctively served by the content limitation is that of displaying the city council's special hostility towards the particular biases thus singled out. That is precisely what the First Amendment forbids. The politicians of St. Paul are entitled to express that hostility—but not through the means of imposing unique limitations upon speakers who (however benightedly) disagree.[43]

If it was not clear from *Hudnut* alone, it should be clear from the combination of *Hudnut* and *R.A.V.* that the feminist attempt to restrict pornography, as defined by the feminists, is likely to fall short of complete success. Yet despite the setbacks, there is still the prospect for some success, and the recognition that violence can be obscene may help in the effort. The ability to restrict violence would have an effect on the film use of violence against women, whether sexual depictions are involved or not. If material that is pornographic, because of the mixture of sex and violence, can be restricted because of its violence, at least that variety of pornography may be suppressed.

It is also possible that material that would not be sexually obscene, if the decision were based solely on sexual content, nor violently obscene, if the decision were based solely on the violent content, could be obscene when the two occur in combination. It is not an isolated scene that makes a film obscene. It is the level of offensiveness and the overall value of the entire film that makes for obscenity. If sex alone were considered and did not rise to the required level of offensiveness, the addition of offensive violence might push the film over the threshold. At the very least, the violent material, even if only nearly obscene, is less likely to add to the value of the film taken as a whole. The recognition that violence can be obscene may then allow an attack on that variety of pornography that combines sex and violence against women.

The Effects of Erotica and of Violence

The feminist concern over pornography is based on the harmful effects such materials are seen as having on women. While the concern extends to materials that depict women in submissive positions, the greatest concern seems to be on material that depicts violence against women. The attack has often been limited, however, to material that combines violence against women with sexual images, even though depictions of violence without sex may also be harmful. If media violence is recognized as potentially obscene, due solely to its violent content and without regard to its sexual content, some of the feminist concerns may be addressed because they will be included within a broader attack on harmful images.

While there has been a great deal of concern expressed over the possibility of pornography causing violence, that concern has been misdirected at pornography, at least as "pornography" is defined by the courts rather than by feminists. Concerns over the violent effects of pornography, as defined by feminists, seem not so misdirected. That class of material that feminists would consider pornographic, because of the violence against women that is mixed with sexual images, may lead to violence. Even there, though, the effort is somewhat misdirected. Once it is recognized that violence may be obscene, the focus may be shifted from depictions of sex to depictions of violence. Such a redirection would be beneficial, because it is the depiction of violence, not the depiction of sex, that appears to cause aggressive behavior.

The 1970 President's Commission on Obscenity and Pornography examined sexually obscene material without focusing specifically on sexually violent obscenity or pornography. The commission concluded, "[E]mpirical research . . . has found no evidence to date that exposure to explicit sexual materials plays a significant role in the causation of delinquent or criminal behavior among youth or adults. The Commission cannot conclude that exposure to erotic materials is a factor in the causation of sex crime or sex delinquency." [44]

In 1987, Professors Edward Donnerstein, Daniel Linz, and Steven Penrod examined the experimental evidence on the question and agreed with the 1970 Commission that causation could not be shown. [45] They found the laboratory studies to be inconsistent, with male aggressiveness against women increasing after exposure to pornography only when given multiple opportunities to be aggressive in the "permission-giving" situation of the laboratory. One study in the commission's research that did purport to show an increase in verbal aggression toward women after exposure to an erotic film, did so only when the male subjects were told that they would see another erotic film, if they increased their verbal abuse.[46]

Donnerstein, Linz, and Penrod also examined research outside the laboratory and found it "even less conclusive."[47] They noted difference in studies on the comparison of rape rates as Denmark eliminated its antipornography laws. Studies by Professor John Court claimed to find an increase there and decreases where pornography restrictions were adopted,[48] while studies by Professor Berl Kutchinsky showed no such rise.[49] Donnerstein, Linz, and Penrod suggest that Court's data is "basically uninterpretable" and that the Kutchinsky research is on a sounder methodological footing, though limited to Danish society.[50] Kutchinsky has been less charitable in his analysis of Court's work, pointing out various instances of the misuse or misreport of statistics.[51] Kutchinsky also points to research reaching his conclusions, based on data from other countries.[52]

The Donnerstein, et al, analysis also suggests that at first glance there might seem to be a correlation between the circulation of sex magazines and rape rates in the United States. However, they suggest caution in this conclusion. The better explanation might be that both increase with the level of "hypermasculinity" in the states' populations, as shown by the fact that the best relation to rape reports was the circulation of *Field and Stream* and *American Rifleman*.[53] In sum, they support the conclusion of the 1970 Commission that the evidence does not show that exposure to sexual obscenity leads to violence against women.

Just one year prior to the 1970 President's Commission on Obscenity and Pornography's inability to conclude that sexual obscenity leads to violence against women, the National Commission on the Causes and Prevention of Violence was able to find a link between television violence and violent behavior in viewers.[54] Later studies and reports supported that view.[55]

Against the background of these reports, the 1986 Attorney General's Commission on Pornography convened to consider anew the issues faced by the 1970 Commission. This time, in looking at violent effects, the 1986 Commission stressed violent pornography, which it believed to be, increasingly, the most prevalent form of pornography.[56] While there may be some question whether or not the violent variety is becoming or has become the most prevalent form,[57] the question addressed is important.

The conclusion of the 1986 Commission was that "substantial exposure to sexually violent materials . . . bears a causal relationship to antisocial acts of sexual violence and, for some subgroups, to unlawful acts of sexual violence." [58] As Professor Frederick Schauer, who served on the 1986 Commission, points out, this conclusion is not inconsistent with the findings of the 1970 Commission.[59] The 1970 Commission considered sexually explicit materials generally, while the 1986 Commission focused on sexually violent materials. It would be a misreading of the 1986 Report to "make the unsupportable connection between sexual explicitness and sexual violence." [60]

Professor Schauer sums up the scientific evidence on the violent effects of sexually violent and sexually explicit depictions:

> The results of these experiments, which try to exclude the spurious by first isolating sex without the violence and then isolating violence without the sex, indicate most importantly that the violence is clearly not spurious. That is, if the violence disappears and we are testing only for the relationship between sex and sexual violence, there is *no* causal relationship, as the Report expressly announces. But if the sexualization (and not just the sexual explicitness) of the violence is eliminated, the evidence indicates that the strength of the causal relationship diminishes. Thus, although the studies indicate some relationship between non-sexualized violence and attitudes about sexual violence, or aggressive tendencies toward women, this relationship, in probabilistic terms, becomes stronger when the sexualization is added.[61]

Donnerstein, Linz, and Penrod describe the studies in the area of media sex, media violence, and violent effects.[62] The most telling of the studies presented is one by Donnerstein, Berkowitz, and Linz.[63] The subjects, male college students, were angered by one of the researchers. They then watched one of four films — aggressive pornography, nonaggressive/noncoercive pornography, a film that depicted aggression against women but with no sexual content, and a neutral film. The subjects were then given the opportunity to behave aggressively against one of the researchers' confederates. There were no differences in aggression against a female target between those who watched the sex-only film and those who watched the neutral film. Those who watched the aggression-only film were more aggressive against a female target than those who watched the sex-only film or the neutral film. Violence in a film increased the likelihood of aggression, while sex did not.

The authors do point out that the group most willing to be aggressive against the female target was the group that had seen the aggressive pornography.[64] While it may be that violence, rather than sex, causes violence, violence with sex is the most violence-provoking. "[T]he sexual context of material is . . . relevant because the sexual context has a synergistic effect with violence that results in the greatest likelihood of harm."[65]

Donnerstein, Linz, and Penrod discuss desensitization to violence, saying sex plays a role that could explain the synergistic effect. They suggest that:

[I]f a film maker were to continually pair violent scenes with relaxing music, or continually pair violence with pleasing stimuli such as mildly erotic scenes, building from the least fearful scenes to a climax of great fearfulness, desensitization may occur very efficiently. The viewer would come to associate, through conditioning, the previously anxiety-provoking stimulus (violence) with the neutral or positive response elicited by [a] neutral scene or a mildly erotic scene.[66]

Their description of "slasher films" fits this desensitization model.

The carnage is usually preceded by some sort of erotic prelude: footage of pretty young bodies in the shower, or teens changing into nighties for a slumber party, or anything that otherwise lulls the audience into a mildly sensual mood. When the killing begins, this eroticism is abruptly abandoned, for it has served its purpose, that of lowering the viewer's defenses and heightening the films [sic] physical effectiveness. The speed and ease with [sic] one's feelings can be transformed from sensuality into viciousness may surprise even those quite conversant with the links between sexual and violent urges.[67]

Violence, then, remains the culprit. Sex, explicit or not, is simply used to amplify the effect of that violence or to make the violence more acceptable by associating it with positively received sexual images. If violence is the true culprit, it makes more sense to ban material based on its violence than based on the level of sexual explicitness. "*[T]he most reasonable conclusion that one can reach from the [1986] commission's own statement is that depictions of violence against women, whether in a sexually explicit context or not, should be the focus of concern.*"[68]

The only shortcoming of this conclusion is that it is too limited. The conclusion of the National Commission on the Causes and Prevention of Violence that violence in media causes violence was not limited to violence against women. While the presence of sexual content with violence may focus against women any resulting violence and may increase the likelihood of violent effects, it is violence that causes violence, and the victim of that violence may be either female or male.

Providing Some Relief for Feminist Concerns

It is possible that the recognition that violence can be legally obscene would provide at least some relief to feminist concerns by reducing the level of violence in society. There are also other potential effects of violent media that could be lessened by the reduction in media violence by such recognition, furthering more feminist goals.

The psychologist Ronald Slaby has identified four effects of media violence.[69] The first, the "aggressor effect," is the increase in willingness to act aggressively by those who watch depictions of violence. A second, the "bystander effect," is an increase in callousness and apathy with regard to violence, a desensitization that leads to increased willingness to accept violence. Feminists, and others, have noted an increased tolerance of rape and a willingness to blame the victim by those who watch violent pornography. If a reduction in media depictions of violence would reduce the "bystander effect," a decrease in tolerance of violent crime, including rape, could affect the climate in which these crimes seem to be increasing in frequency. A third effect, the "increased appetite effect," is the desire induced by media violence to view additional violent material and material that is still more violent. While the effect itself may not be as directly negative, the increased viewing or increased violence in what is viewed may lead to the other direct negative effects. The "increased appetite effect" is then also at least indirectly negative.

The fourth effect is what Slaby calls the "victim effect." As he explains the effect: "Some viewers of television violence, particularly those who identify with the victim, are more likely to show fear, mistrust, and self-protective behavior such as carrying a gun. They display an exaggerated belief that they are extremely vulnerable to violence by strangers."[70] The victim effect is a separate harm beyond that of increased violence. Even if violence were not increased by media depictions of violence, people may come to believe that the world is a more violent place than it is. That belief could have a disabling effect in that people might be led to isolate themselves and lead less active lives. In fact, it would appear that the victim effect could relate to the aggressor effect. A person who believes the world is more violent than it is would seem more likely to take steps to protect himself or herself, including, potentially, the use of violence in response to a perceived but specious threat.

The victim effect appears related to the cultivation hypothesis developed and tested by George Gerbner and his associates in the late 1970s.[71] The cultivation hypothesis suggested that heavy viewers of television, being exposed to violence and crime-related stories, would view the world as more violent and criminal than it really is, would be alienated and more fearful generally, and would take excessive precautions in their everyday lives. The theory was that television would provide an experiential structure through which heavy viewers would interpret reality. Gerbner did find evidence to confirm his hypothesis. Heavy viewers were more fearful of walking alone in their neighborhoods at night and were more likely than light viewers to believe that they would be the victim of violence.

Gerbner's conclusions quickly received support from the work of others. A 1982 meta-analysis of research in the field concluded that the evidence was relatively supportive of the position that television influenced some aspects of social reality and that this was especially so in areas related to violence.[72] The same meta-analysis, however, also suggested the possibility that, when other variables were controlled, the cultivation hypothesis might not be confirmed.

Even before the 1982 meta-analysis, some work had already been done in an attempt to control for other variables. In a 1979 study, Anthony Doob and Glenn Macdonald examined one variable they thought might account for the correlation between heavy television viewing and fear of violence.[73] They recognized Gerbner's controls for variables such as age, sex, education level, news reading, prime-time viewing, and television-news viewing and the result that, within each group, heavy viewers were more fearful than light viewers. However, they suggested that another variable could explain the correlation. Their hypothesis was that the fear of violence on the part of people who watch a lot of television may be greater because they live in more violent neighborhoods. They found that, if the variable of neighborhood was controlled, the effect of heavy television was negligible.[74] They did, however, still find an effect of watching violent television. Heavy viewing of violence was related to the perception of the vulnerability of females and children in certain settings but not to the likelihood of the viewers themselves being victims of violent crime.[75]

While Doob and Macdonald were willing to conclude that television itself did not appear to be a direct cause of fear of violence, they expressed some caution in noting that the correlation did appear to hold in high-crime neighborhoods.[76] They suggested that this correlation may result from the fact that the television violence present in crime drama takes place mostly in high-crime areas. People who live in lower-crime neighborhoods might not see television violence as having any relevance to themselves. Heavy viewing would not make the low-crime neighborhood resident fearful for himself or herself. Interestingly, heavy viewing by residents of low-crime areas might still lead such viewers to believe that others are vulnerable, and that appears related to the correlation that was found.

Doob and Macdonald expressed a second caution in that heavy viewing was correlated, even after control for neighborhood, to responses to certain questions about facts associated with violence and crime. They suggest that television may serve as a source of belief about the world, making the heavy viewer believe the world is a more violent place than it is, yet not affect the viewers' perceptions of how afraid they should be.[77] This distinction was examined by Sparks and Ogles in a 1990 study.[78] They distinguished two kinds of questions that they thought were often confused in other studies. While purporting to measure fear of violence, some studies instead asked questions regarding the likelihood of being a victim of violence. Sparks and Ogles asked questions of both varieties, (1) the respondent's perceived chance of being involved in violence, and other measures typically used in cultivation studies, and (2) questions regarding the respondent's fear of being a victim of certain violent acts. They controlled for both sex and high-crime versus low-crime environment. While they found no evidence of media cultivation using the traditional measures, they did find a "quite modest" relationship between television viewing and the fear of violence.

In Sparks's and Ogles's explanation of the conceptual difference between likelihood and fear, they suggested that an individual who has confidence in his or her ability to cope with violence might believe violence to be likely but would not have an elevated fear of violence. The fact that fear turned out to be correlated with heavy viewing, while assessment of probability did not, is the opposite of their example. This raises the interesting, though untested, possibility that an effect of heavy viewing could be an increased perception of the inability to cope with violent situations. While the heavy viewer may not consider violence more likely than would the light viewer, the heavy viewer may believe that there is nothing to be done to save oneself in such a situation. That, it would seem, is a true "victim effect."

As the prior discussion would indicate, there has been dispute over the existence of the cultivation effect. There is some indication that it does not exist in all viewers and may not be tied to total exposure. A 1986 study by W. James Potter was controlled for beliefs about or attitudes toward television. He found that those who take television to be a "magic window," an accurate, unaltered picture of real life, or who seek instruction from television, or identify with the characters on television, exhibit a stronger belief that the world is a mean and violent place.[79]

Potter also offers a suggestion that would explain some of the evidence against cultivation. The cultivation studies generally compared heavy viewers and light viewers, and while Gerbner showed a correlation between heavy viewing and the belief in a mean and violent world, others have argued that the correlation does not stand up when adequate controls are introduced. Potter suggests that the violent-world belief is cultivated by television but that the amount of television watched is not an important factor. The subjects in his study did show an exaggerated belief in the level of violence in the world.[80] These unrealistic beliefs must come from somewhere, but he found no correlation to amount of viewing. He did find correlation to the attitudes toward and beliefs about television discussed. "It appears that cultivation of beliefs may take place, but the process is much more complex than that specified in the cultivation hypothesis as it is now framed. The amount of exposure to television seems far less important than the attitudes and perceptions of the individuals being exposed."[81] It may be that media violence simply does its work more quickly than had been believed.

Ronald Slaby's victim effect, with his emphasis on the effect on those who identify with the victim, is consistent with Potter's analysis. His particular concern with the effects of media violence on children also appears justified. As he expresses the problem:

> Particularly high levels of unrealistic television violence are presented to those most vulnerable to its distorting effects—children. Children are generally more susceptible than adults because they lack the real-world experience and the critical judgment necessary to evaluate how unrealistic and irrelevant to their own lives the distorted portrayals of violence may be.[82]

Children, lacking real-world experience, would seem more likely to take television to be a "magic window" and to perceive television as instructional.

The correlation between identification with victims of media violence and the cultivation of a violent-world view should have special relevance to feminists. The relevance need not rely on any gender differences in identification with victims. The special concern arises from the female characters that become the victims of media violence. The victims of many of the slasher films are women who show any inclination toward independence and autonomy, sexual or otherwise.[83] Particularly likely to be victims are single women exhibiting such independence.[84] A woman who identifies with such an independent female may be influenced not to express or act on that independence. Further, the lesson may be learned that marriage is necessary for protection in a violent world.

The recognition that media violence can be obscene and subjected to regulation can then address feminists' concerns in at least two ways. A reduction in media violence may decrease violence against women and may also reduce feelings of vulnerability and victimization in women. It also does so without making the concern solely a gender issue. While identifying issues as gender issues may help in the development of gender interest and in the formation of an activist group, recognition that an issue is of direct and personal concern to all may bring more pressure to bear for a solution. Violence is not solely a concern of women. While women may be more likely to be the victims of domestic abuse and of rape, deadly violence seems to have more impact on young males than on any other group. While males may be more likely to be the perpetrators of violence, men and women are both the victims of violence. Neither men nor women can escape the effects of media violence and by working together can make the world safer for all.

Drafting a Statute

Guidance in drafting a statute banning depictions of excessive and graphic violence may be drawn from the Supreme Court's treatment of sexual obscenity. The experience gained in that effort may shorten the time required to develop a mature consideration of the area of violent obscenity. The Court first held sexual obscenity to be unprotected in *Roth v. United States*[1] in 1957. The Court noted with approval lower court standards for obscenity requiring that the material at issue deal with sex in a manner that appeals to the prurient interest, judged by the average person applying contemporary community standards. *Roth* presumed obscene material to be "utterly without redeeming social importance,"[2] but did not explicitly make the complete lack of social importance a part of the test for obscenity. It was nine years later, in *Memoirs v. Massachusetts*,[3] when the "utterly without redeeming social importance" factor became a part of the test for obscenity.[4]

It took an additional seven years, before the Court adopted the current definition in *Miller v. California*.[5] Thus, sixteen years passed between the recognition that sexually obscene material lacked constitutional protection and the adoption of the current test. Even then, the development was not complete. Still another fourteen years later, the *Miller* test required further explanation in the *Pope v. Illinois*[6] examination of the third prong of the *Miller* test. Given Justice Scalia's concerns over how the *Pope* refinement is to be applied, it is not clear that, even with *Pope*, the definition of sexual obscenity is now complete.

This difficulty in defining sexual obscenity, as indicated by the time required in the effort, speaks to the difficulty of setting out such limits on free speech. Whether development is now complete or not, it would be wise to draw as much guidance as possible from the law of sexual obscenity in developing law for the regulation of violent obscenity.

The *Miller* test requires only minor changes to shift the focus from sex to violence.[7] Part (a) of the *Miller* may require no change. The *Roth* Court had defined "prurient" as "[i]tching; longing; uneasy with desire or longing; of persons, having itching, morbid, or lascivious longing; of desire, curiosity, or propensity, lewd"[8] and as "a shameful or morbid interest in nudity, sex, or excretion, and if it goes substantially beyond customary limits of candor in description or representation of such matters."[9] Parts of that definition can certainly carry over to violence. A depiction of violence can go beyond community standards and appeal to morbid longings or curiosity or to shameful or morbid interests and thus appeal to the prurient interest. However, since "prurient" seems to have developed an attachment to sexual activities, the best approach might be to substitute "morbid or shameful" for "prurient."

The second factor must change to reflect the concern with violence rather than sex. Rather than depicting sexual conduct, the test should be whether the work depicts or describes, in a patently offensive way, acts of violence specifically defined by the applicable state law. The state statute must indicate clearly what depictions are banned—murder, rape, aggravated assault, mayhem, and torture would all appear to be good candidates. Not all depictions of such acts would be banned, just as not all depictions of sexual acts are banned. Only depictions of sex and only depictions of violence that are patently offensive could be banned.

The third factor in *Miller* need not change at all. If the work, taken as a whole, lacks serious literary, artistic, political, or scientific value and meets the other factors it is violent obscenity. As is true for sexual obscenity, the "serious value" prong should be judged on the basis of a reasonable person, and not a local values, standard. It is this factor that would protect the violence in Shakespeare from prosecution, even in a jurisdiction with an overzealous approach to banning violence.

A test for the constitutionality of a ban on, or otherwise regulating, material on the basis of violent obscenity would then be:

> (a) whether the average person, applying contemporary community standards, would find that the work, taken as a whole, appeals to a morbid or shameful interest in violence; (b) whether the work depicts or describes, in a patently offensive way, violence specifically defined by the applicable state law; and (c) whether the work, taken as a whole, lacks serious literary, artistic, political, or scientific value.

Even with this test, drawn from the experience with sexual obscenity law, it would be profitable to examine the failed state attempts at regulating violence to see what guidance can be found there. While the recognition that violent material may be obscene, as a result of the violence alone, may cure some of the faults found with the state attempts, other defects must be addressed.

When Missouri attempted to ban the distribution of violent videos to minors, it was attempting to follow the dictates of *Miller*.[10] By using the test presented there, substituting references to violence in place of *Miller*'s references to sex, they hoped to arrive at a constitutional statute. While the Tennessee statute did not directly employ the *Miller* definition as part of its language,[11] the Colorado statute followed Missouri's lead in employing such a definition.[12] When the Missouri statute was struck down in *Video Software Dealers Association v. Webster*,[13] among the flaws noted was the vagueness of the statute as to the material addressed. The recognition of violence as potentially obscene does not overcome that flaw. While less certainty may be required in the regulation of unprotected speech, vagueness concerns and notice requirements do not disappear. The error on the part of the State of Missouri was in treating the *Miller* test as an example of a constitutional statute, rather than as a test for constitutional application of a statute. Substituting violence for sex in *Miller* may serve to turn the test for a constitutional sexual obscenity statute into a test for the constitutionality of a violent obscenity statute. It will not produce such a statute.

The Missouri statute did not meet the *Miller* requirements. *Miller* requires that the sexual conduct banned as obscene be specifically defined in the statute or in construction by state courts. Missouri's statute provided no definition of the violent material banned, nor did the court find a readily apparent construction of the statute that would avoid the vagueness concern. That is the lesson to be found in Missouri's experience. Bans on violent materials must not only meet the first and third prongs of the *Miller* test. There must be an adequate statutory description of the kinds of depictions that are barred.

The lessons learned from the treatment of the Missouri statute are also taught by the treatment afforded the Tennessee statute. Tennessee's definition of "excess violence" as "the depiction of acts of violence in such a graphic and/or bloody manner as to exceed common limits to custom and candor, or in such a manner that it is apparent that the predominant appeal of the material is portrayal of violence for violence's sake"[14] was also found unconstitutionally vague by the Supreme Court of Tennessee.[15] *Miller* and an analogous test for violent obscenity will require a description of the acts the depictions of which are banned. That description requires more specificity than Tennessee provided.

The difficulty with vagueness had earlier led to the Supreme Court invalidation of a state statute in *Winters v. New York*.[16] That case was decided in

1947, before *Miller* provided any guidance in the drafting of statutes. New York's courts had recognized a vagueness problem in the statute's ban on the distribution of "any book, pamphlet, magazine, newspaper or other printed paper devoted to the publication, and principally made up of criminal news, police reports, or accounts of criminal deeds, or pictures, or stories of deeds of bloodshed, lust or crime." [17] The Appellate Division of the New York Supreme Court limited the statute to "matter which presents tales of bloodshed, crime or lust in a manner that would have a tendency to demoralize its readers and would be likely to corrupt the morals of the young and lead them to immoral acts." [18] When the conviction was again appealed, the New York Court of Appeals also adopted its own construction limiting the scope of the statute to "[c]ollections of pictures or stories of criminal deeds of bloodshed or lust unquestionably . . . so massed as to become vehicles for inciting violent and depraved crimes against the person." [19] Even with the attempted limitations on scope, the United States Supreme Court still found the statute unacceptably vague and declared it unconstitutional. *Miller* now provides guidance as to just what is needed to avoid this vagueness—a listing within the statute of the acts the depictions of which are subject to the statute.

A particularly strong insight into the problem of drafting may be found in the Los Angeles County ordinance struck down by the California Supreme Court in *Katzev v. County of Los Angeles.* [20] The ordinance addressed the distribution of crime comics to minors and defined comic books in terms of the number of drawings or photographs involved and the existence of captions or narration balloons. [21] The ordinance also defined "crime," for purposes of the statute, as:

> The commission or attempted commission of an act of arson, burglary, kidnapping, mayhem, murder, rape, robbery, theft, trainwrecking, or voluntary manslaughter; or the commission of an act of assault with caustic chemicals or assault with a deadly weapon[,] includ[ing] but . . . not limited to, acts by human beings, and further includ[ing] acts by animals or any non-human, part human, or imaginary beings, which if performed by a human would constitute any of the crimes named. [22]

There were exceptions for religious works and true stories.

The California court found several constitutional problems with the statute. One problem was that already addressed. Because the court believed violent materials to be constitutionally protected, it required that the type of crime addressed be narrowly tailored to the problem of juvenile delinquency. The ordinance's inclusion of all fictional crime within the listed categories was overly broad.

The court was also troubled by the difficulty of drawing lines as to what is and what is not a comic book. Since many children's books contain illustrations that could bring them within the statute's definition of a comic book, yet were said to be outside the intent of the statute, standards for application of the statute were found lacking. Even if the distinction could have been made more clear, other courts have been troubled by attacks on violence in one medium, while leaving other, equally violent, media unregulated.[23] These problems may be lessened by the recognition that sufficiently violent material may be unprotected by the First Amendment and by the use of *Miller*'s guidance in drafting a statute, but it may still be unwise to let the inclusion of material depend on how many frames of a cartoon are presented. A test of the nature and offensiveness of the violence involved, and the value of the work taken as a whole, provides a better test than counting frames.[24]

The California court also found an Equal Protection violation in the exemptions for true stories and religious works. No difference was seen between nonreligious fiction and tales of real-life gangsters. The better approach is to allow the nonfiction nature of a work to play a role only in the third prong of a *Miller*-like test. Certainly, a religious work would, taken as a whole, have serious value. Similarly, a historical account on the bloody deeds of some real-life character might be more likely to have serious value than would a fictional account of the same deeds, unless the fictional work is saved by its serious literary value.

An additional difficulty raised by the California court may also provide insight. The court objected to the inclusion of acts by animals which would be among the named crimes, had they been performed by humans. Since the ordinance addressed comics, the need to include animals, part-animals, and other beings should be obvious. The characters in comics are often anthropomorphized animals. Violence involving such characters may appeal strongly to children and may be as real for them as violence by and against human characters. While the greatest problem may be presented by the anthropomorphic animal, the ordinance did not require that the animal or other creature be humanlike. As the court pointed out, the ordinance seemed to include such instances as a shark biting off a person's arm, since a similar attack by a person would constitute mayhem or cannibalism.

The best approach here may be simply to list the crimes addressed as the second part of a *Miller*-based statute. There is probably no need specifically to include acts by animals. If an animal bites off a person's arm, that would not be a crime, since animals cannot possess the mental states required for criminal liability. However, if an anthropomorphic cartoon animal does the same, a court could conclude that the fictional animal-human had committed a fictional crime, since such a fictional creature could have the required mental state.

The issue of animals raises another concern. Should a graphic presentation of a violent attack by an animal on a person or other animal be considered violent obscenity? If violence were protected by the First Amendment, and any restrictions had to be based on a compelling governmental purpose of preventing whatever violence is caused by media violence, it might be difficult to establish that animal attacks cause person-on-person violence. If violence may be obscene, it is possible that a film of an animal attack on a person or even on another animal might, if sufficiently offensive and if lacking in overall value, be considered obscene. The result should parallel that for sexual obscenity. Since a film of a human-animal sexual act can be obscene, if the state statute includes bestiality, there is no reason why a graphic film of an animal attack on a human could not be violent obscenity. Since statutes do not seem to address film of animal-animal sexual acts with the regularity that they address bestiality, the issue with regard to animal-animal violence may be less clear. However, since it would seem that the former could be included in a sexual obscenity statute, there is no reason why the latter could not be included in a violent obscenity statute.

There is one other distinction between movies containing explicit sexual activity and movies containing explicit depictions of violence that deserves mention. Sexually explicit movies, at least those falling into the hard-core category, present film of actual sex acts. Violent movies, at least those from major producers, do not present film of actual violence but rather of simulated violence. That distinction, however, is insufficient to protect the violent film. The *Miller* opinion provided, as an example of what a state statute could define as obscene, under the second prong of the *Miller* test, "[p]atently offensive representations or descriptions of ultimate sexual acts, normal or perverted, *actual or simulated.*"[25] Statutes and case law agree that simulation or description can be obscene.[26]

The conclusion that simulation or description can be obscene should easily carry over to animation. If the description can be sufficiently offensive as to be sexually obscene, the addition of animation cannot make it less obscene. The realism of the images present in the advanced graphics of systems that approach virtual reality may well evoke a response that is the same as it would be to actual film or videotape footage of a real sexual encounter. Certainly, the reaction will be stronger than it would be to a print description. The same ought to be true for violent obscenity. Even animated violence may be sufficiently offensive as to be obscene.

With the guidance provided by sexual obscenity law and the failed attempts to regulate depictions of violence, an attempt may be made to write a statute addressing violent obscenity.

Violent Obscenity [27]

I. Violent Obscenity Proscribed: A person is guilty of violent obscenity when, knowing its content and character, he or she:

1. Promotes, or possesses with intent to promote, any material that constitutes violent obscenity; or

2. Produces, presents, or directs a performance constituting violent obscenity.

Violent obscenity is a [misdemeanor in the ____ degree] [felony in the ____ degree].[28]

II. Definitions of Terms

1. "Violent Obscenity." Any material or performance constitutes "violent obscenity" if (a) the average person, applying contemporary community standards, would find that considered as a whole, its predominant appeal is to a morbid or shameful interest in violence, and (b) it depicts or describes in a patently offensive manner, actual or simulated: murder, manslaughter, rape, mayhem, battery, or an attempt to commit any of the preceding crimes, and (c) considered as a whole, it lacks serious literary, artistic, political, or scientific value. Predominant appeal shall be judged with reference to ordinary adults unless it appears from the character of the material or the circumstances of its dissemination to be designed for children or other specially susceptible audience. An act done by or to a part-human/part-animal character, an animal character depicted as possessing humanlike mental character, or a fictional creature depicted as possessing humanlike mental characteristics and otherwise meeting the definitions for the crimes included in clause (b) of this subsection, satisfies the definitional requirements of clause (b).

2. "Material" means anything tangible which is capable of being used or adapted to arouse interest, whether through the medium of reading, observation, sound, or in any other manner.

3. "Performance" means any play, motion picture, or other exhibition performed before an audience.

4. "Promote" means to manufacture, issue, sell, give, provide, lend, mail, deliver, transfer, transmute, publish, distribute, circulate, disseminate, present, exhibit, or advertise, or to offer or agree to do the same.

5. "Simulated" means the explicit depiction or description of any of the types of conduct set forth in clause (b) of subdivision one of this section, which creates the appearance of such conduct. Simulations may include animated presentations.

A state might also choose to ban certain depictions of violence by or against non-anthropomorphized animals. That could be accomplished either by amending clause (1)(b) of the definitions to include attacks by animals on persons or other animals, or by drafting a separate statute.

Once it is recognized that violence may be obscene, a statute such as that presented should withstand constitutional attack. The statute banning distributions of depictions of violence that was struck down in *Winters* was declared unconstitutional because of its vagueness. The violent obscenity statute presented here should not suffer the same fate. The definition tracks the requirements set forth in *Miller* for a constitutional sexual obscenity statute. With regard to concerns that the *Roth* definition of sexual obscenity was too vague, the Court said:

> Many decisions have recognized that these terms of obscenity statutes are not precise. This Court, however, has consistently held that lack of precision is not itself offensive to the requirements of due process. "[T]he Constitution does not require impossible standards"; all that is required is that the language "conveys sufficiently definite warning as to the proscribed conduct when measured by common understanding and practices. . . ." These words, applied according to the proper standard for judging obscenity, already discussed, give adequate warning of the conduct proscribed and mark . . . "boundaries sufficiently distinct for judges and juries fairly to administer the law. . . . That there may be marginal cases in which it is difficult to determine the side of the line on which a particular fact situation falls is no sufficient reason to hold the language too ambiguous to define a criminal offense."[29]

That analysis carries over to *Miller,* and there is no reason why such an approach to vagueness should be applicable to sexual obscenity but inappropriate for violent obscenity.

Variable Obscenity and Indecency

Professor Cass Sunstein notes that sexual obscenity prosecutions are rather rare.[30] He sees the combination of offensiveness and appeal to the prurient interests required by the *Miller* test as unlikely to occur. For him, that unlikely required combination and the additional requirement that the material taken as a whole lack serious value makes the test very protective of speech. With the exception of materials he classifies as masturbatory aids, he suggests that it will be quite difficult to win sexual obscenity prosecutions.

Whatever difficulties may be present in obtaining convictions for sexual obscenity are likely to carry over to violent obscenity. The combination of offense and attraction in the *Miller* test, that Sunstein finds to be an "odd psychological state," becomes no less odd in a test for violent obscenity. The ability of a depiction to appeal to a shameful or morbid interest in violence and at the same time to be offensive must be just as "odd" as the ability to appeal to the prurient interest in sex, while also being offensive.

The combination may not be as psychologically odd as Sunstein indicates.[31] Nonetheless, he is correct in his observation that there is much less than a flood of sexual obscenity prosecutions. Whether the *Miller* test is so restrictive that very little is obscene or instead prosecutors are simply not making such cases a priority, Sunstein may well be correct in his assertion that "most people involved in the production of sexually explicit work have little to fear from the *Miller* test."[32]

The limited application and enforcement of the sexual obscenity statutes may or may not carry over to the arena of violent obscenity. If the lack of prosecution for sexual obscenity is due to prosecutorial disinterest, the interest in prosecuting violent obscenity might not be so lacking. While it has not been established that sexually explicit films or materials cause any actual harm, the causal effect of violent material is better established. The harmful effects of violent materials may not have been sufficiently demonstrated to meet the strict scrutiny that would be required were such materials protected by the First Amendment. However, once it is recognized that such materials may be obscene and unprotected, a clear demonstration of harmful effect is not required for proscription. Neither must the harmful effect speak to a compelling governmental purpose. It need only increase the interest of the state in prosecuting the production and distribution of such material. Prosecutors may be more likely to be motivated by citizens fearful for the safety of themselves and their children than by citizens expressing moral concern over the sexual climate.

If the limited number of prosecutions is instead the result of the difficulty in meeting the requirements of the *Miller* test, that difficulty is likely to be present in prosecuting violent obscenity. It may be that at least the major movie producers, television networks, and cable program providers have little to fear from a violent obscenity prosecution, under a *Miller*-like test. However, the evolution of community standards, as shown by growing public concern, may increase the possibility of prosecution and conviction. Furthermore, even if prosecution for violent obscenity remains unlikely, the existence of violent obscenity statutes could have other legal and moral effects on the amount of violence present in the media.

The change in obscenity law to recognize the existence of violent obscenity would have two immediate legal consequences. Sexual obscenity law has been accompanied by a doctrine of variable obscenity and the possibility of regulating indecency. Violent obscenity should have the same accompaniment. There would develop a doctrine of variable violent obscenity and a concept of violent indecency. Even if the actual law of violent obscenity were to have little effect, these other legal theories would be likely to have great effect. The recognition that violence can be obscene might also affect the moral climate and further bring about a reduction in the availability of such material.

Variable Obscenity

The concept of variable obscenity allows the regulation of material that would not be obscene to one group to be considered obscene as marketed and distributed to particular groups. Of relevance here is the fact that material may be found obscene to youth, if it appeals to the prurient interests of youth, as recognized in *Ginsberg v. New York*.[33] The recognition that materials may be obscene because of the violence they contain should, by analogy to *Ginsberg*, speak to the distribution of violent materials to minors. There should be a category of "violent obscenity to minors." While the fact that material is violent obscenity to minors would not allow the government to proscribe the distribution of such materials to adults,[34] it should allow the adoption of restrictions on the distribution to minors. Thus far, the concern over violent materials expressed by legislatures and the public has been directed at the exposure of youth to such materials. This concern is better-founded than concerns over exposure to sexually explicit materials, given the better establishment of correlation to violence in the general population. Special protections are also required for youth because research indicates that children often do not perceive distinctions between fantasy and reality in media presentations.[35] Even cartoon depictions of violence appear to cause aggressive behavior in children.[36] It may be difficult to find most cartoon depictions to be violently obscene under the test as applied to adults, but such material might well be found violently obscene for minors.

The current version of the New York statute that was at issue in *Ginsberg* can provide guidance in drafting a statute protecting children from exposure to violence.

Disseminating Excessively Violent Material to Minors[37]

I. Disseminating Excessively Violent Material to Minors Proscribed: A person is guilty of disseminating excessively violent material to minors when:

1. With knowledge of its character and content, he sells or loans to a minor for monetary consideration:

(a) Any picture, photograph, drawing, sculpture, motion picture film, or similar visual representation, or image which depicts actual or simulated: murder, manslaughter, rape, mayhem, battery, or an attempt to commit any of the preceding crimes and which, taken as a whole, is harmful to minors; or

(b) Any book, pamphlet, magazine, printed matter however reproduced, or sound recording which contains any matter enumerated in paragraph (a) hereof and which, taken as a whole, is harmful to minors; or

2. Knowing the character and content of a motion picture, show, or other presentation which, in whole or in part, depicts crimes enumerated in paragraph (1)(a) hereof and which is harmful to minors, he:

(a) Exhibits such motion picture, show, or other presentation to a minor for a monetary consideration; or

(b) Sells to a minor an admission ticket or pass to premises whereon there is exhibited or to be exhibited such motion picture, show, or other presentation; or

(c) Admits a minor for a monetary consideration to premises whereon there is exhibited or to be exhibited such motion picture show or other presentation.

3. An act done by or to a part-human/part-animal character, an animal character depicted as possessing humanlike mental character, or a fictional creature depicted as possessing humanlike mental characteristics and otherwise meeting the definitions for the crimes included in this clause satisfies the definitional requirements of clause (1)(a) hereof.

Disseminating excessively violent material to minors is a [misdemeanor of the ____ degree][felony of the ____ degree].[38]

II. Definition of Terms

The following definitions are applicable to subsection I hereof:

1. "Minor" means any person less than eighteen years old.

2. "Harmful to minors" means that quality of any description or representation, in whatever form, of violence, when it:

(a) Considered as a whole, appeals to the shameful or morbid interest in violence of minors; and

(b) Is patently offensive to prevailing standards in the adult community as a whole with respect to what is suitable material for minors; and

(c) Considered as a whole, lacks serious literary, artistic, political, and scientific value for minors.

3. "Simulated" means the explicit depiction or description of any of the types of conduct set forth in section I(1)(a) of this statute, which creates the appearance of such conduct. Simulations may include animated presentations.

Here too, a state might also choose to ban certain depictions of violence by or against non-anthropomorphized animals, by amending subsection I(3) to include attacks by animals on persons or other animals.

Indecency

Another way in which the recognition of violent obscenity could have an effect, even if prosecution under an obscenity statute is unlikely, is in the effect such a recognition would have on the regulation of indecency. The recognition that material may be obscene due to its violent depictions opens up the possibility of material being considered not sufficiently violent to be obscene but nonetheless being indecent. The broadcast of such indecent material could be the subject to regulation by the Federal Communications Commission.

Federal Communications Commission v. Pacifica Foundation[39] upheld the Commission's authority to channel the broadcast of indecent material into hours when children were unlikely to be in the audience. While the Court defined "indecent" as "nonconformance with accepted standards of morality,"[40] the arguments of Professors Thomas Krattenmaker and L. A. Powe Jr.[41] that the concept of indecency must be tied to the concept of obscenity seem strong. While they used that position to argue that the FCC's authority to channel did not reach violent material, the recognition of violent obscenity moots the argument.

Krattenmaker and Powe's position that *Pacifica* is limited to material that focuses on sexual or excretory matters rests on the position that only sexual or excretory depiction or descriptions can be obscene. Once it is recognized that material may be obscene because of its violent content, a lesser level of violence can serve as the basis for holding material indecent. The tie of indecency to obscenity, that they believe is required to reconcile *Pacifica* with the earlier cases they examine, will still exist. The Commission, under the *Pacifica* rationale, could channel the broadcast media's use of such material into hours when children are unlikely to be watching. The only restrictions on such channeling would be those that also restrict the ability of the Commission to channel sexually indecent material.

While the possibility of the Commission restricting violence in the same way it may restrict sexual indecency would seem to address much of the public concern over media violence, it has become unclear just what the extent of the Commission's authority is, even in the arena of sexual indecency. The United States Court of Appeals for the District of Columbia Circuit has, several times since *Pacifica*, examined the scope of the authority recognized by that case.[42] In the D.C. Circuit's view, the Commission, in the decade after *Pacifica*, took a limited view of its authority and restricted itself to enforcing the indecency ban only against material involving the repeated use, for shock value, of language similar to that at issue in *Pacifica* and taking no action against the broadcast of indecent material after 10 P.M. In 1987 the Commission expanded its regulation of indecency by limiting the broadcast of such materials to the hours between midnight and 6 A.M. and addressing all indecent material, no longer limiting the application to matter like Carlin's monologue.

The Commission's new regulations were challenged in the first of several cases titled *Action for Children's Television v. Federal Communications Commission,*[43] and referred to in the D.C. Circuit as *ACT I*. The court found the reduction of the "safe harbor period" to midnight through 6 A.M. not to be justified in the record. Specifically, the court noted the Commission had not explained its expansion of the definition of protected "children" from those below twelve years old to adolescents up to seventeen and had only estimated the numbers of teenagers in the audience.[44]

While *ACT I* would only have required further development of the record to support the more restrictive, shorter safe harbor and the increase of the age levels addressed, Congress entered the fray and directed the Commission to enforce the indecency regulations twenty-four hours per day.[45] The round-the-clock restrictions were struck down by the D.C. Circuit in a case referred to as *ACT II*.[46] The court determined that some safe-harbor period was required and directed the Commission to conduct the rulemaking inquiries required under *ACT I*.

Before the Commission could begin the hearings required by *ACT I* and *ACT II*, Congress again intervened, requiring the Commission to establish rules barring indecent material between the hours of 6 A.M. and midnight.[47] The Commission, taking Congress's determination that a midnight to 6 A.M. safe-harbor properly balanced the interests of protections against indecency and the free exchange of ideas as determinative, proceeded with further rule-making to update the record with regard to the government interest in restricting the broadcast of indecent materials. The Commission adopted the congressionally directed restrictions, finding sufficient interests in "(i) 'ensuring that parents have an opportunity to supervise their children's listening and viewing of over-the-air broadcasts,' (ii) 'ensuring the well being of minors' regardless of parental supervision, and (iii) protecting 'the right of all members of the public to be free of indecent material in the privacy of their homes.' "[48]

The newly adopted rules were again challenged, in still another action titled *Action for Children's Television v. Federal Communications Commission*[49] and presumably destined to be referred to as *ACT III*. Because indecent, but not obscene, speech is constitutionally protected, the court applied strict scrutiny and required that the government establish a compelling governmental interest for the restriction of such speech and adopt the least restrictive means to further that interest. The court also found the Commission's articulated interests insufficient to support the rule it had adopted.

With regard to the third interest asserted, that of protecting the interest of even adults to be free from indecent material broadcast into their homes, the court refused to recognize the existence of such an interest. Despite the *Pacifica* Court's concern over the intrusion of the broadcast media into the home and the position that changing the channel after exposure to indecency was an insufficient remedy, the D.C. Circuit concluded that the *Pacifica* decision rested on the effects of indecent material on children. Consulting programming guides was seen as adequate protection for adults, and any occasional unwilling exposure was seen as no different than exposure to offensive material in a bookstore.[50]

The court did recognize the compelling interests asserted in the Commission's two rationales based on the protection of children. Nonetheless, neither was capable of supporting the rules promulgated, because the rules were not sufficiently narrowly tailored to the interests. Narrow tailoring would require the widest safe-harbor period consistent with the protection of children, and the need for a ban from 6 A.M. to midnight was not established.

The court also questioned the Commission's inclusion of all minors in the group needing protection against indecency. The court recognized "a compelling interest in preventing exposure to indecent material of children 'both old enough to understand and young enough to be adversely affected' by the indecent material,"[51] but saw the grounds for restrictions fading as the minor matures. The court concluded:

> When the government affirmatively acts to suppress constitutionally protected material in order to protect teenagers as well as younger children, it must remain sensitive to the expanding First Amendment interests of maturing minors. . . . [E]ven where "patently offensive" material is involved, a seventeen year old does not generally warrant the same degree of governmental protection that may be appropriate for an eight year old.[52]

Lastly, the court could find no evidence in the record that the Commission had tailored its rules sufficiently narrowly to avoid unnecessary infringement on adult First Amendment rights.

Over the following two years *ACT III* was rewritten. The D.C. Circuit vacated the opinion of the three-judge panel and reheard the case *en banc*.[53] In the *en banc* opinion the court largely upheld the FCC's channeling decision. The court noted that while restrictions on broadcast must meet strict scrutiny, factors that make the broadcast media unique must be taken into account. Turning to the issue of a compelling interest, support of parental supervision of children and the government's own interest in the well-being of minors were each seen as meeting that standard. The court rejected the position that psychological harm to minors had to be scientifically demonstrated.[54]

The court was also untroubled by the other issues raised by the panel opinion. The definition of "children" as including those seventeen and under was seen as consistent with other statutes, held to be constitutional, protecting children as similarly defined. The channeling was also held to protect adequately the First Amendment rights of adults and not to create an impermissible chilling effect on "prime time" broadcasts. Further, FCC studies demonstrated that viewing by children drops rapidly as midnight approaches, justifying the FCC delineation of the safe-harbor.

The only aspect of the congressionally directed FCC rule that was altered had the effect of increasing the safe-harbor period. The rule had contained a midnight-to-6 A.M. period but had provided an exception for public television and radio stations that sign off the air at or before midnight. Such stations would have no safe-harbor period, and it had been determined that they should be allowed to broadcast indecent material after 10 P.M. The court determined that the public broadcasting exception could not be justified under the interests that provided the constitutional support for channeling. While a midnight to 6 A.M. period could have been justified, the exception could not. The result was that the court increased the safe-harbor period to 10 P.M. to 6 A.M. for all broadcasters.

It remains to be seen whether this is a play in three *ACT*s. The precise contours of rules for the channeling of indecent broadcasts may not be finally determined. Nonetheless, whatever rules do result for the restriction of sexually indecent material should allow similar restrictions on the broadcast of material that is not violently obscene but sufficiently violent as to be indecent.

Modifying the Moral Climate

The recognition that excessively violent materials may be obscene could also have extralegal effects on the prevalence of violence in the media. The sexual climate in the media is not the maximum the law would allow. While there are producers of very explicit sexually oriented films that border on, or cross the border into, obscenity, the films of major studios do not even approach the legal limits on sexual explicitness. Similarly, the sexual climate on television falls far below the levels mandated by law. Some late-night cable films might be considered indecent, but broadcast fare, even in the early morning hours, does not seem indecent.

It is speculative to suggest the cause of this adherence to standards higher than those imposed by law. For some, the determination not to produce even near-obscene films or broadcast indecent material in the time period allowed may be purely a business decision. While there is a market for obscene and near-obscene films and a television audience for indecent material, there is also a market that insists on less-explicit fare. Some studios and broadcasters may find more profit in the latter market and may believe that consistency in their choice of material helps in the maintenance of a position in that market.

There is, however, a possibility that people simply want to be disassociated from the negative connotations of involvement in even near-obscenity or indecency. Studios or broadcasters that could make a profit from sexually explicit materials may decide not to purvey such material, because if they did so, society would hold them in low regard. It should be noted that concern over lower regard differs from the chilling effect that has concerned the Court. The insistence on clarity in First Amendment law is motivated by a concern that vagueness would lead speakers, publishers, producers, and broadcasters to limit their own speech, even though that speech is in fact protected. It is true that, as a result of societal-regard concerns, there may be some self-suppression of protected speech. There is, however, a major difference, a constitutional difference, between chilling effect and self-suppression over societal regard. Chilling effect is the fear of legal sanctions. The effect suggested here is simply the recognition that such things are simply not done; they are in a sense impolite.

The recognition that excessive violence may be obscene, and lesser levels of violence may be indecent, may bring about similar self-suppression of media violence. It is certainly not inconceivable that an individual, who would never even consider producing or broadcasting sexual obscenity, would have no reticence toward producing or broadcasting excessively violent material. After all, the former is obscene, and obscenity mongers are not well thought of, while the latter has not been considered obscene. The recognition that excessively violent material is, in fact, obscene may lead such a person to avoid violent content for the same reason he or she avoids sexual content.

The same effect might be found among parents. Most parents would not allow their children to view sexually obscene films and, depending on the child's age, will tolerate only some levels of sexual indecency. Despite recent concerns over media violence, the statistics on children's exposure to violence indicate that parents do not exercise as much control in that area. Again the recognition that depictions of violence can be obscene or indecent may lead to more parental restriction on the exposure of their children. Few parents would want to admit that they allow their children to view the near-obscene or even indecent material.

The change in the moral climate that could accompany the recognition of violent obscenity may be more valuable than the legal effects of the law itself. If Sunstein is correct, it is unlikely that there would be many prosecutions under a violent obscenity statute. Given the Federal Communications Commission's difficulties before the D.C. Circuit, it may even be unlikely that the Commission would sanction violent indecency. Nonetheless, those who protest the level of violence in the media would have strength added to their moral stance.

It should be mentioned, once again, that the effects of any change in moral climate are not of legal moment. If the moral climate leads to self-restriction below the limits set by violent obscenity statutes or violent indecency regulations, such discretion is not caused directly enough by the changes in the law as to result in the law's unconstitutionality. The change in the law would simply have caused people to recognize the true obscene or indecent nature of some violent depictions and to decide to avoid depictions that even border on the regulable categories. Their decisions would be moral, not legal, and it would be the improved moral climate, and not the law directly, that would make the world a better place.

Violent Obscenity and the Arts

The arts community is likely to be concerned over the suggestion that violence can be obscene. Certainly, television and motion picture executives have indicated a fondness for First Amendment protections when called to answer for the violent content of their broadcasts and films.[55] Those who would argue against the regulation of violence often point out that even Shakespeare contains violence. The inference seems to be that, since few would argue for restrictions that could affect the works of Shakespeare,[56] violence should be left unrestricted. The argument is faulty for two reasons. First, the violence present in many modern films and television programs goes far beyond most of that present in Shakespeare.[57] More importantly, Shakespeare's works have characteristics that should lead to protection of even the most offensive violence.

The test for a violent obscenity statute capable of standing constitutional muster matches the *Miller* test for the constitutionality of a sexual obscenity statute. Only material, which "taken as a whole lacks serious literary, artistic, political, or scientific value,"[58] may be proscribed as obscene, either as sexual obscenity or violent obscenity. Shakespeare's works clearly have serious literary value and can not be considered obscene.

While writers of Shakespeare's caliber have nothing to fear, those of lesser talent might reasonably be concerned. Their work might not have sufficient value to protect the level of violence they wish to depict. But what is lost from their inability to portray violence in an explicit and offensive way? It might be suggested that violence is necessary to drama, but it is really conflict that would lay the better claim to be foundational. Just as filmmakers have had to learn that the love that is the basis for many literary works is distinguishable from sex, producers of material based on conflict will need to learn the difference between conflict and violence. While love often leads to sex, it is love as a dimension of the human spirit that makes for a literary work, while concentration on sex may make for obscenity. Similarly, while conflict may lead to violence, it is the conflict that makes good drama. The concentration on violence makes for gore and, in the extreme, violent obscenity.

Just as the media can differentiate between a love scene and sexual obscenity, they will come to distinguish between conflict and even a death scene and the butchery that makes a work violently obscene. There should be little lost from the ability to tell a story. It is clear that the First Amendment will not allow an attack on a story line or the position espoused in a book or film. In *Kingsley International Pictures Corp. v. Regents*,[59] the Court held invalid a decision to deny a license to show the film *Lady Chatterley's Lover*. New York law had required such a denial for a film depicting immorality as desirable or proper behavior. The Court said that the message the state found unacceptable could not be the basis for proscription. It is the medium of offensive sexual explicitness, not the message of the acceptability of adultery, that may lead to a finding of obscenity. Much the same distinction was drawn in *Pacifica*. The Court noted that the monologue at issue there did present a point of view, but that "[t]he Commission objects, not to this point of view, but to the way in which it is expressed."[60]

It is difficult to think of a story that cannot be told without offensive levels of violence. It is true that sometimes impact is lost, when the writer or filmmaker is not free to choose his or her medium. The Court, in *Cohen v. California*,[61] recognized that the commentary on the draft emblazoned on Cohen's jacket would have had less emotive impact had the four-letter word been lacking. The Court refused to "indulge the facile assumption that one can forbid particular words without also running a substantial risk of suppressing ideas in the process."[62] That message was, however, protected political commentary. The Court has not shown the same concern over sexually obscene materials. It seems to have recognized that the message can be expressed, even when the medium is suppressed. The same should be true of violent obscenity. The message can be conveyed through a medium of less-violent depictions. While it is admittedly the case that some impact may be lost, that cost has not stopped the development of sexual obscenity law, and violent obscenity law should be treated in the same way.

An important response to this claim is Professor Schauer's observation that violent material is regularly used to make a political point. Despite his recognition that violence might be considered obscene,[63] he argues that, because violence is frequently used to emphasize moral or political arguments, citing as an example the use of vivid depictions of a violent death to stress the horrors of war, it should come within his Free Speech Principle.[64] Once again, however, it must be noted that any work, which, taken as a whole, has serious political value, would not be obscene. The situation is again the same as it is for sexual obscenity, which has also often served as a tool for political and social criticism.[65] While impact may be lost, stories can be told. The loss of that impact is a price the Court has found to be constitutionally acceptable in the area of sexual obscenity, and there is no reason to treat violent obscenity differently.

Violence and the News

It is possible that the recognition of violent obscenity, and its accompanying recognition of violent indecency, could have some effect on news broadcasts. Legitimate news broadcasts should not fear violent obscenity prosecutions. The news certainly has sufficiently serious value to protect even the offensive depiction of violence from such a prosecution. It is unclear how indecency law would interact with the importance of the news. George Carlin's monologue, at issue in *Pacifica*, was social commentary on society's difficulty accepting certain words, yet it was held to be indecent and subject to channeling. It is possible that indecency restrictions might have some effect on how news stories are presented. Furthermore, any change in moral climate making violent depictions less acceptable might have an effect on the broadcasters' decisions on what should be depicted on news broadcasts.

Whatever restrictions, other-imposed or self-imposed, may result probably also exist in the area of sexual obscenity and indecency. If the news media were challenged to uncover evidence of sexual activity of a candidate for office, the media would be likely to show film or photos they might obtain of a meeting between the candidate and a believed sex partner. Suppose, however, that the media came into possession of videotape of an actual sex act involving the candidate and a partner. The question of whether or not that tape would be broadcast or still photos published is more difficult. It is unlikely, given the importance of the political impact such photos might have, that such a broadcast or publication would lack the serious value required to protect against a sexual obscenity prosecution. While indecency regulations might limit broadcast of the tape, such regulations would not speak to newspapers or safe-harbor broadcast. Yet, it is uncertain that the tape or photos would appear. Broadcasters and newspapers have their own standards, and such material might not be deemed to be within the boundaries of "all the news that's fit to print."

The suggested reticence to print what would be sexual obscenity, had value been lacking, may carry over to the issue of violence. News broadcasts already warn viewers of the graphic nature of the depictions of violence or the effects of violence that they are about to broadcast. The warnings would seem to reflect a recognition that some segment of the viewing population finds such depictions at least uncomfortable and perhaps unacceptable. The recognition that violent materials are not simply in bad taste, but that they may be obscene, could lead news broadcasts to choose not to show such footage. Again, it would be unlikely that such a depiction within a legitimate news broadcast could be found violently obscene, but indecency regulations and a changed moral climate might lead to suppression.

This possibility is not untroubling. The depiction of violence or the effects of violence may have extremely important political consequences. A magazine photo of a young, unclothed Vietnamese girl fleeing in terror the destruction of her village brought home the horror of the war to the American people in a way that data on civilian casualties could not. More recently, video of destruction in Bosnia resulted in a call for greater involvement by the rest of the world. Whatever regulations or self-censorship may result from the recognition of violent obscenity and violent indecency must be protective of such depictions.

On the other hand, there appears to be a growing trend in the news to choose stories based on the existence of videotaped violence. Robberies of convenience stores occur with regularity all over the country. Often they go unreported or receive minor mention, even in the cities in which they occur. Yet, if a robbery, especially one that culminates in murder, is captured on videotape, it receives nationwide airing. It might be argued that the issue is the same as that presented by the Vietnam photo. Only the video brings home the impact of crime to the degree necessary to mobilize the public. It may be, however, that the competition the news feels from the entertainment media leads it to choose stories based on their appeal to the public's shameful interest in violence. As has been said, "If it bleeds, it leads." The news would not choose to satisfy the public's interest in sex, even with sexual depictions that are news-relevant but not necessary to the story, because that interest is related to obscenity. Perhaps the recognition that violence can be obscene will lead to different choices in the news' presentation of, in that sense gratuitous, violence as well.

The dangers involved in government control of the news would probably best be addressed by the refusal to regulate in that area. News broadcasts or publications are of sufficient value so as to be protected against obscenity prosecutions. Whatever indecency rules result with regard to sexual indecency and the news may carry over to violence. Whatever those rules may be, a place for serious news reporting and the sex or violence that may be necessary to bring home the impact of the news must be protected. Perhaps the best result is to allow the change in moral climate that might follow the recognition of violent obscenity and violent indecency to do its work. If broadcasters and publishers come to realize that such depictions are morally or socially unacceptable, they will impose some degree of self-regulation. With self-regulation, however, the exceptional story that requires the depiction of violence may be broadcast, while the viewer will, at the same time, be relieved of the burden of seeing every murder that can be found on tape.

Conclusion

The concern the public has come to feel over violence in the media is well-founded. The psychological evidence strongly indicates that the constant exposure to portrayals of violence is a causal factor in aggressive behavior by viewers. The evidence is clearly better than any corresponding evidence on any negative effects from exposure to depictions of sex. Despite the showing of negative effects of media violence, various levels of government have faced difficulty in regulating the amount of violence in the media or even in limiting the exposure of youth to such depictions.

The difficulty has arisen from the belief that depictions of violence, unaccompanied by sufficiently explicit and offensive sex so as to make the material sexually obscene, are protected by the First Amendment. If such depictions are constitutionally protected, restrictions must face strict scrutiny. They must be necessary to, or narrowly tailored to, a compelling governmental interest. While the avoidance of actual violence to the citizenry and the protection of the psychological and moral development of youth appear to be compelling interests, courts have found regulatory statutes lacking in sufficiently close tailoring. There has been an insistence on precision with regard to exactly which depictions lead to the harmful results, and the present state of psychological research appears not to have provided legislators with sufficient understanding to make the fine distinctions required.

The recognition that material may be sufficiently violent so as to be obscene, removes these seemingly insurmountable legislative hurdles. Because sexual depictions that violate community standards for offensiveness and lack value are obscene and unprotected, close tailoring to any supposed effects has not been required. As a result, sexual obscenity law has been allowed to develop, although not without growing pains, and even sexual indecency has been regulated in the broadcast media. Once the category of violent obscenity is established, violent obscenity law can similarly develop, and violent indecency can be regulated in the broadcast media.

Obscenity is a well recognized exception to First Amendment protection. Society has, however, lost sight of what is truly obscene. With regard to sex, the acts themselves are not offensive or disgusting. It is only the public display of those acts or depictions of those acts that society finds offensive. With regard to violence, the acts themselves are offensive and disgusting. Public display or depiction of such acts cannot make them anything but even more offensive.

Obscenity speaks even better to violence than it does to sex. The history of the concept shows the earliest concerns to have been over the depiction of violence. The legal history, at all constitutionally relevant times, fails to distinguish between sex and violence for purposes of obscenity law. It is only the Victorian-era obsession with limiting masturbation, and sex generally, that led to the capture of the word "obscene," and the claim of exclusive use of the word in legal contexts, by the forces opposed to depictions of sex. Those opposed to depictions of violence have just as good a claim to the term and to the legal implications of such a label.

A culture in which sexual expression is suppressed, while violent depictions are permitted, is not a better place than a culture in which the exposure to violence is limited, whatever treatment is accorded sex. It may not be certain that limiting media violence will lead to a more peaceful society. It is certainly likely that any resultant decrease in actual violence would take years to develop. Nonetheless, it is rational to believe that the violence that is pandemic in our society would decrease as a result of a decrease in media violence, and the benefits seem worth the attempt. Something must be done. Restrictions on media violence seem a reasonable step, though not a cure-all, and the recognition that violence may be obscene provides a constitutional basis for such restrictions.

The goal of this work has been to establish a basis in constitutional law and theory for the inclusion of violence within the concept of obscenity. While it has been argued that it would be constitutional to regulate depictions of violence in a way similar to that in which depictions of sex and excretion are now regulated, no list of films thought to be obscene has been presented. It did not seem reasonable to generate such a specific list in an abstract, theoretical work such as this. To be legally obscene, a film must depict acts specifically described by statute. While a statutory form has been presented here, the actual decision on the obscenity of a work will depend on the acts listed in a real statute. A concern for freedom of expression would indicate that that list should be generated with the help of behavioral scientists. Such consultation would not be required, once violence is recognized as obscene, but still would seem wise, as a matter of policy. It is important, however, to note that the conclusions of the scientists would not have to be as certain as has been required by courts operating under the assumption that violence cannot, absent sexual content, be obscene.

A second obstacle to the development of a list of violently obscene films is the role played by community standards. To be obscene, a film or other work must, taken as a whole, appeal to a morbid or shameful interest in violence of the average person, applying contemporary community standards. Similarly, the patent offensiveness of the depiction is also a matter of the community's toleration for violent images. Whatever level of skill in constitutional analysis may be demonstrated in the argument presented in this book probably does not serve to provide the basis for a claim of expertise in community values. The task of developing such standards is left not to the First Amendment theorist but to the community.

The Constitution must, as with sexual materials, set some limitations on governmental attempts to regulate media depictions of violence. As with sexual material, a work which, taken as a whole, has serious artistic, literary, educational, political, or scientific value should be protected. It is in that context that it was indicated that the works of Shakespeare had nothing to fear, since even if they were found to reach offensive levels in their violence, they have serious literary value. That seemed to be an appropriate conclusion to offer in a work of scholarship, since the value of a book, play, or film is not a matter of community standards.

As with sexual obscenity, there will also be the opportunity for the courts to place some limits on the community's setting of standards for prurient interest and offensiveness. In reviewing jury decisions, some standard equivalent to the "hard core" requirement of sexual obscenity will develop. While knowing it when we see it may be the only test, some guidelines will be available as cases are decided. It is true that there may well be some speech chilled, until the lines become clear. However, that concern did not curtail the development of sexual obscenity law and should not do so here. In both cases it is only speech at the periphery of First Amendment protection that faces any potential threat. Core speech relating to the citizen's role in government, all speech with serious value, and even entertainment lacking serious value but not coming close to offensive levels of violence, will remain unaffected.

Notes

Introduction

1 *See* Charles S. Clark, "TV Violence," 3 *CQ Researcher* 167, 175 (no. 12, March 26, 1993).

2 *See id.* at 168.

3 American Psychological Association, *Big World Small Screen: The Role of Television in American Society* 53-54 (1992).

4 *Id.* at 54.

5 *See* Brandon S. Centerwall, "Television and Violence: The Scale of the Problem and Where to Go From Here," 267 *J. of the Am. Med. Assn.* 3059 (no. 22, June 10, 1992).

6 Federal Bureau of Investigation, *Crime in the United States 1991* 10-13 (1992).

7 C. Everett Koop & George D. Lundberg, "Violence in America: A Public Health Emergency," 267 *J. of the Am. Med. Assn.* 3075 (1992).

8 See *Statistical Abstract of the United States 1992* 180 (112th ed.) (comparing 1980 and 1990 data).

9 American Psychological Association, *supra* note 3, at 55 (citing studies published in 1961 and 1963 as the "major initial experimental studies").

10 National Commission on the Causes and Prevention of Violence, *To Establish Justice, To Insure Domestic Tranquility: Final Report of the National Commission on the Causes and Prevention of Violence* (1969).

11 Robert Baker & Sandra Ball, *Mass Media and Violence, Vol. IX: A Report to the National Commission on the Causes and Prevention of Violence* 376 (1969).

12 National Institute of Mental Health, *Television and Behavior: Ten Years of Scientific Progress and Implications for the Eighties* (1982).

13 William H. Deitz & Victor C. Strasburger, "Children, Adolescents, and Television," *Current Problems in Pediatrics* 14 (January 1991).

14 354 U.S. 476 (1957).

15 438 U.S. 726 (1978).

16 This is the position taken in Thomas G. Krattenmaker & L. A. Powe Jr., "Televised Violence: First Amendment Principles and Social Science Theory," 64 *Va. L. Rev.* 1123 (1978).

1   The Public Debate over Media Violence

1   Charles S. Clark, "TV Violence," 3 *CQ Researcher* 167, 168 (no. 12, March 26, 1993).

2   The evidence for a relationship between media violence, particularly television violence, and real world violence is the subject of chapter 2.

3   American Academy of Pediatrics Committee on Communications, "Children, Adolescents, and Television," 85 *Pediatrics* 1119, 1120 (1990).

4   *Id.* at 1119.

5   Testimony of William H. Dietz before the Oversight Hearing on the Television Improvement Act of 1990 of the Senate Judiciary Committee Constitution Subcommittee and Juvenile Justice Subcommittee 5 (June 8, 1993).

6   1993 *AMA Policy Compendium* 428.

7   *See* American Psychological Association, *Big World Small Screen: The Role of Television in American Society* 2 (1992).

8   National PTA, *Position Statement: Mass Media XIV.7B* (Revised and reaffirmed, 1989) (emphasis in original).

9   Statement of Parker Page before the Senate Judiciary Subcommittee on Juvenile Justice and the Government Affairs Subcommittee on Regulation and Government Information Joint Hearing on Video Games: What Parents Need to Know 2 (December 9, 1993).

10   Statement of Robert Chase before the Senate Judiciary Subcommittee on Juvenile Justice and the Government Affairs Subcommittee on Regulation and Government Information Joint Hearing on Video Games: What Parents Need to Know (December 9, 1993).

11   Charles S. Clark, *supra* note 1, at 173.

12   Testimony of Leonard D. Eron before the Oversight Hearing on the Television Improvement Act of 1990 of the Senate Judiciary Committee Constitution Subcommittee and Juvenile Justice Subcommittee 5 (June 8, 1993).

13   Statement of Robert S. Peck before the Senate Judiciary Subcommittee on Juvenile Justice and the Government Affairs Subcommittee on Regulation and Government Information Joint Hearing on Video Games: What Parents Need to Know (December 9, 1993).

14   Statement of Jack Valenti before the Oversight Hearing on the Television Improvement Act of 1990 of the Senate Judiciary Committee Constitution Subcommittee and Juvenile Justice Subcommittee 7 (June 8, 1993).

15   Editorial, "Protected Violence," *Chicago Tribune* Perspective sec. 15 (June 14, 1993) (quoting Mr. Valenti's comments to the Subcommittee on the Constitution of the Senate Judiciary Committee).

16   Robert L. Jackson, "TV Execs Vow Stronger Effort to Reduce Violence," *Los Angeles Times* F2 (May 22, 1993) (quoting Mr. Murphy's comments to the Subcommittee on the Constitution of the Senate Judiciary Committee).

17   Testimony of Stephen W. Palley before the Oversight Hearing on the Television

Improvement Act of 1990 of the Senate Judiciary Committee Constitution Subcommittee and Juvenile Justice Subcommittee 5 (June 8, 1993).

18 Board of Directors, National Association of Broadcasters, *Statement of Principles of Radio and Television Broadcasting* 4 (January 16, 19, 1993).

19 "Turner Blasts TV: Cable Magnate Calls Medium Cause of Violence," *St. Louis Post Dispatch* 1A (June 26, 1993) (quoting Mr. Turner).

20 Charles S. Clark, *supra* note 1, at 175.

21 Oversight Hearing on the Television Program Improvement Act of 1990, U.S. Senate Judiciary Committee, Constitution Subcommittee, May 21, 1993; Oversight Hearing on the Television Program Improvement Act of 1990, U.S. Senate Judiciary Committee Joint Hearing, Constitution Subcommittee, Juvenile Justice Subcommittee, June 8, 1993.

22 Charles S. Clark, *supra* note 1, at 174–75.

23 S. Rep. 62, *Comic Books and Juvenile Delinquency: Interim Report of the Committee on the Judiciary*, 84th Cong., 1st Sess. 7 (1955).

24 *Id.* at 32.

25 *See, e.g., Los Angeles Times, supra* note 16, F2 ("At a House hearing earlier this month, several members of Congress signaled a growing impatience with the industry's effort to police itself. Even Congressional liberals who traditionally oppose censorship have said government restraints may be enacted.").

26 47 U.S.C. sec. 303c (1992).

27 47 U.S.C. 303c(c) (1992). The legislation was necessitated by a federal court ruling that industry self-regulatory rules adopted under Federal Communications Commission persuasion violated both the First Amendment and antitrust law. *See Writers Guild of America v. Federal Communications Commission,* 423 F.Supp. 1064 (C.D.Cal. 1976).

28 S. 973, 103d Cong., 1st Sess. (1993); H.R. 2159, 103d Cong., 1st Sess. (1993).

29 S. 943, 103d Cong., 1st Sess. (1993).

30 H.R. 2883, 103d Cong., 1st Sess. (1993).

31 S. 1383, 103d Cong., 1st Sess. (1993); H.R. 2837, 103d Cong., 1st Sess. (1993).

32 That question will be addressed in chapter 3.

33 S. Rep. 62, *supra* note 23, at 23.

34 Daniel Cerone, "Caging the Beast: Are the Networks Serious About Curbing Violence? An Upcoming Meeting Looms as a Key Test, as a Wary Congress Awaits Action," *Los Angeles Times* Calendar sec. 3 (July 18, 1993).

35 Sen. Paul Simon, Editorial, "If the Broadcasters Won't Dial Down TV Violence, Who Will? Congress is Honing the Sword," *Philadelphia Enquirer* A15 (August 26, 1993).

36 *See* Joel Cooper & Diane Mackie, "Video Games and Aggression in Children," 16 *J. of Applied Social Psych.* 726 (1986).

37 Patricia Brennan, "The Link Between TV and Violence," *Washington Post* Y6 (January 8, 1995).

38   Foundation to Improve Television, *Petition for Rule Making, In the Matter of The Foundation to Improve Television's Proposal to Amend the Commission's Rules to Regulate Television Programming Containing an Excessive Amount of Dramatized Violence and to Alleviate the Harmful Effects of Such Programming* (filed with the Federal Communications Commission, March 25, 1993).

39   Foundation to Improve Television, *Petition for Rulemaking*, RM-1515 (filed with the Federal Communications Commission, October 7, 1969).

40   *See* In re Corey, 37 FCC 2d (1972); In re Grace, 18 Rad. Req. 2d (P&F) 1017 (1970).

41   *Petition of V.I.O.L.E.N.T.*, RM-2140 (filed with the Federal Communications Commission, February 20, 1973).

42   H.R. Rep. No. 1139, 93d Cong., 2nd sess. 15 (1974); S. Rep. No. 1056, 93d Cong., 2nd Sess. 17 (1974).

43   *Report on the Broadcast of Violent, Indecent, and Obscene Material*, 51 FCC 2d 418 (February 19, 1975).

44   47 U.S.C. sec. 326.

45   18 U.S.C. sec. 1464.

46   423 F.Supp. 1064 (C.D.Cal. 1976).

47   The court also found antitrust law problems in the agreement of the NAB and networks to so limit broadcasts. The antitrust aspects were addressed years later, when Congress granted an antitrust exception for discussions among the networks aimed at reducing televised violence. *See* The Television Program Improvement Act of 1990, 47 U.S.C. sec. 303c (1992).

48   Alan M. Schlein, "Quello Talks Tough on Violence," *Hollywood Reporter* (June 18, 1993).

49   Cindy Skrzycki, "FCC Nominee Backs Wider Telecommunications Competition," *Washington Post* C13 (September 23, 1993).

50   Paul Farhi, "Rulemaker for a Revolution: FCC's Reed Hundt Takes on Critics — and a Key Role in Building the Data Highway," *Washington Post* H1 (May 1, 1994).

51   Nat Hentoff, "The FCC and the First Amendment," *Washington Post* A23 (November 26, 1994).

52   *See generally*, Note, "State Restrictions on Violent Expression: The Impropriety of Extending an Obscenity Analysis," 46 *Vand. L. Rev.* 473 (1993).

53   Mo. Rev. Stat. sec. 573.090 (Supp. 1992).

54   413 U.S. 15 (1973).

55   The Supreme Court's decision in *Miller v. California* will be discussed in Chapter 3.

56   Tenn. Code Ann. sec. 39-17-911 (1991).

57   Colo. Rev. Stat. Ann. sec. 18-7-601 (1992).

58   *See* Anne Swardson, " 'Power Rangers' Fight for Life on Canadian TV: TV Network Drops 'Violent' Children's Show," *Washington Post* A1 (November 3, 1994).

59   1884 N.Y. Laws 464-65.

60   1887 N.Y. Laws 899-900.

61 333 U.S. 507 (1948).

62 S. Rep. No. 62, *supra* note 23, at 2-3.

63 Margaret A. Blanchard, "The American Urge to Censor: Freedom of Expression Versus the Desire to Sanitize Society—From Anthony Comstock to 2 Live Crew," 33 *Wm. & Mary L. Rev.* 741, 793 (1992).

64 *See* David Altaner, "Super (Violent) Heroes Plain Old Justice is Out; Brutality is In. Today's Comic Book Good Guys Don't Just Hurt Crooks, They Slaughter Them," *Ft. Lauderdale Sun Sentinel* 1D (August 7, 1993).

65 *See* Paula Span, "The Squeaky-Clean Comics: In a World of Violent Superheroes, Archie is an Anachronism, and His Publishers are Making Sure the Image Sticks," *Washington Post* C1 (July 22, 1989).

66 Blanchard, *supra* note 63, at 792-3.

67 *Id.* at 797.

68 *See supra* notes 46–47 and accompanying text.

69 *See, e.g.,* Judith Barra Austin, "TV Industry Responds to Cranked-Up Volume of Protests of Violence," *Houston Post* A20 (January 16, 1994).

70 Christopher Scanlan, "Networks 'Break Vows' on Violence: Critics Say TV Moguls Ignoring Advisories," *Arizona Republic* E1 (September 19, 1993).

71 Kathleen Best & Tim Poor, "Flood Washed Away Last Year's Priorities: Area Congressional Delegation Returning to Other Issues," *St. Louis Post Dispatch* 1B (January 23, 1994).

72 *See* Ellen Edwards, "Reno: End TV Violence Regulation not Unconstitutional, Panel Told," *Washington Post* A1 (October 21, 1993).

73 S. 332, 104th Cong., 1st Sess. (1995). As this volume went to press, the v-chip portions of S. 332 had been incorporated in both the Senate and House telecommunications bills, S. 652, 104th Cong., 1st Sess. (1995), and H.R. 1555, 104th Cong., 1st Sess. (1995). Both bills passed in their respective houses and have gone to conference. Since the v-chip portions are identical, they should survive conference and become law.

2 The Social Science Debate on the Causative Effect of Media Violence

1 *See* Frederick Schauer, "Causation Theory and the Causes of Sexual Violence," 1987 *Am. B. Found. Res. J.* 737, 754.

2 Robert Baker & Sandra Ball, *Mass Media and Violence, Vol. IX: A Report to the National Commission on the Causes and Prevention of Violence* 376 (1969).

3 *Id.* at 376–77.

4 The Surgeon General's Scientific Advisory Committee on Television and Social Behavior, *Television and Growing Up: The Impact of Televised Violence: Report to the Surgeon General* 7 (1972).

5 National Institute of Mental Health, *Report of the National Institute of Mental Health* 6 (1982).

6   *See* Albert Bandura, Dorothea Ross, & Sheila Ross, "Imitation of Film-Mediated Aggressive Models," 66 *J. of Abnormal & Social Psych.* 3 (1963).

7   Leonard Berkowitz & Joseph T. Alioto, "The Meaning of an Observed Event as a Determinant of Its Aggressive Consequences," 28 *J. of Personality & Social Psych.* 206 (1973).

8   The article reporting the study refers to the track film as "our standard 6-minute movie of a track race." *Id.* at 209. This would appear to be the film of a race between the first two runners to break the four-minute mile that Berkowitz used in other studies. *See, e.g.,* Leonard Berkowitz & Russell G. Geen, *Film Violence and the Cue Properties of Available Targets,* 3 *J. of Personality & Social Psych.* 525, 527 (1966).

9   Leonard Berkowitz & Russell G. Geen, *supra* note 8.

10 *See* Marcia Pally, *Sex & Sensibility: Reflections on Forbidden Mirrors and the Will to Censor* 28–29, 88–93 (1994).

11 *Id.* at 28–29.

12 *Id.* at 95.

13 Leonard Berkowitz & Joseph T. Alioto, *supra* note 7, at 210–12.

14 Marcia Pally, *supra* note 10, at 95.

15 Jonathan L. Freedman, "Effect of Television Violence on Aggressiveness," 96 *Psych. Bulletin* 227 (1984).

16 Lynette Friedrich-Cofer & Aletha C. Huston, "Television Violence and Aggression: The Debate Continues," 100 *Psych. Bulletin* 364 (1986). This article is written in part as a response to Professor Freedman.

17 The studies are cited as J. P. Leyens, R. D. Parke, L. Camino & L. Berkowitz, "Effects of Movie Violence on Aggression in a Field Setting as a Function of Group Dominance and Cohesion," 32 *J. of Personality & Social Psych.* 346 (1975), and R. D. Parke, L. Berkowitz, J. P. Leyens, S. G. West, & R. J. Sebastian, "Some Effects of Violent and Nonviolent Movies on the Behavior of Juvenile Delinquents" in 10 *Advances in Experimental Social Psych.* 135 (L. Berkowitz, ed. 1977).

18 Lynette Friedrich-Cofer & Aletha C. Huston, *supra* note 16, at 365.

19 Jonathan Freedman, *supra* note 15, at 231.

20 *Id.*

21 *Id.* at 234.

22 Lynette Friedrich-Cofer & Aletha C. Huston, *supra* note 16, at 366.

23 *Id.*

24 *See* Brandon S. Centerwall, "Television and Violence: The Scale of the Problem and Where to Go From Here," 267 *J. Am. Med. Assn.* 3059 (no. 22, June 10, 1992). Centerwall's article discusses his 1989 paper's findings and predictions and later evidence he believes backs up both.

25 L. A. Joy, M. M. Kimball, & M. I. Zabrack, "Television and Children's Aggressive Behavior" in *The Impact of Television: A Natural Experiment in Three Communities* 303 (T. M. Williams, ed. 1986).

26   This point is made by Marcia Pally in her criticism of the social science evidence for television-induced aggression. *See* Marcia Pally, *supra* note 10, at 108–9.

27   *Id.* at 109.

28   *Id.* at 112.

29   Monroe M. Lefkowitz, Leonard D. Eron, Leopold O. Walder, & L. Rowell Huesmann, "Television Violence and Child Aggression: A Followup Study" in *Television and Social Behavior: Reports and Papers, Vol. III: Television and Adolescent Aggressiveness* 35 (George Comstock & Eli Rubinstein, eds. 1972).

30   *Id.* at 49. The statistical methods used in arriving at this conclusion were questioned by Professor David Kenny. He did, however, also conclude that the data, using what he took to be the proper approach, did demonstrate that violent television causes aggression, but with a lesser degree of statistical significance. David Kenny, "Threats to the Internal Validity of Cross-Lagged Panel Inference, as Related to 'Television Violence and Child Aggression: A Followup Study'" in *Television and Social Behavior: Reports and Papers, Vol. III: Television and Adolescent Aggressiveness* 136 (George Comstock & Eli Rubinstein, eds. 1972). Professor John Neale, using still different techniques, also found support for the original conclusion. John Neale, "Comment on 'Television Violence and Child Aggression: A Followup Study'" in *Television and Social Behavior: Reports and Papers, Vol. III: Television and Adolescent Aggressiveness* 141 (George Comstock & Eli Rubinstein, eds. 1972).

31   This argument is similar to that made by Professor William McGuire, who expresses concern that a murder scores no higher as an incidence of violence than pushing or restraining a person, slapstick comic violence, and cartoon conflicts. *See* William J. McGuire, *The Myth of Massive Media Impact: Savagings and Salvagings* in 1 *Public Communication and Behavior* 173, 191 (George Comstock, ed. 1986).

32   *See* Jonathan L. Freedman, *supra* note 15, at 243.

33   *See* Lynette Friedrich-Cofer & Althea C. Huston, *supra* note 16, at 368.

34   Stanley Milgram & R. Lance Shotland, *Television and Antisocial Behavior: Field Experiments* (1973).

35   The Milgram and Shotland experiment may be criticized for its choice of antisocial behavior to measure. The authors needed a "crime" that did not do any real harm, and the box was not really the charity's, but was still significant. However, "robbing the poorbox" may be viewed more seriously by the subjects than the experimenters may have realized.

36   George Comstock & Haejung Paik, *Report to the National Research Council: The Effects of Television Violence on Aggressive Behavior: A Meta-Analysis* (1990).

37   George Comstock & Haejung Paik, *The Effects of Television Violence on Aggressive Behavior: A Meta-Analysis*, 21 *Communications Res.* 516 (1994).

38   *See* Marcia Pally, *supra* note 10, at 93–97.

39   *See id.* at 110–11.

40   Even the examination of the direction of causation offered by Lefkowitz, et al.,
     see supra notes 29–30 and accompanying text, is really an examination of dif-
     ferences in correlation. While it speaks to causation, what is demonstrated is a
     difference in correlation.
41   *See, e.g.,* P. Mandel, L. Ciesielski, M. Maitre, S. Simler, G. Mack, & E. Kempf,
     "Involvement of Central GABA-ergic Systems in Convulsions and Aggressive Be-
     havior" in *GABA — Biochemistry and CNS Function* 475 (Paul Mandel & Francis
     DeFeudis, eds. 1979).
42   *Id.* at 484–88.
43   The result is reported in a book by two-time Pulitzer-Prize-winning science
     writer Jon Franklin, now a professor at the University of Oregon. Jon Franklin,
     Molecules of the Mind 157 (1987). Franklin's report is based on an interview with
     Professor Mandel. Carl Sagan and Ann Druyan also report Mandel's result but
     base their report on Franklin. Carl Sagan & Ann Druyan, *Shadows of Forgotten
     Ancestors* 236 (1992).
44   Donald Roberts & Christine Bachen, "Mass Communication Effects," 32 *Ann.
     Rev. Psych.* 307, 342 (1981).
45   S. 332, 104th Cong., 1st Sess. (1995).
46   140 Cong. Rec. S2035 (daily ed. Feb. 2, 1995) (Statement of Sen. Conrad) (quoting
     a Guggenheim Foundation study titled "Violence in Society").
47   *Id.*

3   First Amendment Limitations

1   315 U.S. 568 (1942).
2   343 U.S. 250 (1952).
3   376 U.S. 254 (1964).
4   *See, e.g., Curtis Publishing Co. v. Butts,* 388 U.S. 130 (1967).
5   354 U.S. 476 (1957).
6   354 U.S. at 482. The decisions cited are discussed in chapter 5.
7   The statutes, cases, and policy arguments are discussed in detail in chapter 5.
8   354 U.S. at 487 n.20 (quoting *Webster's New International Dictionary* (Unabridged,
     2d ed., 1949).
9   *Id.* (quoting *American Law Institute, Model Penal Code* sec. 207.10(2) (Tent. Draft
     No. 6, 1957)).
10   354 U.S. at 489.
11   383 U.S. 413 (1966).
12   383 U.S. at 418.
13   383 U.S. 463 (1966).
14   413 U.S. 15 (1973).
15   413 U.S. at 24 (citations omitted).
16   481 U.S. 497 (1987).

17   481 U.S. at 501.

18   The academic criticism of the obscenity exception will be discussed in chapter 7.

19   William B. Lockhart & Robert C. McClure, "Censorship of Obscenity: The Developing Constitutional Standards," 45 *Minn. L. Rev.* 5 (1960).

20   *Id.* at 85.

21   383 U.S. 502 (1966).

22   The James-Lange theory of the experience of emotions, discussed in chapter 7, is of interest here. The theory holds that the pathway from visual stimulus to effect on the conscious brain is from stimulus to the limbic portions of the brain, then directly to the body, and finally back to the brain in the conscious brain's recognition of the effects of the stimulus on the body. With material designed for a sexually deviant group, the pathway is the same for a member of that group as it would be for ordinary obscenity and an average person. As a result, the deviant group could have their prurient interests aroused and still find the material offensive. The average person may well be offended, but the limbic response would be lacking and the combination of appeal to the prurient interest and offense would be missing.

23   390 U.S. 629 (1968).

24   390 U.S. at 633 (quoting N.Y. Penal Law sec. 484(h)). The statute also addressed, in the same section, the sale of magazines containing such pictures. The Court also cited obscenity statutes from thirty-five states containing provisions regarding distribution to minors. *See* 390 U.S. at 647 (App. B).

25   *Id.* (quoting N.Y. Penal Law sec. 484-h(f)(1)). The subsection in its entirety read as follows:

1. Definitions. As used in this section:

. . .

(f) "Harmful to minors" means that quality of any description or representation, in whatever form, of nudity, sexual conduct, sexual excitement, or sadomasochistic abuse, when it:

(i) predominantly appeals to the prurient, shameful or morbid interest of minors, and

(ii) is patently offensive to prevailing standards in the adult community as a whole with respect to what is suitable material for minors, and

(iii) is utterly without redeeming social importance for minors.

N.Y. Penal Law sec. 484-h (quoted in 390 U.S. at 645–46).

26   There was also a challenge based on vagueness, but the Court noted that the statutory definition matched the requirements for defining adult obscenity as presented in *Memoirs v. Massachusetts,* 383 U.S. 413 (1966).

27   390 U.S. at 641 (quoting N.Y. Penal Law sec. 484-e).

28   390 U.S. at 641.

29   390 U.S. at 643 (quoting Noble State Bank v. Haskell, 219 U.S. 104, 110 (1911)).

30   The actual charges in *Schenck v. United States,* 249 U.S. 47 (1919), and *Debs v.*

United States, 249 U.S. 211 (1919), involved obstruction of recruitment in violation of espionage laws, but the claim of obstruction was based on leaflets and speeches, and the complaint appears more one of sedition.

31   395 U.S. 444 (1969).

32   458 U.S. 747 (1982).

33   773 F.Supp. 1275 (W.D. Mo. 1991), aff'd, 968 F.2d 684 (8th Cir. 1992).

34   *Video Software Dealers Ass'n v. Webster,* 968 F.2d 684 (8th Cir. 1992).

35   No. 90-1893-III(I) (Tenn. Chanc. Feb. 14, 1992).

36   Tenn. Code Ann. sec. 39-17-901(4) (1991).

37   *Allied Artists Pictures Corp. v. Alford,* 410 F.Supp. 1348, 1357 (W.D. Tenn. 1976) (emphasis added).

38   Tenn. Code Ann. secs. 39-17-911(b), 39-17-914 (1991).

39   *See, e.g., Hamling v. United States,* 418 U.S. 87, 123–24 (1974).

40   *Mishkin v. New York,* 383 U.S. at 511.

41   *Davis-Kidd Booksellers, Inc. v. McWherter,* 866 S.W.2d 520 (Tenn. 1993).

42   866 S.W.2d at 532.

43   438 U.S. 726 (1978).

44   438 U.S. at 731 (citing 18 U.S.C. sec. 1464 (1976)).

45   438 U.S. at 731 (citing sec. 303(g) of the Communications Act of 1934, 48 Stat. 1082, as amended, as set forth in 47 U.S.C. sec. 303(g)).

46   438 U.S. at 739 (citing the *Webster's Third New International Dictionary* (1966), defining "indecent" as "altogether unbecoming: contrary to what the nature of things or what circumstances would dictate as right or expected or appropriate: hardly suitable: UNSEEMLY . . . : not conforming to generally accepted standards of morality.").

47   438 U.S. at 735.

48   438 U.S. at 739.

49   S. 1383, 103d Cong., 1st Sess. (1993); H.R. 2837, 103d Cong., 1st Sess. (1993); S. 332, 104th Cong., 1st Sess. (1995).

50   Thomas G. Krattenmaker & L. A. Powe Jr., "Televised Violence: First Amendment Principles and Social Science Theory," 64 *Va. L. Rev.* 1123 (1978).

51   393 U.S. 503 (1969).

52   422 U.S. 205 (1975).

53   *See, e.g.,* Note, "View at Your Own Risk: Gang Movies and Spectator Violence," 12 *Loyola L.A. Ent. L.J.* 477 (1992) (detailing incidents in which gang violence has arguably been triggered by gang movies).

54   *See, e.g., Pope v. Illinois,* 481 U.S. 497 (1987); *Erznoznik v. Jacksonville,* 422 U.S. 205 (1975); *Miller v. California,* 413 U.S. 15 (1973); *Memoirs v. Massachusetts,* 383 U.S. 413 (1966).

55   403 U.S. 15 (1971).

56   403 U.S. at 20.

57   422 U.S. 205, 213 n.10 (1975).

4   The Concept of Obscenity

1   William B. Lockhart & Robert C. McClure, "Literature, the Law of Obscenity, and the Constitution," 38 *Minn. L. Rev.* 295, 320–21 (1954).

2   *Id.* 320–21.

3   354 U.S. 476 (1957).

4   Joel Feinberg, *Offense to Others*, 2 *The Moral Limits of the Criminal Law* 97–98 (1985).

5   *Id.* at 98.

6   *Id.* at 127.

7   *Id.* at 97–126.

8   *Id.* at 107 (citing Peter Glassen, " 'Charientic' Judgments," *Philosophy* 138 (April, 1958)).

9   *Id.* at 109 (emphasis in original).

10 *Id.*

11 *Id.* at 124–25 (emphasis in original).

12 *Id.* at 115.

13 *Id.* at 112.

14 *Id.* at 113.

15 David A. J. Richards, "Free Speech and Obscenity Law: Toward a Moral Theory of the First Amendment," 123 *U. Pa. L. Rev.* 45, 51 (1974).

16 *Oxford English Dictionary* (1971).

17 Samuel Johnson, *A Dictionary of the English Language* (4th ed. London 1773).

18 *See, e.g.,* Harry M. Clor, *Obscenity and Public Morality: Censorship in a Liberal Society* 210 (1969); Andrea Dworkin, "Against the Male Flood," 8 *Harv. Women's L.J.* 1, 7 (1985).

19 Harry M. Clor, *supra* note 18, at 210 (citing Havelock Ellis, *On Life and Sex* 100 (1947)). *See also* William B. Lockhart & Robert C. McClure, *supra* note 1, at 321 (citing Havelock Ellis, "The Revaluation of Obscenity" in Havelock Ellis, *More Essays in Love and Virtue* 100 (1931)).

20 *See, e.g.,* Walter Allen, *To Deprave and Corrupt* 147 (1962) ("Obscenity seems originally to have meant that which could not be represented upon the stage. It is related to ancient Greek theories of drama.") (quoted in Richard H. Kuh, *Foolish Figleaves? Pornography in — and out of — Court* 335–36 n.1 (1967)).

21 Sheldon H. Nahmod, "Adam, Eve and the First Amendment: Some Thoughts on the Obscene as Sacred," 68 *Chi.-Kent L. Rev.* 377, 378 (1992). Interestingly, Professor Nahmod's justification is perhaps unique in not being applicable to depictions of violence, which few would argue are sacred experiences that would be cheapened by media depictions.

22 Harry M. Clor, *supra* note 18, at 225.

23 *Id.* at 231 (quoting Joseph Heller, *Catch 22* 449–50).

24 *Id.* at 234.

25   That is not to say that subhuman, animal life is garbage. Films can quite movingly depict the death of an animal, but do so most effectively when they focus on the spirit of the animal. To the degree that the animal has spirit, that is in the higher animals, scenes of animal mutilation, like slasher films, might be viewed as obscene.

26   Harry M. Clor, *supra* note 18, at 225.

27   *Id.*

28   *Id.*

29   *Id.* at 226.

30   *Id.* at 225.

31   *Id.* at 230.

32   *See* Joel Feinberg, *supra* note 4, at 125 (arguing that public executions are obscene spectacles, because they intrude on privacy and violate personal dignity).

33   Harry M. Clor, *supra* note 18, at 245.

34   *Id.*

35   Joel Feinberg, *supra* note 4, at 117 (citing Havelock Ellis, *On Life and Sex* 175 (1947)).

36   *Id.*

37   David Tribe, *Questions of Censorship* 32 (1973) (quoting D. Lawrence, *Pornography and Obscenity* 5–6 (1929)).

38   Aristophanes, *The Clouds* in *Four Plays by Aristophanes* 71 (William Arrowsmith, Richard Lattimore, & Douglass Parker, trans. 1984).

39   *Id.* at 127.

40   *Id.* at 157–58 n.63.

41   The lines spoken by Aristophanes in Arrowsmith's translation may instead be assigned to the Chorus speaking for the author. *See id.* at 156–57 n.61.

42   *Id.* at 63.

43   *Id.* at 160 n.90.

44   *Id.* at 90–91.

45   *Id.* at 91.

46   Aristophanes, *Lysistrata* in *Four Plays by Aristophanes, supra* note 38.

47   *Id.* at 406–7.

48   *Id.* at 419.

49   *Id.* at 434–35.

50   *Id.* at 444–45.

51   H. Montgomery Hyde, *A History of Pornography* 10 (1964).

52   Aristophanes, *Lysistrata* (Robert Henning Webb, trans. 1963).

53   *Id.* at 85. The German accent appears to have been employed to indicate that the Spartan dialect differed from the Athenian. *See id.* at 7 n.10. Parker's translation employs a back-woods accent to the same end.

54   *Id.* at 91.

55   *Id.* at 94.

56 H. Montgomery Hyde, *supra* note 51, at 40 (citing James C. N. Paul & Murray L. Schwartz, *Federal Censorship* 104 (1961)).

57 *See, e.g.,* H. C. Baldry, *The Greek Tragic Theatre* 50 (1971) ("The ancient Greeks were not squeamish about violence or death: from the *Iliad* onwards bloodshed was a commonplace in narrative poetry.").

58 Sophocles, *Electra* in *The Complete Plays of Sophocles* 37 (Sir Richard Claverhouse Jebb, trans., Moses Hadas, ed. 1967).

59 *Id.* at 71.

60 *See, e.g.,* Charles Segal, "Violence and Dramatic Structure in Euripides' *Hecuba,*" in *Violence in Drama* 35, 35 (James Redmond, ed. 1991) ("Greek drama, on the whole, avoids the direct visual depiction of violence on the stage.").

61 Roy C. Flickinger, *The Greek Theater and Its Drama* 127–28 (4th ed. 1936).

62 Peter D. Arnott, *An Introduction to the Greek Theatre* 22 (1959).

63 Peter D. Arnott, *Greek Scenic Conventions in the Fifth Century B.C.* 130 (1962); Roy C. Flickinger, *supra* note 61, at 129.

64 Comments are based on Rex Warner's translation found in *Euripides* (David Grene & Richard Lattimore, eds. 1955).

65 Peter D. Arnott, *supra* note 62, at 22 ("It is usually held that Greek taste forbade the representation of death in view of the audience.").

66 Roy C. Flickinger, *supra* note 61, at 130.

67 The translation employed here is that of William Arrowsmith and is found in *Euripides III* (David Grene & Richard Lattimore, eds. 1958).

68 J. Michael Walton, *Greek Theatre Practice* 135 (1980).

69 *Id.* at 135–36.

70 *See* Lionel Cassen, "Introduction" in *Aeschulus, The Orestea Trilogy and Prometheus Unbound* xi–xii (Michael Townsend, trans. 1966).

71 *See* Sophocles, *Ajax,* in *The Complete Plays of Sophocles* 1 (Sir Richard Claverhouse Jebb, trans., Moses Hadas, ed. 1967).

72 Comments are based on Philip Vellacott's translation. *See Euripides, Orestes and Other Plays* 189 (Philip Vellacott, trans. 1972).

73 Roy C. Flinkinger, *supra* note 61, at 129 ("The rule of Greek dramaturgy which has just been described is liable to one notable exception—the dramatic characters may not commit murder before the eyes of the spectators but they may commit suicide there."); *id.* at 132 ("[T]he taboo . . . prevented one actor from murdering another upon the stage. But this taboo did not protect an actor against himself or against the assaults of nature or of the gods. Hence suicides and natural deaths were permissible within the audience's sight, though homicides were not.").

74 Notes to *Ajax* in *The Complete Plays of Sophocles, supra* note 71, at 1.

75 Richard C. Beacham, *The Roman Theatre and Its Audience* (1991).

76 *Id.* at 4–5.

77 *Id.* at 129.

78 *Id.* at 54.

79   *Id.* at 30.
80   *Id.* at 91.
81   *Id.* at 124.
82   *Id.* at 31.
83   Sheldon Cheney, *The Theatre: Three Thousand Years of Drama, Acting and Stagecraft* 102 (4th ed. 1972).
84   Richard C. Beacham, *supra* note 75, at 136.
85   Sheldon Cheney, *supra* note 83, at 104.
86   Richard C. Beacham, *supra* note 75, at 136.
87   *Id.* at 137.
88   Sheldon Cheney, *supra* note 83, at 103–4.
89   John S. Gatton, " 'There Must Be Blood': Mutilation and Martyrdom on the Medieval Stage," in *Violence in Drama, supra* note 60, at 79, 79.
90   *Id.* at 80.
91   While public execution as entertainment would speak to the issue of what has historically been considered obscene, it may still be argued on other grounds that such execution is obscene. Feinberg takes such a position. *See* Joel Feinberg, *supra* note 4, at 117. Feinberg also finds double obscenity in public reaction to a public execution. "Public hangings before huge crowds are obscene spectacles even when the crowd is appropriately solemn, insofar as they are intrusions upon privacy and violations of personal dignity. When the crowd is boisterous and lustful for blood, the spectacle is doubly obscene, as both intrusive and inappropriately responsive." *Id.* at 125.
92   John S. Gatton, *supra* note 89, at 80.
93   *See generally* Jonas Barish, "Shakespearean Violence: A Preliminary Survey" in *Violence in Drama, supra* note 60, at 101.
94   *Id.* at 102.
95   *Id.* at 110.
96   *See id.* at 102.
97   *Id.*
98   *Id.* at 104–7.
99   *See* Roy C. Flickinger, *supra* note 61, at 131.
100   *See* Jonas Barish, *supra* note 93, at 102.
101   Eberhard & Phyllis Kronhausen, *Pornography and the Law* 66–67 (1964).
102   Roy C. Flickinger, *supra* note 61, at 130 (quoting Thomas R. Lounsbury, *Shakespeare as a Dramatic Artist* 175 (1902)) (emphasis in Flickinger).
103   John M. Callahan, "The Ultimate in Theatre Violence," in *Violence in Drama, supra* note 60, at 165, 165 (quoting "Speaking of Pictures," 22 *Life* 15 (April 28, 1947)).
104   Frederick F. Schauer, *Free Speech: A Philosophical Enquiry* 179 (1982).
105   *See* Joel Feinberg, *supra* note 4, at 122–23.
106   *Id.* at 125.

107   *Id.* at 115–16.

108   *Id.* at 116.

109   Harry M. Clor, *supra* note 18, at 234.

110   *Id.* at 225.

111   Richard C. Beacham, *supra* note 75, at 25.

112   *Id.* at 133.

113   249 U.S. 47 (1919).

114   249 U.S. 211 (1919).

115   341 U.S. 494 (1951).

116   354 U.S. 298 (1957).

117   367 U.S. 203 (1961).

118   367 U.S. 290 (1961).

119   *See United States v. Spock,* 416 F.2d 165 (1st Cir. 1969).

120   Richard C. Beacham, *supra* note 75, at 25.

121   Leonard Levy, *Blasphemy: Verbal Offense Against the Sacred, from Moses to Salman Rushdie* (1993).

5   The History of Obscenity Law and the Development of Its Limitation to Depictions of Sex

1   It has, for example, been suggested that the Eighth Amendment ban on cruel and unusual punishment is meant to evolve along with changing perceptions of humane justice. *See, e.g., Gregg v. Georgia,* 428 U.S. 153, 171–73 (1976); Furman v. Georgia, 408 U.S. 238, 429–30 (Powell, J., dissenting).

2   463 U.S. 783 (1983).

3   403 U.S. 602 (1971).

4   463 U.S. at 790.

5   463 U.S. at 790–91.

6   276 U.S. 394 (1928).

7   276 U.S. at 412.

8   423 U.S. 411 (1976).

9   389 U.S. 347 (1967).

10   428 U.S. 153 (1976).

11   315 U.S. 568 (1942).

12   315 U.S. at 571–72.

13   343 U.S. 250 (1952).

14   354 U.S. 476 (1957).

15   354 U.S. at 482.

16   *See* 354 U.S. at 482 n.12.

17   354 U.S. at 483 (citing 1712 Mass. Bay Acts & Laws, ch. CV, sec. 8, 1814 Mass. Bay Colony Charters & Laws 399).

18   1784 Conn. Pub. Acts 66, 67.

19   *Id.*

20   1737 Act Against Drunkenness, Blasphemy; and to Prevent the Grevious Sins of Prophane Cursing, Swearing and Blasphemy, secs. 4, 5, 1797 Del. Laws 173, 174.

21   *Id.* at sec. 4.

22   *Id.* at sec. 5.

23   1786 Act to Regulate Taverns, and to Suppress Vice and Immorality, Digest of the Laws of Ga. 512, 513 (Prince 1822).

24   Act of 1723, ch. 16, sec. 1, Digest of the Laws of Md. 92 (Herty 1799).

25   *Id.*

26   1646 Mass. Bay General Laws & Liberties, ch. XVIII, sec. 3, 1814 Mass. Bay Colony Charters & Laws 58.

27   *Id.*

28   Act of 1782, ch. 8, 1836 Mass. Rev. Stat. 741, sec. 15.

29   Act of 1798, ch. 33, secs. 1, 3, 1836 Mass. Rev. Stat. 741, sec. 16.

30   *Id.*

31   1791 Act for the Punishment of Certain Crimes Not Capital, 1792 N.H. Laws 252, 256.

32   1791 Act for the Punishment of Profane Cursing and Swearing, 1792 N.H. Laws 258.

33   *Id.*

34   The word "profane" is said to be derived from "in front of a temple." *See* David Tribe, *Questions of Censorship* 19 (1973).

35   1798 Act for Suppressing Vice and Immorality, secs. VIII, IX, 1800 N.J. Rev. Laws 329, 331.

36   1788 Act for Suppressing Immorality, sec. IV, 2 N.Y. Laws 257, 258 (Jones & Varick 1777-89).

37   8 Johns. 290 (N.Y. 1811).

38   1741 Act for the Better Observation and Keeping of the Lord's Day, Commonly Called Sunday, and for the More Effectual Suppression of Vice and Immorality, sec. III, 1 N.C. Sess. Laws 52 (Martin Rev. 1715-1790).

39   *Id.* at sec. II.

40   *Id.* at secs. IV, V.

41   1700 Act to Prevent the Grievous Sins of Cursing and Swearing, II Pa. Statutes at Large 49 (1700-1712).

42   *Id.*

43   1794 Act for the Prevention of Vice and Immorality, sec. II, 3 Pa. Laws 177, 178 (1791-1802).

44   *Id.*

45   1798 Act to Reform the Penal Laws, secs. 33, 34, 1798 R.I. Pub. Laws 584, 595.

46   1703 Act for the More Effectual Suppressing of Blasphemy and Prophaneness, 1790 S.C. Laws 4.

47   *Id.*

48 *Id.*

49 1797 Act, for the Punishment of Certain Capital, and Other High Crimes and Misdemeanors, sec. 20, 1 Vt. Laws 332, 339 (Tolman 1808).

50 *Id.*

51 1797 Act, for the Punishment of Certain Inferior Crimes and Misdemeanors, sec. 20, 1 Vt. Laws 352, 361 (Tolman 1808).

52 1792 Act for the Effectual Suppression of Vice, sec. 1, 1794 Va. Acts 286.

53 354 U.S. at 483 (quoting 1712 Mass. Bay Acts & Laws, ch. CV, sec. 8, 1814 Mass. Bay Colony Charters & Laws 399).

54 1712 Mass. Bay Acts & Laws, ch. CV, sec. 8, 1814 Mass. Bay Colony Charters & Laws 399.

55 Frederick F. Schauer, *The Law of Obscenity* 1–2 (1976).

56 Morris Ernst & Alan Schwartz, *The Search for the Obscene* 8–9 (1964).

57 David Tribe, *supra* note 34, at 19.

58 Frederick F. Schauer, *supra* note 55, at 2.

59 David Tribe, *supra* note 34, at 19–20. Tribe does note an alternate derivation of "obscene" as adverse or ill-omened and that "pornography" is more focused on sexual material as derived from writing about harlots.

60 Frederick F. Schauer, *supra* note 55, at 3.

61 *See, e.g.*, Frederick F. Schauer, *supra* note 55, at 4; Leo M. Alpert, "Judicial Censorship of Obscene Literature," 52 *Harv. L. Rev.* 40, 40–41 (1938).

62 83 Eng. Rep. 1146 (K.B. 1663). The case is also reported at 82 Eng. Rep. 1036 (K.B. 1663).

63 Leonard Levy, *Blasphemy: Verbal Offense Against the Sacred, from Moses to Salman Rushdie* 214 (1993).

64 Accounts of the acts leading up to the case may be found in Leo M. Alpert, *supra* note 61, at 41–42; Frederick F. Schauer, *supra* note 55, at 4; Leonard Levy, *supra* note 63, at 214.

65 Frederick F. Schauer, *supra* note 55, at 4.

66 83 Eng. Rep. at 1146.

67 88 Eng. Rep. 953 (Q.B. 1708). The rule set forth in *Read* was later overruled by *Dominus Rex v. Curll*, 93 Eng. Rep. 849 (K.B. 1727).

68 Leo M. Alpert, *supra* note 64, at 43.

69 88 Eng. Rep. at 953.

70 Fortescue's Reports 98, 92 Eng. Rep. 777 (1708) (second report of *Queen v. Read*).

71 Leonard Levy, *supra* note 63, at 306.

72 93 Eng. Rep. 849 (K.B. 1727).

73 Frederick F. Schauer, *supra* note 55, at 5.

74 Leo M. Alpert, *supra* note 64, at 44.

75 Leonard Levy, *supra* note 63, at 307.

76 *Id.*

77 Frederick F. Schauer, *supra* note 55, at 6.

78   The *King v. John Wilkes*, 95 Eng. Rep. 737 (K.B. 1764).

79   Frederick F. Schauer, *supra* note 55, at 6.

80   Leo M. Alpert, *supra* note 64, at 44.

81   *Id.* at 45.

82   Leo M. Alpert, *supra* note 64, at 47. Alpert's summary might be read so as not to conclude that there was not even a focus on sex. Even after the focus on sexual and excretory activities became clear in *Roth* and its progeny, Justice Stewart still could not define obscenity, but knew it when he saw it rather than smelled it. *See Jacobellis v. Ohio*, 378 U.S. 184, 197 (1964) (Stewart, J., concurring).

83   354 U.S. at 483.

84   1798 Act for Suppressing Vice and Immorality, sec. XII, 1800 N.J. Rev. Laws 329, 331.

85   *Id.* The statute did allow the exhibition of natural curiosities and of plays found by three justices of the peace to be innocent and of useful end. *Id.*

86   *Id.*

87   1821 Act Concerning Crimes and Punishments, sec. 69, 1824 Conn. Stat. Laws 109.

88   *Id.*

89   1835 Mass. Rev. Stat., ch. 130, sec. 10, 1836 Mass. Rev. Stat. 740.

90   1842 Rev. Stat., ch. 113, sec. 2, 1843 N.H. Rev. Stat. 221.

91   *Id.*

92   3 Day 103 (Conn. 1808).

93   3 Day at 103 (emphasis in original).

94   3 Day at 103 (emphasis in original).

95   3 Day at 107.

96   3 Day at 108.

97   3 Day at 108.

98   Harry M. Clor, *Obscenity and Public Morality: Censorship in a Liberal Society* 225 (1969).

99   *Id.* at 234.

100   2 Serg. & Rawle (Pa.) 91 (1815).

101   2 Serg. & Rawle at 91–92.

102   2 Serg. & Rawle at 91.

103   2 Serg. & Rawle at 101. Chief Justice Tilghman relied on the English conviction of Sir Charles Sedley for standing naked on a balcony in London. While the Chief Justice recognized that Sir Charles had also thrown down bottles of urine on the crowd below, he concluded that the conviction rested primarily on his "exposure of his person." *Id.* This reading of the case may be questioned, and in any case, simple nudity would not fit current definitions of obscenity.

104   2 Serg. & Rawle at 102.

105   2 Serg. & Rawle at 103.

106   17 Mass. 335 (1821).

107   Frederick F. Schauer, *supra* note 55, at 6.

108   *Id.* at 7.

109   L.R. 3 Q.B. 360 (1868).

110   3 Q.B. at 371.

111   *Id.*

112   Frederick F. Schauer, *supra* note 55, at 7.

113   *Id.* at 10–11 (quoting *State v. Rose*, 32 Mo. 560 (1862); *State v. Gardner*, 28 Mo. 90 (1859)).

114   354 U.S. at 481.

115   96 U.S. 727, 736–37 (1877).

116   135 U.S. 255, 261 (1890).

117   194 U.S. 497, 508 (1904).

118   227 U.S. 308, 322 (1913).

119   327 U.S. 146, 158 (1946).

120   165 U.S. 275, 281 (1897).

121   283 U.S. 697, 716 (1931).

122   315 U.S. 568, 571–72 (1942).

123   343 U.S. 250, 266 (1953).

124   333 U.S. 507, 510 (1948).

125   *See* 354 U.S. at 481 n.9.

126   161 U.S. 446 (1896).

127   354 U.S. at 485.

128   5 Stat. 548, 566 (1842).

129   11 Stat. 168 (1857).

130   13 Stat. 504, 507 (1865).

131   17 Stat. 302 (1872).

132   17 Stat. 598 (1873).

133   *Id.*

134   *Id.*

135   19 Stat. 90 (1876).

136   25 Stat. 187, 188 (1888).

137   25 Stat. 496 (1888).

138   26 Stat. 567, 614–15 (1890).

139   *Id.*

140   29 Stat. 512 (1897).

141   33 Stat. 705 (1905).

142   35 Stat. 1129 (1909).

143   35 Stat. 1138 (1909).

144   41 Stat. 1060 (1920).

145   46 Stat. 688 (1930).

146   *Id.*

147   48 Stat. 1091 (1934).

148   48 Stat. 1100 (1934).

149   62 Stat. 768 (1948). Section 1461 of the statute codified 35 Stat. 1129, sec. 211. The statute also codified 33 Stat. 705 (1905), as amended by 35 Stat. 1138 (1909) and 41 Stat. 1060 (1920), and 35 Stat. 1129, sec. 212 (1909). The statute became 18 U.S.C. secs. 1461–64, *see infra* note 153 and accompanying text.

150   64 Stat. 194 (1950).

151   64 Stat. 451 (1950).

152   69 Stat. 183 (1955).

153   18 U.S.C. sec. 1461.

154   354 U.S. at 485 (citing Agreement for the Suppression of the Circulation of Obscene Publications, 37 Stat. 1511; Treaties in Force 209 (U.S. Dept. State October 31, 1956)).

155   Agreement for the Repression of the Circulation of Obscene Publications, signed at Paris, May 4, 1910, entered into force, September 15, 1911, 37 Stat. 1511.

156   Morris Ernst, *The First Freedom* 17 (1946).

157   17 Stat. sec. 598 (1973). The current version of the statute is found at 18 U.S.C. sec. 1461. As noted, there are earlier federal obscenity statutes.

158   Morris Ernst, *supra* note 156, at 17–18.

159   Frederick F. Schauer, *supra* note 55, at 18 (citing *United States v. Davis*, 38 F. 326 (W.D. Tenn. 1889); *United States v. Olney*, 38 F. 328 (W.D. Tenn. 1889)).

160   161 U.S. 446 (1896).

161   Frederick F. Schauer, *supra* note 55, at 19.

6   The Law and Depictions of Violence

1   354 U.S. 476 (1957).

2   354 U.S. at 482–83 (citation and footnotes omitted).

3   354 U.S. at 483.

4   3 Day 103 (Conn. 1808).

5   3 Day at 103.

6   354 U.S. at 482.

7   354 U.S. at 485.

8   161 U.S. 446 (1896).

9   Frederick F. Schauer, *The Law of Obscenity* 19 (1976).

10   Morris L. Ernst, *The First Freedom* 17 (1946).

11   Morris L. Ernst & Alan U. Schwartz, *Censorship: The Search for the Obscene* 29 (1964).

12   See *Winters v. New York*, 333 U.S. 507, 520 n.1 (Frankfurter, J., dissenting).

13   Frederick F. Schauer, *supra* note 9, at 12.

14   1884 N.Y. Laws 464–65.

15   1887 N.Y. Laws 899–900.

16   333 U.S. 507 (1948). The statute was found at the time of *Winters* at New York Consolidated Laws, ch. 40, sec. 1141.

17   1885 Mass. Acts 758.

18   1885 Minn. Laws 330–31.

19   1885 Mo. Laws 146–47.

20   1885 Me. Laws 291.

21   1885 Ohio Laws 184.

22   *Id.*

23   1885 Or. Laws 126–27 (banning the distribution to minors of "any book, pamphlet, magazine, newspaper or other printed paper devoted to the publication, or principally made up of criminal news, police reports, or of criminal deeds or pictures and stories of deeds of bloodshed, lust or crime.").

24   1885 Mich. Pub. Acts 155–56.

25   1885 Conn. Pub. Acts 433 (banning the distribution of "any book, magazine, pamphlet or paper devoted wholly or principally to the publication of criminal news, or pictures and stories of deeds of bloodshed, lust or crime.").

26   1885 Colo. Sess. Laws 172–73.

27   1886 Iowa Acts 217–19.

28   1886 Kan. Sess. Laws 137.

29   1887 Neb. Laws 671–74.

30   1887 Pa. Laws 84–85 (barring materials "devoted to the publication, or principally made up of criminal news, police reports, or accounts of criminal deeds, or pictures and stories of deeds of bloodshed, lust or crime.").

31   1889 Ill. Laws 114 (barring materials "devoted to the publication, or principally made up of criminal news, police reports, or accounts of criminal deeds, or pictures and stories of deeds of bloodshed, lust or crime.").

32   1891 Mont. Laws 255–56 (barring materials "devoted to the publication or principally made up of criminal news, police reports or accounts of criminal deeds or pictures and stories of lust or crime.").

33   1894 Ky. Acts 3–4.

34   1894 Md. Laws 360–61.

35   1895 N.D. Laws 122.

36   *Id.*

37   1895 Ind. Acts 230.

38   161 U.S. 446 (1896).

39   Frederick F. Schauer, *supra* note 9, at 19.

40   1897 Tex. Gen. Laws 160–61.

41   333 U.S. 507, 523 (Frankfurter, J., dissenting).

42   1901 Wis. Laws 348–49 (barring materials "devoted principally to the publication of criminal news, police reports, or accounts of criminal deeds, or pictures and stories of bloodshed, lust or crime.").

43   1909 Wash. Laws 951.

44   1913 S.D. Laws 334–35.

45   161 U.S. at 449 (citing Revised Statutes sec. 3893).

46 161 U.S. at 450.

47 161 U.S. at 451.

48 161 U.S. at 451.

49 N.Y. Penal Law, sec. 1141(2) (1941).

50 *People v. Winters*, 48 N.Y.S.2d 230, 231 (App. Div., 1st Dept. 1944).

51 *Id.*

52 48 N.Y.S.2d at 232.

53 48 N.Y.S.2d at 233 (quoting *People v. Most*, 171 N.Y. 423, 431 (1902)).

54 63 N.E.2d 98 (N.Y. Ct. App. 1945).

55 63 N.E.2d at 100 (citations omitted).

56 63 N.E.2d at 100–101.

57 333 U.S. 507 (1948).

58 333 U.S. at 513.

59 333 U.S. at 519.

60 333 U.S. at 519.

61 333 U.S. at 520.

62 333 U.S. at 520.

63 333 U.S. at 519.

64 333 U.S. at 520.

65 43 N.E. 622 (1896).

66 333 U.S. at 511–12.

67 46 A. 409 (Conn. 1900).

68 333 U.S. at 522–23 (Frankfurter, J., dissenting). As Justice Frankfurter noted, the Connecticut statute he cited had been repealed by the time the *Winters* decision issued.

69 333 U.S. at 523 (Frankfurter, J., dissenting).

70 333 U.S. at 523–24 (Frankfurter, J., dissenting).

71 Ill. Ann. Stat. ch. 720, sec. 670(1) (Smith-Hurd 1995).

72 Mich. Comp. Laws Ann. sec. 750.41 (1995).

73 S. Rep. 62, *Comic Books and Juvenile Delinquency: Interim Report of the Committee on the Judiciary* 84th Cong., 1st Sess. 2–3 (1955).

74 *Id.* at 7.

75 *Id.* at 8–10.

76 *See* John Hoskins, "Comment, Delinquency, Comic Books and the Law," 18 *Ohio St. L.J.* 512, 521 (1957) (citing Council of State Governments, *Suggested Legislative Program for 1957* 105–7).

77 *Id.*

78 Maryland Code, 1957, article 27, secs. 420–25, as amended by ch. 197 of the Acts of 1959.

79 162 A.2d 727 (Ct. App. Md. 1960).

80 162 A.2d at 727.

81 1955 Wash. Laws, ch. 282, 1231.

82   322 P.2d 844 (Wash. 1958).

83   354 U.S. 436 (1957).

84   341 P.2d 310 (Cal. 1959).

85   *See* 341 P.2d at 313.

86   *See* 341 P.2d at 313.

87   341 P.2d at 315.

88   354 U.S. at 437.

89   1950 N.Y. Laws 1450-52.

90   *Id.*

91   354 U.S. at 438 (emphasis added).

92   *Burke v. Kingsley Books,* 142 N.Y.S.2d 735, aff'd, 134 N.E.2d 461 (N.Y. App.), aff'd, 354 U.S. 437 (1957).

93   142 N.Y.S.2d at 741 (quoting *United States v. Kennerley,* 209 F. 119, 121 (S.D.N.Y. 1913)).

94   142 N.Y.S.2d at 741.

95   142 N.Y.S.2d at 742.

96   142 N.Y.S.2d at 742.

97   142 N.Y.S.2d at 742.

98   142 N.Y.S.2d at 742.

99   142 N.Y.S.2d at 742.

100   142 N.Y.S.2d at 742.

101   *See, e.g., Kingsley Int'l Pictures v. Regents,* 360 U.S. 684 (1959) (portraying sexual immorality as acceptable or proper behavior not in itself obscene); *American Booksellers Ass'n v. Hudnut,* 771 F.2d 323 (7th Cir. 1985) (pornography statutes may not select among viewpoints), aff'd, 475 U.S. 1001 (1986).

102   354 U.S. at 438.

103   Richard H. Kuh, *Foolish Figleaves? Pornography in—and out of—Court* 44 (1967) (footnote omitted).

104   773 F.Supp. 1275 (W.D. Mo. 1991), aff'd, 968 F.2d 684 (8th Cir. 1992).

105   *Video Software Dealers Association v. Webster,* 968 F.2d 684 (8th Cir. 1992).

106   333 U.S. at 508, 510.

107   968 F.2d at 688.

108   333 U.S. at 520.

109   413 U.S. 15, 24 (1973).

110   354 U.S. at 487.

111   422 U.S. 205 (1975).

112   968 F.2d at 688 (quoting *Erznoznik v. Jacksonville,* 422 U.S. at 213 n.10).

113   968 F.2d at 688 (citation omitted).

114   866 S.W.2d 520 (Tenn. 1993).

115   410 F.Supp. 1348 (W.D. Tenn. 1976).

116   410 F.Supp. at 1350 (citing Memphis Code of Ordinances, secs. 22-23.1 to 22-23.4).

117   *Id.*

118   410 F.Supp. at 1355–56.

119   410 F.Supp. at 1357.

120   448 F.Supp. 306 (N.D. Ohio 1977), remanded on other grounds, 610 F.2d 428 (1979).

121   Ohio Revised Code sec. 2907.32.

122   Ohio Revised Code sec. 2907.01(F).

123   448 F.Supp. at 400 (citation omitted).

124   413 U.S. at 20 n.2.

125   *Id.*

126   403 U.S. 15 (1971).

7   Sex, Violence, and First Amendment Policy

1   354 U.S. 476, 484 (1957).

2   354 U.S. at 484 (quoting 1 *Journals of the Continental Congress* 108 (1774)).

3   Alexander Meiklejohn, *Free Speech and Its Relation to Self-Government* 22–26 (1948).

4   *Id.* at 36–37.

5   Meiklejohn suggests that members of Congress did more damage to President Wilson's peace plans than was, or could have been, done by those charged in the dissident trials of the era. *Id.* at 36.

6   *Id.* at 38–39.

7   *Id.* at 39.

8   Vincent Blasi, "The Checking Value in First Amendment Theory," 1977 *Am. B. Found. Res. J.* 521, 527. Blasi cites the same letter to the inhabitants of Quebec cited by the *Roth* opinion. *Id.* at 535.

9   *Id.* at 527.

10   *Id.* at 548.

11   *Id.* at 551–52.

12   *Id.* at 561–62. Professor Blasi's view fits nicely with the examination of the role of the people in government presented by Bruce Ackerman in his book *We the People: Foundations* (1991). According to Ackerman the people are not regular participants in government. Ordinarily the people let the government take care of the business of running the country, and even such participation as voting is most often done with little real reflection. It is only in extraordinary situations that the people become involved in constitutional moments in which we speak as "We the People" and take the reins of government. While Blasi's checking value appears to visualize more frequent application than Ackerman's constitutional moments, Ackerman's views do seem to favor a Blasi approach to that of Meiklejohn.

13   *Id.* at 528.

14   *Id.*

15   *Id.* at 553.

16   Vincent Blasi, "The Pathological Perspective and the First Amendment," 85 *Colum. L. Rev.* 449 (1985).

17   *Id.* at 449–50.

18   *Id.* at 476–77.

19   *Id.* at 478.

20   *Id.* at 477.

21   *Id.* at 479 (footnote omitted).

22   *See* Zechariah Chafee, *Free Speech in the United States* 33 (1941). "The First Amendment protects two kinds of interests in free speech. There is an individual interest, the need of many men to express their opinions on matters vital to them if life is to be worth living, and a social interest in the attainment of truth, so that the country may not only adopt the wisest course of action but carry it out in the wisest way."

23   Alexander Meiklejohn, *supra* note 3, at 62.

24   It should be noted that Meiklejohn's protections based on self-government did have a fairly wide scope. The protection went beyond the public discussion of governance issues to include all phases of education, philosophy, science, literature, and the arts. *See* Alexander Meiklejohn, "The First Amendment Is an Absolute," 1961 *Sup. Ct. Rev.* 245, 257.

25   That is not to say that sexually obscene material never has any social or political content. Pornography has often been a vehicle for challenging the social status quo and questioning government, often mixing issues of sex with political questions. The conviction of John Wilkes, discussed in chapter 5, is illustrative. While he was convicted of publishing sexual obscenity, he was a political critic of the government, and that criticism seems to have provided the real motive to prosecute.

26   494 U.S. 624 (1990).

27   494 U.S. at 632.

28   501 U.S. 1030 (1991).

29   501 U.S. at 1034–35 (quoting *Butterworth v. Smith,* 494 U.S. at 632).

30   491 U.S. 397 (1989).

31   491 U.S. at 411 (citations omitted).

32   391 U.S. 563 (1968).

33   391 U.S. at 573.

34   376 U.S. 254 (1964).

35   391 U.S. at 574.

36   487 U.S. 474 (1988).

37   487 U.S. at 479 (quoting *New York Times Co. v. Sullivan,* 376 U.S. at 270, other citations omitted).

38   458 U.S. 886 (1982).

39   458 U.S. at 915 (quoting *Henry v. First National Bank of Clarksdale,* 595 F.2d 291, 303 (1979)).

40   424 U.S. 1 (1976).
41   424 U.S. at 39 (quoting *Williams v. Rhodes*, 393 U.S. 23, 32 (1968)).
42   333 U.S. 507 (1948).
43   333 U.S. at 510.
44   438 U.S. 726 (1978).
45   438 U.S. at 743 (footnote and citations omitted).
46   501 U.S. 560 (1991).
47   501 U.S. at 566.
48   413 U.S. 15 (1973).
49   413 U.S. at 24.
50   354 U.S. at 484 (footnote omitted).
51   *Id.*
52   315 U.S. 568 (1942).
53   354 U.S. at 485 (quoting 315 U.S. at 571–72 (emphasis added in *Roth v. United States*)).
54   Frederick F. Schauer, *Free Speech: A Philosophical Enquiry* (1982).
55   *Id.* at 89–90.
56   *Id.* at 92–95.
57   Schauer does not argue that all communication is within the scope of his Free Speech Principle. He suggests that most performative uses of language are not so protected. In fact, it could even be argued that such utterances are not communicative or at least are only in part communicative, in which case only the communicative portion would be within the scope of the Free Speech Principle. Also excludable, he suggests, are what he calls "propositional wrongs," such as perjury or fraud. *See id.* at 102.
58   Frederick F. Schauer, *supra* note 55, at 109.
59   *Id.* at 110.
60   *Id.* at 104–5.
61   *Id.* at 181.
62   *Id.*
63   *Id.* (footnote omitted). Joel Feinberg takes a similar position. He classifies hardcore pornographic pictures as nothing more than devices designed to excite the sex organs and says "it would be as absurd to think of them as speech or art as it would to think of . . . mechanical devices made solely to stimulate erotic feelings, in the same manner." Joel Feinberg, *The Moral Limits of the Criminal Law, Volume Two: Offense to Others* 169 (1985).
64   Frederick F. Schauer, *supra* note 55, at 182.
65   Havelock Ellis, "The Revaluation of Obscenity" in Havelock Ellis, *More Essays in Love and Virtue* 100, 130 (1931).
66   Frederick F. Schauer, *supra* note 55, at 182.
67   *Id.*
68   *Id.* (emphasis in original).

69 See, e.g., Neil R. Carlson, *Physiology of Behavior* 350–51 (5th ed. 1994).

70 As scientific evidence for the theory Professor Carlson cites studies of individuals with spinal cord injuries. The intensity of their emotional feelings was weaker the higher in the spine the injury occurred and thus the larger the part of the body to which they were insensitive. *Id.* at 350. While Carlson does not explain why that effect might not be due to a lack of physical effects in the body, resulting from the spinal injury, rather than the lack of sensitivity to the effects, the conclusion would appear to be the same. The process by which emotions are felt is not self-contained within the brain but requires feedback from physiological responses.

71 Schauer's position has been characterized as arguing "that because pornography goes straight to the genitals without passing through intellectual processes it is better characterized as sex than speech." Deana Pollard, "Regulating Violent Pornography," 43 *Vand. L. Rev.* 125, 135–36 (1990).

72 Frederick F. Schauer, *supra* note 55, at 179.

73 *Id.* at 185.

74 See, e.g., Cass Sunstein, *Democracy and the Problem of Free Speech* 210 (1993). There are many puzzles in the *Miller* test. For one thing, the test seems to require an odd psychological state from the judge and jury. In order to be regulable, the materials must be simultaneously sexually arousing (the "prurient interest" part of the test) and "patently offensive." This is not an unrecognizable psychological state, but it entails a certain dissonance, and a certain attitude about sexuality, that are likely to be unusual or at least to be rarely confessed.

75 *Id.*

76 See *id.* at 8–11.

77 *Id.* at 130 (emphasis omitted).

78 *Id.* at 11.

79 Cass Sunstein, "Pornography and the First Amendment," 1986 *Duke L.J.* 589, 603–4 (footnotes omitted).

80 *Id.* at 606; Cass Sunstein, "Low Value Speech Revisited," 83 *Nw. U. L. Rev.* 555, 560 n.18 (1989).

81 Larry Alexander, "Low Value Speech," 83 *Nw. U. L. Rev.* 547, 550 (1989).

82 *Id.*

83 Cass Sunstein, *supra* note 74, at 155.

84 *Id.* at 211.

85 *Id.*

86 *Id.* at 209.

87 *Id.* at 224–25.

88 *Abrams v. United States*, 250 U.S. 616, 630 (1919) (Holmes, J., dissenting).

89 Lee C. Bollinger, *The Tolerant Society* 107 (1986).

90 *Id.* at 185.

91 *Id.*

92   366 U.S. 36 (1961).

93   366 U.S. at 61 (Black, J., dissenting). Justice Black added a footnote on Madison's view:

> James Madison . . . indicated clearly that he did not understand the Bill of Rights to permit any encroachments upon the freedoms it was designed to protect. "If they [the first ten amendments] are incorporated into the Constitution, independent tribunals of justice will consider themselves in a peculiar manner the guardians of those rights; they will be an impenetrable bulwark against every assumption of power in the Legislative or Executive; they will be naturally led to resist every encroachment upon rights expressly stipulated for in the Constitution by the declaration of rights." *Id.* at 61 n.11 (citing 1 *Annals of Congress* 439 (1789)).

94   *Id.* at 64.

95   *Id.* at 68.

96   *Id.* at 66–67.

97   Alexander Meiklejohn, *supra* note 24.

98   Cass Sunstein, *supra* note 74, at 126.

99   *Id.* at 127–28.

100 Edward de Grazia, *Girls Lean Back Everywhere: The Law of Obscenity and the Assault on Genius* (1992).

101 *See* C. Edwin Baker, *Human Liberty and Freedom of Speech* (1989); C. Edwin Baker, "Scope of the First Amendment Freedom of Speech," 25 *UCLA L. Rev.* 964 (1978).

102 C. Edwin Baker, *Human Liberty and Freedom of Speech, supra* note 101, at 54.

103 Even if Baker's position with regard to sexual obscenity were to become the law, it is possible that a violent obscenity exception could survive. Professor Baker would not protect all speech. He recognizes exceptions for coercive speech, forms of espionage, and other varieties of speech that cause more direct harm. *Id.* at 56–66. His basis for protecting speech is that speech furthers autonomy in a non-violent manner. C. Edwin Baker, "Scope of the First Amendment Freedom of Speech," *supra* note 101, at 990. Perhaps the tie of violent obscenity to violence in viewers could distinguish the two varieties of obscenity, although it is a distinction Baker would seem unlikely to accept, since whatever violence results does so through an effect on the mind and emotions of the viewer.

8   Violence and the Feminist Concern with Pornography

1   *See* Caryn Jacobs, "Patterns of Violence: A Feminist Perspective on the Regulation of Pornography," 7 *Harv. Women's L.J.* 5, 23 (1984); *see also* Andrea Dworkin, "Against the Male Flood: Censorship, Pornography, and Equality," 8 *Harv. Women's L.J.* 1, 9 (1985) ("The insult pornography offers, invariably, to sex

is accomplished in the active subordination of women: the creation of a sexual dynamic in which the putting down of women, the suppression of women, and ultimately the brutalization of women, *is* what sex is taken to be.").

2   Caryn Jacobs, *supra* note 1, at 24.

3   Richard Delgado & Jean Stefancic, "Pornography and Harm to Women: 'No Empirical Evidence?,'" 53 *Ohio St. L.J.* 1037, 1045 (1992).

4   *American Booksellers Ass'n v. Hudnut,* 771 F.2d 323, 328 n.1 (7th Cir. 1985), aff'd, 475 U.S. 1001 (1986) (quoting Catharine A. MacKinnon, "Pornography, Civil Rights, and Speech," 20 *Harv. C.R.-C.L. L. Rev.* 1, 17–18 (1985)).

5   Caryn Jacobs, *supra* note 1, at 19.

6   Catharine A. MacKinnon, "Pornography as Defamation and Discrimination," 71 *B.U. L. Rev.* 793, 802 (1991).

7   *Id.* at 804.

8   *Id.* at 798.

9   *Id.* at 799.

10 *Id.* at 800 (footnotes omitted).

11 Nadine Strossen, "A Feminist Critique of 'The' Feminist Critique of Pornography," 79 *Va. L. Rev.* 1099 (1993).

12 *Id.* at 1103.

13 *Id.* at 1107 (footnotes omitted).

14 *Id.* at 1111–12.

15 771 F.2d 323 (7th Cir. 1985), aff'd, 475 U.S. 1001 (1986).

16 475 U.S. 1001 (1986).

17 771 F.2d at 324 (quoting Indianapolis Code sec. 16-3(q)).

18 771 F.2d at 325.

19 771 F.2d at 326 (quoting Indianapolis Code sec. 16-3(g)(7)).

20 771 F.2d at 326 (quoting Indianapolis Code sec. 16-17(b)).

21 771 F.2d at 324.

22 771 F.2d at 325.

23 *Id.* (quoting Catharine A. MacKinnon, *supra* note 4, at 21).

24 *Id.*

25 771 F.2d at 328.

26 771 F.2d at 329.

27 771 F.2d at 330–31.

28 771 F.2d at 331. The court offered several Supreme Court opinions in support of this proposition. It took as such a case the Court's determination in *Buckley v. Valeo,* 424 U.S. 1 (1976): it is unconstitutional to limit campaign expenditures, even though the rules were designed to make it easier for candidates to answer each other's speech. Similarly, the Court noted that *Mills v. Alabama,* 384 U.S. 214 (1966), held unconstitutional a statute prohibiting election day editorials, even though the statute was designed to prevent speech that was printed so late as to be unanswerable.

29   771 F.2d at 331.

30   The court also briefly considered the possibility that the materials affected by the ordinance could be considered group libel. While *Beauharnais v. Illinois,* 343 U.S. 250 (1952), allowed proscription of group libel, the court concluded that later cases had so weakened *Beauharnais* that it could no longer be considered authoritative. The court also said that, even if *Beauharnais* is still authoritative, it was not clear that the materials addressed by the ordinance constituted group libel. "Work must be an insult or slur for its own sake to come within the ambit of *Beauharnais,* and a work need not be scurrilous at all to be 'pornography' under the ordinance." 771 F.2d at 332 n.3.

31   112 S.Ct. 2538 (1992).

32   112 S.Ct. at 2541 (quoting St. Paul, Minn. Legis. Code sec. 292.02 (1990)).

33   In re Welfare of R.A.V., 464 N.W.2d 507, 510 (Minn. 1991).

34   315 U.S. 568 (1942).

35   464 N.W.2d at 511.

36   112 S.Ct. at 2543.

37   112 S.Ct. at 2545.

38   112 S.Ct. at 2547.

39   *Id.*

40   112 S.Ct. at 2548.

41   112 S.Ct. at 2549.

42   475 U.S. 41 (1986).

43   112 S.Ct. at 2549 (footnote omitted).

44   *The Report of the Commission on Obscenity and Pornography* 27 (1970).

45   Edward Donnerstein, Daniel Linz, & Steven Penrod, *The Question of Pornography: Research Findings and Policy Implications* 72 (1987).

46   *Id.* at 51.

47   *Id.* at 107.

48   Edward Donnerstein, Daniel Linz, & Steven Penrod, *supra* note 45, at 62–65, provide an overview of the Court's results.

49   *Id.* at 61–62.

50   *Id.* at 73.

51   Berl Kutchinsky, "The Politics of Pornography Research," 26 *Law & Society Rev.* 447 (1992).

52   *Id.*

53   *Id.* at 66–68, 73.

54   Edward Donnerstein, Daniel Linz, & Steven Penrod, *supra* note 45, at 118 (citing the report of National Commission on the Causes and Prevention of Violence (1969)).

55   The scientific studies on the aggression-causing effects of media violence are discussed in chapter 2.

56   Attorney General's Commission on Pornography, *Final Report* 323 (1986).

57   *See, e.g.,* Daniel Linz, Steven Penrod, & Edward Donnerstein, "The Attorney General's Commission on Pornography: The Gaps Between 'Findings' and Facts," 1987 *Am. B. Found. Res. J.* 713, 716.

58   Attorney General's Commission on Pornography, *supra* note 56, at 326.

59   Frederick F. Schauer, "Causation Theory and the Causes of Sexual Violence," 1987 *Am. B. Found. Res. J.* 737, 750.

60   *Id.* at 758–59 n.49.

61   *Id.* at 765 (emphasis in original) (footnotes omitted).

62   Edward Donnerstein, Daniel Linz, & Steven Penrod, *supra* note 45, at 108–36. For a more concise overview of the research and a discussion of their work, *see* Steven Alan Childress, "Reel 'Rape Speech': Violent Pornography and the Politics of Harm," 25 *Law & Society Rev.* 177 (1991).

63   Edward Donnerstein, Daniel Linz, & Steven Penrod, *supra* note 45, at 110.

64   *Id.*

65   Deana Pollard, "Regulating Violent Pornography," 43 *Vand. L. Rev.* 125, 129 (1990).

66   Edward Donnerstein, Daniel Linz, & Steven Penrod, *supra* note 45, at 118.

67   *Id.* at 114 (quoting J. Maslin, "Bloodbaths Debase Movies and Audiences," *N.Y. Times* (Nov. 11, 1982)).

68   Daniel Linz, Steven Penrod, & Edward Donnerstein, *supra* note 57, at 721 (emphasis in original).

69   Ronald Slaby, "Combating Television Violence," *Chronicle of Higher Education* sec. 2, p. 1, 2 (January 5, 1994). Dr. Slaby was a member of the American Psychological Association Commission on Youth and Violence.

70   *Id.* Dr. Slaby notes that the belief with regard to strangers does not correspond to reality, where the main source of violence is one's partner, family, and acquaintances.

71   *See, e.g.,* George Gerbner & Larry Gross, "Living with Television: The Violence Profile," 26 *J. of Communication* 173 (1976); George Gerbner, Larry Gross, Michael Eleey, Marilyn Jackson-Beeck, Suzanne Jeffries-Fox, & Nancy Signorielli, "Violence Profile No. 8: The Highlights," 27 *J. of Communication* 171 (1977); George Gerbner, Larry Gross, Michael Eleey, Marilyn Jackson-Beeck, Suzanne Jeffries-Fox, & Nancy Signorielli, "Cultural Indicators: Violence Profile No. 9," 28 *J. of Communication* 176 (1978).

72   W. James Potter, "Perceived Reality and the Cultivation Hypothesis," 30 *J. of Broadcasting & Electronic Media* 159, 159 (1986) (citing R. P. Hawkins & S. Pingree, "Television's Influence on Social Reality" in *Television and Behavior: Ten Years of Scientific Progress and Implications for the Eighties* 224, 244 (D. Pearl, L. Bouthilet, & J. Lazar, eds. 1982)).

73   Anthony Doob & Glenn Macdonald, "Television Viewing and Fear of Victimization: Is the Relationship Causal?," 37 *J. of Personality & Social Psych.* 170 (1979).

74   *Id.* at 175.

75   *Id.* at 177.

76 *Id.*

77 *Id.* at 179.

78 Glenn Sparks & Robert Ogles, "The Difference Between Fear of Victimization and the Probability of Being Victimized: Implications for Cultivation," 34 *J. of Broadcasting & Electronic Media* 351 (1990).

79 W. James Potter, *supra* note 72, at 168.

80 While the chance of being a murder victim in the relevant year was actually 11 in 100,000, adolescents estimated the chances as 4,251 in 100,000, and college-age subjects estimated the chances as 563 in 100,000. *Id.* at 169–70.

81 *Id.* at 171–72.

82 Ronald Slaby, *supra* note 69, at 1.

83 *See* Elayne Rapping, "Make Room for Daddy," 57 *Progressive* no. 11, p. 1 (Nov. 1993).

84 *See* Nina Burleigh, "Backlash May Indicate Success," *Chicago Tribune* Tempo-woman section p. 2 (April 21, 1991) (reviewing Joan Smith, *Misogynies: Reflections on Myths and Malice* (1989)).

9 Statutes and Implications

1   354 U.S. 476 (1957).

2   354 U.S. at 484.

3   383 U.S. 413 (1966).

4   The *Memoirs* test was presented in a plurality opinion. There were, however, other justices who would have been even more protective of material charged to be obscene. Since the justices in the plurality had to be drawn away from the justices who would protect obscene material in order to affirm a conviction, the *Memoirs* test provided a working definition for a period of seven years, until it was replaced by a majority definition.

5   413 U.S. 15 (1973).

6   481 U.S. 497 (1987).

7   Professor Childress notes that only a two-word change in the usual obscenity test is required to include materials that are "patently offensive *violent* images which appeal to an unhealthy interest in *violence* and are without serious social value." Steven Alan Childress, "Reel 'Rape Speech': Violent Pornography and the Politics of Harm," 25 *Law & Society Rev.* 117, 204 (1991) (emphasis in original).

8   354 U.S. at 487 n.20 (quoting *Webster's New International Dictionary* (Unabridged, 2d ed., 1949)).

9   354 U.S. at 486 n.20 (quoting A.L.I., Model Penal Code, sec. 207.10(2) (Tent. Draft No. 6, 1957)).

10 Mo. Rev. Stat. sec. 573.090 (Supp. 1992). The Missouri statute is discussed in chapters 1 and 3.

11 Tenn. Code Ann. sec. 39-17-911 (1991).

12   Colo. Rev. Stat. Ann. sec. 18-7-601 (1992).

13   773 F.Supp. 1275 (W.D. Mo. 1991), aff'd, 968 F.2d 684 (8th Cir. 1992).

14   Tenn. Code Ann. sec. 39-17-901(4) (1991).

15   *Davis-Kidd Booksellers, Inc. v. McWherter*, 866 S.W.2d 520 (Tenn. 1993).

16   333 U.S. 507 (1948).

17   N.Y. Penal Law, sec. 1141(2) (1941).

18   48 N.Y.S.2d 230, 232 (1944).

19   63 N.E.2d 98, 100 (N.Y. Ct. App. 1945).

20   341 P.2d 310 (Cal. 1959).

21   *See* 341 P.2d at 312-13.

22   *See* 341 P.2d at 312.

23   *See Police Commissioner v. Siegel Enterprises*, 162 A.2d 727 (Ct. App. Md. 1960); *Adams v. Hinkle*, 322 P.2d 844 (Wash. 1958).

24   The fact that violence is presented in comic-book format may have some effect on the application of a test for violent obscenity. Where material is aimed at juveniles, a different standard, the "obscene as to youth" standard, may apply. The presentation in comic form may well speak to the intended audience.

25   413 U.S. at 25 (emphasis added).

26   For example, Louisiana defines the crime of obscenity to include:

Participation or engagement in, or management, operation, production, presentation, performance, promotion, exhibition, advertisement, sponsorship, or display of, hard core sexual conduct when the trier of fact determines that the average person applying contemporary community standards would find that the conduct, taken as a whole, appeals to the prurient interest; and the hard core sexual conduct, as specifically defined herein, is presented in a patently offensive way; and the conduct taken as a whole lacks serious literary, artistic, political, or scientific value.

La. Rev. Stat. Ann. sec. 14-106(A)(2)(a) (West 1995). To provide the specificity required by *Miller*, the statute goes on to define "hard core sexual conduct":

(b) Hard core sexual conduct is the public portrayal, for its own sake, and for ensuing commercial gain of:

(i) Ultimate sexual acts, normal or perverted, actual, simulated, or animated, whether between human beings, animals, or an animal and a human being; or

(ii) Masturbation, excretory functions or lewd exhibition, actual, simulated, or animated, of the genitals, pubic hair, anus, vulva, or female breast nipples.

La. Rev. Stat. Ann. sec. 14-106(A)(West 1995).

Montana also defines "obscene" in terms of the *Miller* test. The code states:

A thing is obscene if:

(a)(i) it is a representation or description of perverted ultimate sexual acts, actual or simulated;

(ii) it is a patently offensive representation or description of normal ultimate sexual acts, actual or simulated; or

(iii) it is a patently offensive representation or description of masturbation, excretory functions, or lewd exhibition of the genitals.

Mont. Code Ann. sec. 45-8-201(2)(a)(1993). The definition is meant to address the requirement that the materials addressed be described by statute. The code goes on to address the first and third prongs of the test. *Id.* at sec. 45-8-201(2)(b).

Oklahoma, in defining "obscene material" for purposes of obscene performances, also tracks the *Miller* requirements. In that state's approach to the second requirement, that the statute describe the depictions that are barred, the code addresses "sexual conduct" which it defines to include "[a]cts of sexual intercourse including any intercourse which is normal or perverted, actual or simulated." Ok. Stat. tit. 21, sec. 1024.1(3)(a)(1994).

In addition to these statutes, all prosecutions based on nonpictorial obscene publications may be considered to be aimed at simulations.

27 The statute is modeled very roughly after the New York sexual obscenity statute, N.Y. Penal sec. 235.00 *et seq.*

28 A state might choose to grade offenses based on prior convictions, the wholesale nature of the distribution involved or various other factors. *See, e.g., id.* at secs. 235.05 *et seq.*

29 354 U.S. at 491–92 (quoting *United States v. Petrillo,* 332 U.S. 1, 7–8 (1947)) (other citations and footnotes omitted).

30 Cass Sunstein, *Democracy and the Problem of Free Speech* 210 (1993).

31 In the examination of Professor Schauer's Free Speech Principle in chapter 7, the James-Lange theory on how the conscious brain experiences emotions was used to explain why the combination might not be so odd as Professor Sunstein thinks.

32 Cass Sunstein, *supra* note 30, at 211. A recent study indicates that the possibility of prosecuting violent obscenity may be greater than might be supposed. The study shows a disparity between what individuals believe to be acceptable levels of movie violence and what those individuals believe the community's level of toleration to be, with people in the study less tolerant of violence than they believe others to be. Daniel Linz, Edward Donnerstein, Bradley J. Shafer, Kenneth C. Land, Patricia L. McCall & Arthur C. Graesser, "Discrepancies between the Legal Code and Community Standards for Sex and Violence: An Empirical Challenge to Traditional Assumptions in Obscenity Law," 29 *L. & Soc'y Rev.* 127 (1995). If people come to realize that their attitude toward violence is shared, there may be a greater call for prosecution.

33 390 U.S. 629 (1968).

34 *See Butler v. Michigan,* 352 U.S. 380 (1957). *Butler* concerned restrictions on materials the state considered sexually obscene to youth but that were not obscene to adults, under the then-current test.

35 Robert Baker & Sandra Ball, *Mass Media and Violence, Vol. IX: A Report to the National Commission on the Causes and Prevention of Violence* 377 (1969).

36 Richard E. Goranson, "A Review of Recent Literature on Psychological Effects of

Media Portrayals of Violence," Appendix III-A in Robert Baker & Sandra Ball, *supra* note 35, at 395, 401.

37   The statute is based roughly on *N.Y. Penal Law* sec. 235.20 *et seq.* (McKinney 1994).

38   A state may wish to grade the offense depending on prior convictions, etc.

39   438 U.S. 726 (1978).

40   438 U.S. at 739 (citing the *Webster's Third New International Dictionary* (1966), defining "indecent" as "altogether unbecoming: contrary to what the nature of things or what circumstances would dictate as right or expected or appropriate: hardly suitable: UNSEEMLY . . . : not conforming to generally accepted standards of morality.").

41   Thomas G. Krattenmaker & L. A. Powe, Jr., "Televised Violence: First Amendment Principles and Social Science Theory," 64 *Va. L. Rev.* 1123 (1978). A more in-depth examination of Krattenmaker and Powe's argument may be found in chapter 3.

42   The history of the issue in the D.C. Circuit may be found in *Action for Children's Television v. Federal Communications Commission,* 11 F.3d 170, 171–73 (D.C. Cir. 1993) vacated, 15 F.3d 186 (D.C. Cir. 1994).

43   852 F.2d 1332 (D.C. Cir. 1988).

44   852 F.2d at 1341.

45   Pub.L. No. 100–459, sec. 608, 102 Stat. 2186, 2228 (1988).

46   *Action for Children's Television v. Federal Communications Commission,* 932 F.2d 1504 (D.C. Cir. 1991), *cert. denied,* 503 U.S. 914 (1992).

47   Public Telecommunications Act of 1992, Pub.L. No. 102–356, 106 Stat. 949. The statute did allow public broadcast stations that do not broadcast after midnight to air indecent material after 10 P.M.

48   *See Action for Children's Television v. Federal Communications Commission,* 11 F.3d 170, 173 (D.C. Cir. 1993) (quoting 1993 Order, 8 F.C.C.R. 704, 705–06) vacated, 15 F.3d 186 (D.C. Cir. 1994).

49   11 F.3d 170 (D.C. Cir. 1993), vacated, 15 F.3d 186 (D.C. Cir. 1994).

50   11 F.3d at 176. The court also noted that the Commission's brief, in admitting that the fact that there was no appreciable audience of children in the time involved could be a defense to a charge of broadcasting indecency outside of the safe-harbor period, indicated that its true concern was over children. *Id.* The Commission also seemed unwilling to sanction a single objectionable reference in an otherwise unobjectionable program. The court saw this as a refutation of the *Pacifica* Court's concern over exposure to indecent material in the interval before the channel could be changed. 11 F.3d at 176 n.10.

51   11 F.3d at 178 (quoting *Pacifica,* 438 U.S. at 750 n. 29).

52   11 F.3d at 180.

53   *ACT III* was vacated in *Action for Children's Television v. Federal Communications Commission,* 15 F.3d 186 (D.C. Cir. 1994), and the new opinion appeared as *Action*

for Children's Television v. Federal Communications Commission, 58 F.3d 654 (D.C. Cir. 1995) (en banc).

54   58 F.3d at 660–63 (citing *Ginsberg v. New York*, 390 U.S. 629 (1968); *Bethel School District v. Fraser*, 478 U.S. 675 (1986)). The court did not address a third suggested compelling interest, the protection of the home from intrusive, offensive broadcasts.

55   *See, e.g.,* the comments to the Senate Judiciary Committee of Jack Valenti, President of the Motion Picture Association of America, and Thomas Murphy, Chairman of Capital Cities/ABC, presented in chapter 1.

56   It is not clear that no one would find the level of violence in Shakespeare unacceptable. At the same time, not everyone has found the level of sex in Shakespeare acceptable. The term "bowdlerize" comes from the efforts of Dr. T. Bowdler to remove what was seen as excessive sexual content from his publication of the works of Shakespeare. *See* II *Oxford English Dictionary* 454 (2d ed. 1989). Just as Bowdler's efforts were excessive, an attack on violent depictions of the level present in Shakespearean works would seem uncalled for.

57   There are exceptions. The violence present in *Titus Andronicus* might well go beyond what would be considered decent for broadcast purposes in periods when children are likely to be in the audience.

58   413 U.S. at 24.

59   360 U.S. 684 (1959).

60   438 U.S. at 746 n.22.

61   403 U.S. 15 (1971).

62   403 U.S. at 26.

63   Frederick F. Schauer, *Free Speech: A Philosophical Enquiry* 179 (1982).

64   *Id.* at 185.

65   The attack on the social fiber present in sexual obscenity has often proceeded as a part of, or at least alongside, an attack on other aspects of the social order. The prosecution in *The Queen v. Hicklin*, L.R. 3 Q.B. 360 (1868), arose over an anti-Catholic pamphlet published during the No Popery campaign of the Orangemen. *See* David Tribe, *Questions of Censorship* 64–65 (1973). While sexually obscene, the pamphlet's antagonism toward the Catholic Church is shown by its title *The Confession Unmasked: Showing the Depravity of the Priesthood, and the Immorality of the Confessional, being the Questions Put to Females in Confession.* The prosecution of John Wilkes for his *Essay on Woman, The King v. Wilkes*, 95 Eng. Rep. 737 (K.B. 1764), 98 Eng. Rep. 327 (K.B. 1770), also appears to have been motivated by a distaste for Wilkes's political views and writings. *See* Leo Alpert, "Judicial Censorship of Obscene Literature," 52 *Harv. L. Rev.* 40, 44–47 (1938).

Index

Kevin W. Saunders is Professor of Law at the University
of Oklahoma.

Library of Congress Cataloging-in-Publication Data
Saunders, Kevin W.
Violence as obscenity : limiting the media's First
Amendment protection / Kevin W. Saunders.
p.   cm. — (Constitutional conflicts)
Includes index.
ISBN 0-8223-1758-3 (cloth : alk. paper). —
ISBN 0-8223-1767-2 (pbk. : alk. paper)
1. Mass media — Law and legislation — United States.
2. Violence in mass media — Law and legislation —
United States.   3. Obscenity (Law) — United States.
4. Freedom of the press — United States.   I. Title.
II. Series.
KF2750.S38   1996
343.7309'9 — dc20
[347.30399]   95-39400 CIP